THE
CHILDREN'S RIGHTS
MOVEMENT

ANCHOR·PRESS·DOUBLEDAY·

BEATRICE AND RONALD GROSS, nationally known leaders in the movement for educational change, are coeditors of *Will It Grow in a Classroom?* and *Radical School Reform* (selected by the New York *Times* as one of the outstanding books of 1970). Their writings have appeared often in major media such as the New York *Times Magazine, Saturday Review,* and *The Christian Science Monitor,* resulting in a Distinguished Achievement Award from the Educational Press Association of America in 1974.

Ms. Gross is a Distinguished Visiting Scholar of the State University of New York and also teaches at New York University. A leading child advocate, she appears frequently throughout the country as a lecturer, workshop leader, and school consultant. Listed in the World Who's Who of Women, Who's Who of Child Development Professionals, and Leaders in Education, she was commissioned by the U. S. Office of Education to coauthor an American Education Bicentennial essay.

Mr. Gross has been associated with The Ford Foundation, the Fund for the Advancement of Education, and the Aspen Institute for Humanistic Studies, and is currently on leave from the Academy for Educational Development to serve as adjunct associate professor of social thought at New York University. Among his previous books are *High School, The New Professionals,* and *Individualism.* He is the founder of Writers in the Public Interest, which encourages writing for social change.

THE
CHILDREN'S RIGHTS
MOVEMENT

Overcoming the Oppression of Young People

EDITED BY

BEATRICE GROSS AND RONALD GROSS

ANCHOR BOOKS

ANCHOR PRESS/DOUBLEDAY

GARDEN CITY, NEW YORK

1977

The Children's Rights Movement grew out of the work of Writers in the Public Interest, which encourages writing for social change. Grateful acknowledgment is made to the following contributors for permission to reprint the material contained in this book:

Andrew Schneider for "Beaten, Burned, Boiled and Starved." Copyright © 1974 by *The New Hampshire Times*.
Lloyd deMause for "The Nightmare of Childhood." Copyright © 1976 by Lloyd deMause.
Bob Greene for "They Tried to Help," from the Chicago *Sun-Times*, June 4, 1974. Reprinted by permission of the Chicago *Sun-Times*. Copyright © 1974 by Bob Greene.
Youth Liberation of Ann Arbor for "Do You Wanna Get Beat Up at Home or in Prison?" Copyright © 1972 by Youth Liberation of Ann Arbor.
Sanford N. Katz for "Who Looks After Laura?" from 1966—

For Elizabeth Gross, who has vowed
not to "lose her childhood" as she grows up.

Contents

4. Young People Act—for Themselves, for Others

5. Bills of Rights

Editors' Note

The following people's work, lives, and counsel have inspired and guided us: Helen Baker, William Bird-Forteza, Robert Coles, Alvin Eurich, the late Paul Goodman, Nat Hentoff, John Holt, and Jonathan Kozol. Leaders in the field have generously shared their expert knowledge and judgment, particularly Jean Reynolds, National Center for Child Advocacy; Dr. Alfred Kahn, New York School of Social Work (Columbia University); Jane Knitzer, Children's Defense Fund; Shirley Soman, author of *Let's Stop Destroying Our Children*; Joan Bel Geddes, UNICEF; Hon. Mary Conway Kohler, National Commission on Resources for Youth; Eda LeShan, dean of American parent educators and author of *The Conspiracy Against Children*; Urie Bronfenbrenner, Cornell University; Hortense Landau, New York Society for the Prevention of Cruelty to Children; Jill Grossman, Carnegie Council on Children.

We also owe much to our superb editor, Marie Dutton Brown, and to the courtesy of Bill Whitehead in leading us to her. Finally, Virginia Kobarg has been the best typist imaginable.

Introduction

THE EDITORS

A movement on behalf of children and young people seems to be taking shape in this country. There is much for it to do.

Such a movement may begin to rectify the shameful conditions that lead to the damage and death of so many children.

It could raise our personal consciousness about our stereotypes and hurtful attitudes toward the young.

It could change our laws and institutions to recognize the fact that age is no precondition to human rights.

It might provide young people with healthier options for learning and growing.

Change is needed everywhere—in our minds and feelings, and in our patterns of work, education, law, and politics. We urgently need to see clearly, articulate precisely, and above all act boldly on issues involving young people.

This book is designed as a contribution to the job that needs to be done.

A good case can be made for the fact that young people are the most oppressed of all minorities. They are discriminated against on the basis of age in everything from movie admissions to sex. They are traditionally the subjects of ridicule, humiliation, and mental torture by adults. Their civil rights are routinely violated in homes, schools, and other institutions. They often cannot own money or property. They lack the right to trial by jury before being sentenced to jail.

These oppressions are inherent in being too young in this society. If a child is spared them, it is because of special privilege and the sufferance of adults, not because as a human being he or she has an inviolable right not to be damaged, sentenced, incarcerated, or discriminated against. "Lucky" children are of course far better off than the children of the poor, who still often work in migrant labor camps for miserable wages, getting deathly sick in the process. But even "lucky" children are often driven to drugs, and sometimes even to suicide, by the depredations of their "protectors."

Among children from birth to ten years it is quite possible that the chief cause of death is murder at the hands of their parents or "protectors." Experts in child abuse point out that "battering" parents come from all social and economic classes.

The second-largest cause of death among people aged fifteen to twenty-four is suicide; many of these deaths derive from the intolerable condition of being a young person in this society, with which some young people—many of them from well-to-do families, as we all know—simply cannot cope.

"What is clear is that in a wide range of areas—education, justice, mental health and retardation, health, products, child abuse, television and many more—children are in need of far greater attention and protection than they have received up to now," wrote Peter Edelman in the New York *Times* recently. The new concern with children as an oppressed minority in our society takes many forms. The field of children's rights and youth liberation comprises a wide range of issues, problems, conditions, concerns, and proposals. It addresses itself to the emerging questions about children, childhood, and our society—questions that will increasingly challenge parents, educators, social workers, psychologists, and of course young people themselves. It includes such questions as: Is there a "special world" of childhood that does more harm than good? Should children enjoy the same rights as other members of society? What rights should parents have over their children and what right does the state have to intervene? What are children's real needs? How do the young feel about themselves and their place in America? Who is really trying to help children, and who is merely saying so? And, most important, what changes must be made in our ideas and in our institutions to better promote the healthy growth of the young into adulthood?

More specifically, the field embraces concern, study, and action on the following fronts:

1. Physical and mental torture of children in reformatories and youth facilities.

2. Medical care for prospective mothers, newborns, babies, and young children.

3. Effects on children's bodies and minds of technology and institutions such as TV, toys, poisonous or non-nutritive food, drugs used by schools on "hyperactive" students.

4. Violation of basic civil rights, such as freedom of speech, protection against search and seizure, and due process, of students in high schools.

5. Discriminatory exclusion of children from numerous environments and experiences in the worlds of work, culture, etc.

6. Compulsory school attendance and lack of choice or options within the process of schooling.

7. Consciousness-raising by us, and by young people, to become aware of what we are really doing to children, what was done to us when we were children and what its effects have been, and where the true needs and interests of young people lie.

8. The history of what children have done and been prior to the historically recent "invention of childhood," including their role in American history and contemporary affairs (e.g., the Children's Lobby within the National Welfare Rights Organization and its organization of the Children's March for Survival a couple of years ago).

9. A bill of rights for children: what rights should be affirmed and implemented through political, social, economic, and cultural means?

10. Patronization and other damaging attitudes toward chil-

dren: "cuteness" as a stereotypical way of not taking children seriously as persons, etc.

The literature of this movement is just beginning to burgeon, and what there is, is largely invisible. "Children" and "youth" are not even major categories in most libraries and bookstores. The situation is similar to that which confronted black people or women before their movements won their own categories, defined in their terms. Ten years ago, if you went into a library or bookstore and asked for the black-studies section or the section of books about, by, and for women, you would have been met with incomprehension. You probably would have been asked what "field" you were interested in. Some books about women, for example, would be found under "Psychology," in which psychologists looked at women through their particular professional glasses. Others would have been found, say, in the section on motherhood, or child care, where women were looked at in terms of how they fitted into those specific roles.

But, in every case, the women being written about were encapsulated in some academic or scientific discipline, which studied them as subjects of its kind of inquiry, or in some institution in which the focus was on how they fitted into a societal role: the family, the schools, business, etc.

There was no place, no category, and indeed little literature (compared to what exists today) in which women spoke in their own voices, *as* women, *to* other women, about their individual and collective conditions and prospects. There was no category in which a woman could find the realities of her life, in all their full complexity and urgency, expressed, portrayed, and advocated.

Today there is a category and a growing body of literature for Blacks and for women. But not, yet, for children and youth. A young person cannot readily find his or her way to a wide range of books that explore the condition of youth in American society. The voices for and of the young are still, as far as a literature goes, difficult to hear. They are scattered, muted, and hidden within other categories. One of the technical problems we faced in preparing this volume was the fact that libraries, bookstores, and other information sources are not yet set up to respond to the need for information about, by, and for young people. Books by Robert Coles might be in sociology or American studies, those by Philippe Ariès in history, those by Lloyd deMause in psychology. And for that growing number of books that speak directly to and from the experience of childhood, such as John Holt's *Escape from Childhood*, Richard Farson's *Birthrights*, or the publications of Youth Liberation of Ann Arbor, there is no place at all in the existing categories.

The most sophisticated writers have recognized this problem. "We have always been interested in children," wrote the editors of one of the nation's leading education journals recently, "but we have usually seen them as subjects for research, objects of pedagogy, or products of the schools. We have been more curious about the impact of the educational process than about the group it presumably serves. While this approach has helped structure academic inquiry, often it has not helped us understand what it is like to be a child growing up in America or how various social institutions, among them the schools, affect children's lives."

This is no mere semantic problem. The way we define children's problems, the way we talk and write about them, limit the answers we come up with and the alternatives we consider. If we see young people only through the spectacles of particular professional disciplines or established institutions, we will be able to imagine only the kinds of solutions—in fact, we will be able to see only the kinds of problems—those professions and institutions care to define. The reality of children's lives escapes us. We miss the point. Their real needs slip through the sieve. We fumble and fall, and the individuals we care about are damaged and sometimes destroyed.

The categories, of course, must and will change. Further growth in the literature, and even more the increasing emphasis in social action on the needs and rights of the young, will ensure that the categories expand to make room for this work and make it more accessible, especially to young people.

Our society's failure with children is intertwined with its larger ethos of discrimination, injustice, and racism. Wherever one looks—at exclusion from school, at the delivery of health services, at the treatment of children in the juvenile justice system, at foster care and institutionalization procedures—the children who get the least are those who need the most. Black children, Indian children, and Spanish-speaking children are the worst-served.

The children of the poor have the least protection of the laws, the poorest services, the most vulnerability to bad treatment. We permit our economic system—the "market"—to determine life and death. The infant mortality rates among the poor are more than one and one half times those for middle-income Americans. Money, in this case, can buy things that should not be for sale. This is capitalism gone berserk, the market become tyrant over the most inviolable human values. It seems clear that any effort on behalf of children must take account of this intertwining of the economic, the political, and the human. The struggle for the welfare of children and the rights of youth must engage the larger issues of equity in our whole society.

The record of the federal government is not encouraging. The last White House Conference on Children, in 1970, "shattered the myth that this is a child-centered society," in the words of its chairman. The conference made some thirty recommendations for urgent implementation, including universal day care, and health and early learning opportunities and services in which parents and the neighborhood would play a major role. Few of the recommendations were ever acted on by then-President Nixon.

In 1971 Congress passed the Child Development Act, which, if it had not been vetoed, would have provided $2 billion a year for everything from prenatal nutrition to federally subsidized day-care centers.

The status of the nation's children was probed again in 1975 by a joint Congressional committee headed by Senator Walter Mondale. "Our national myth is that we love children," Senator Mondale concluded. "Yet we are starving thousands. Other thousands die because decent medical care is unavailable to them. The lives of still other thousands are stifled by poor schools, and some never have a chance to go to school at all. Millions live in substandard and unfit housing in neighborhoods which mangle the human spirit."

The rights of children is an abstract, general, legalistic concept. It is an idea, an ideal, at best an affirmation of principle. It does not help children until it is put into practice. If it is ignored, obstructed, or perverted, it does no good; in fact, it may do harm, because many people will take the words for the act and think that because the words have been spoken the condition of children's lives has changed. "Rights without services are meaningless," says Judge Justine Polier.

So the affirmation of children's rights, even by the Supreme Court, is only the signal to start a long march through the institutions of the society. The schools, the welfare and social service institutions, the health field, the professions that directly deal with young people—all must be reformed, piece by piece, so that their practice is informed by the commitment to treat children humanely, fairly, and equitably. There must be constant monitoring, evaluation, and reconsideration: the institutional patterns of yesterday may be failing today's children. The struggle must be unremitting. The task is the most portentous one imaginable: in working for and with children, we are coming as close as we can to shaping the human future.

There is a compelling mandate here to every professional who works for and with children. It challenges us to do more than accomplish our own jobs honestly, competently, and creatively—a hard enough job! It says that we must also consider ourselves child advocates. As workers closest to the lives of children who need help, we are in the best position to know what conditions are like in the institutions in which we work. We must be willing to speak out, both within and without—

what Ralph Nader calls "whistle-blowing"—to help keep such institutions accountable. And we must enlist in the social movements that are working on behalf of children in other institutions. Otherwise we run the risk of becoming mere technicians. No matter how well we do our individual jobs, the social and economic conditions that blight children's lives will overwhelm our best efforts in many cases. The system must be changed: "One good year isn't enough," Herbert Kohl's Harlem students told him as they left him for a dim future in the public school system. We must become better workers for our souls' sake—but we must become, too, social reformers for the sake of all children.

"Child advocacy" has become a catchword in education over the past five years. As the term has turned up increasingly in federal and state governmental funding provisions, many a routine project has suddenly been renamed a "child-advocacy" project in order to qualify it for this new funding. A community family health project, for example, designed for the worthwhile purpose of giving children free health checkups, may get titled a "child-advocacy health project" to secure funding. Of course, kids need health services. But this does cloud the distinctive *new* concept that the term should designate.

Another way the concept gets muddled is through confusion with what might be called "case advocacy," a commendable but different effort. Here, a dedicated and resourceful adult—or a young person on his or her own behalf—may take up an individual case of a youngster getting abused or neglected by the system, and fight for the rights of that individual. Such efforts are invaluable not only in sparing damage to an individual, which is of course the ultimate aim of the entire enterprise, but also in reminding bureaucrats that they cannot misuse their authority with impunity.

A distinctive role is played by child protective services, such as the New York Society for the Prevention of Cruelty to Children. Such agencies are a special breed in the social-service field: whereas other agencies must wait for a client to ask for help, child protective services have the mandate to investigate whenever there is suspicion, even a mere anonymous complaint, that a child is being mistreated. They consider the child their client. Their job is to find out the facts, and then if necessary file a petition, usually in family court but in any other court of the state as necessary, on behalf of the child.

But there is, over and above these uses of the term, an application of "child advocacy" that is new and distinctive and therefore useful in calling attention to some new possibilities for helping children. This new role is *not* direct services to children. Rather, it addresses another need: to change *systems* and *institutions* and *laws* so that children are better served. There are conditions in our society that trap and destroy children, that no amount of working with individual kids can rectify. *The system* must be changed.

Child advocacy, in this unique sense, means working with, or against, the systems that affect children. It may mean intervening on their behalf in the process by which budget allocations or new legislation is made. It may mean working for new procedures and institutions that strengthen the family and protect children's rights. It may mean demanding that existing legislation be enforced or funded, or that existing institutions that purport to serve children—courts, private agencies, social-service professionals—feel accountable and be indeed called to account. Child advocacy tries to make our systems accountable for their actual effects on the lives of children.

The foremost organization in this field is the Children's Defense Fund, modeled after the NAACP Legal Defense Fund. It is a national advocate on behalf of children, privately funded and staffed mostly by lawyers. It uses a number of strategies to bring about "change for children": investigative reports such as its stunning "Banished Children," litigation, research, model legislation, negotiation, and public education. CDF tries to pick indisputably harmful practices and challenge them head on through court action, as in the case of school "push-outs" or jail detention for children. Its major thrusts are in the areas of the right to an education for all children, the right to privacy (in connection with school and other records), protection of children from medical experimentation and other harmful research, the right to adequate health care, and the right of children to receive fair and humane service in the juvenile justice system.

"Change for children," as the CDF puts it, is an intensely political issue. It involves who gets what, how, and when—in terms of money, power, and service. To make the interests of children felt in the halls of power, therefore, there is great need for a public presence in the society of CDF and other groups like it or working in conjunction with it. "Class-action suits" are required to rectify abuses or inequities of the system, and continuing monitoring, research, and publicity are required to prevent bureaucracies from slipping into self-serving rather than child-serving patterns.

The book spans a very wide age range, from conditions affecting infants to action projects of seventeen-year-olds. Therefore, what is said in one section about people of a certain age may not apply to people of different ages and conditions discussed elsewhere in the book. This is intentional. The commonest response to the term children's liberation is to scoff: "What—two-year-olds driving, voting, having sex!" The assumption is that all young people are "children" and essentially alike in being incapable of adult activities. So such critics assume that if one advocates driving privileges for certain sixteen-year-olds, one is claiming the same thing for two-year-olds, "since they're both children." But one of the basic tenets of this movement is that children and young people are not all the same, and should not be treated all the same, merely on the basis of their being below the age of "adulthood." A two-year-old and a sixteen-year-old are far more different in their capabilities and their needs than many sixteen-year-olds and many twenty-five-year-olds. This belief, John Holt points out, "has divided the curve of life . . . into two parts—one called Childhood, the other called Adulthood, or Maturity. It has made a Great Divide in human life, and made us think that the people on opposite sides of this divide, the Children and the Adults, are very different . . . with respect to the kind of control he has over his own life, the ability to make important choices, the sixteen-year-old is much closer to the two-year-old than he is to someone of twenty-two."

The voices, documents, and experiences in this volume speak more eloquently than we can about the scope and thrust of this burgeoning movement. There are manifestos and case studies, personal memoirs and reflections, and reports on organizations and individual efforts. There is as much material as we could lay our hands on by children and young people themselves. Together, the selections testify to a commitment on behalf of all kinds of people to helping gain for our children the protections, options, and genuine concern they need.

This suggests our answer to the knee-jerk criticism: "Does children's rights mean giving the vote to two-year-olds?" For our whole point is that children should not be treated alike, and we apply this same principle to the movement for children's rights itself. We must consider the potentialities and the needs of each age youngster—in fact, of each *individual* youngster whatever his age—and then have enough options and "give" in our institutions to meet that child, where he or she is, with opportunities for growth and fulfillment.

One purpose we hope this book will serve is to create bridges, make connections, generate mutual strengthening, between quite different individuals and groups involved in this effort. We admire the theoreticians such as John Holt and Richard Farson who probe the roots of our ideology of childhood. But we admire equally those people who commit themselves to concrete advance in a discrete practical area, such as Victoria Reis's struggle against the toy industry's assault on children. Similarly, organizations that have perhaps never been in contact before will find their works side by side between these covers, and perhaps find the company congenial and supportive—and feel impelled to carry it into further direct communication and collaborative action. All too often, major efforts at social change are pressed by people needlessly isolated from each other, organizations unnecessarily unaware that their over-all aims are highly akin. The whole movement may gain strength and momentum from a keener awareness of our common commitment.

As editors, we have viewed our task as simply to place in the reader's hands a varied and representative selection of the best that is being thought and done in this nascent field. We have eschewed imposing our own position on the materials, and have not been afraid to include, if not contradictory viewpoints —for we believe virtually all the contributors take a basically progressive, reformist view of the subject—then certainly pieces that imply quite different emphases. For example, some children need vastly *more* help, protection, and concern, while others need *less* hovering over, channeling, and imposition of adult standards. Similarly as to *levels* of action: we need to change our national policies regarding payments in support of children, but we also need to work ruthlessly on our own benighted attitudes about the "cuteness" of children and the impulsiveness of adolescents.

The approach of the book is frankly pluralistic: we believe that diverse approaches are needed to reform ourselves and our institutions.

1.
Destroying Children

Destruction is not too strong a word for the processing that poor, non-white, brutalized, banished, and "exceptional" children often face in our country today. Much of this destruction is done directly by agencies either *of* the state or accredited *by* the state. Much, too, is done indirectly by our political and economic system, which reduces the parents of poor children to such despair that they are often unable to protect or provide the physical and emotional health their children require.

This section has some very upsetting material in it. It is upsetting to face the horror of our responsibility for a system that not only "picks on" little kids, but kicks them when they're down. We fight dirty through our service institutions—and street kids learn the rules. We don't actively wield the bludgeon, whereas the poor, as always, are engaged in the hand-to-hand battle, getting killed, or killing, or both.

These reports tell how children are denied health care, foster care, schooling. They tell us that many children are sent to brutal institutions to "protect" them from their abusive parents or because they have no parents. They tell us that many children are sent to prison for non-criminal acts such as truancy, for having lost those who can look after them, for being unable to comprehend a teacher's directions, for talking back to an adult. And once in these prisons children are beaten, locked in solitary, deprived of an education, of therapy, of privacy, movement, mail, personal belongings, and all respect. They are deprived of information relating to their futures, and often sent so far away that even the very limited visiting rights of parents are precluded by expense and distance.

Such deprivations prevent most of these children from ever reaching real maturity.

In 1969 The American Humane Association estimated that ten thousand children "are beaten, burned, boiled and deliberately starved in the United States each year by parents, relatives and guardians." Now, in 1975, the estimated numbers of children "abused," according to the U. S. Office of Child Development, is between fifty thousand and five hundred thousand.

Beaten, Burned, Boiled, and Starved
ANDREW SCHNEIDER

Her name was Mary. She had blue eyes, blond hair and the curiosity that comes with being two years old. It was that curiosity that prompted her to rub her mother's lipstick on the clean kitchen floor.

The whistling teapot brought Mary's mother into the kitchen. She paused a moment to look at the red streaks on the floor, walked to the stove, picked up the screaming kettle, and poured the boiling water over the lipstick marks and her young daughter.

Mary was hospitalized with severe burns over 54 per cent of her body. She will carry physical and mental scars for the remainder of her life.

CHILD ABUSE—*Any physical injury or injuries sustained by a child as a result of cruel or inhumane treatment or as a result of a malicious act by a parent, adoptive parent, or other person who has permanent or temporary care, custody, or responsibility for the supervision of a minor.*

Tommy was considered a perfect baby. Although only six months old, he rarely cried. So when neighbors heard crying coming from the third-floor apartment, they were surprised, but after it continued for three days the surprise became concern. Attempts to get anyone to answer the door prompted a call to the police.

When the eleven-year veteran of the Manchester Police Department forced open the door and saw the child in the crib, he promptly vomited.

Tommy was curled up in a corner of the crib amid several bowls of sour milk and hardened baby food. Although the crib was in front of an opened window, the stench was unbearable.

The child was covered with urine and feces, but beneath the caked filth the police officer could see that the baby's skin had a bluish coloring.

When Tommy's mother and her boyfriend returned to the apartment four days later, she was furious that her baby had been removed from the apartment. She threatened to sue everyone in sight for invasion of privacy.

Tommy spent three weeks in the critical-care unit of a Boston hospital, where he was treated for exposure, dehydration, and pneumonia. The doctor suspected permanent brain damage.

NEGLECT—*The failure of a parent or guardian to provide a child proper subsistence, education, medical or surgical care, or other care necessary for his health, morals, or well-being, or allowing the child to exist in a situation or surroundings that may prove injurious.*

Black people and Native Americans have known for years that history has always been written by whites. More recently, women have learned that history ignores or distorts the role of women. Little wonder, then, that the true history of childhood has only lately come to the fore. It is a nightmare hitherto relegated to the margins of our literature.

Abandonment, terrorization, beating, sexual abuse—all these

*are documented in unsparing detail by Lloyd deMause. Here
are infants beaten for crying, little boys buggered and castrated,
children regularly whipped with a cultivated variety of tools
made especially for their tormenting.*

The Nightmare of Childhood
LLOYD DEMAUSE

The history of childhood is a nightmare from which we have
only recently begun to awaken. The further back in history one
goes, the lower the level of child care and the more likely children are to be killed, abandoned, beaten, terrorized, and sexually abused. It is our task here to see how much of this childhood history can be recaptured from the evidence that remains
to us.

*Psychological Principles of Childhood History:
Projective and Reversal Reactions*

In studying childhood over many generations, it is most important to concentrate on those moments which most affect the
psyche of the next generation: primarily, this means what
happens when an adult is face to face with a child who needs
something. The adult has, I believe, three major reactions
available: (1) He can use the child as a vehicle for projection
of the contents of his own unconscious (projective reaction),
(2) he can use the child as a substitute for an adult figure
important in his own childhood (reversal reaction), or (3) he
can empathize with the child's needs and act to satisfy them
(empathic reaction).

The child in the past was so charged with projections that
he was often in danger of being considered a changeling if
he cried too much or was otherwise too demanding. There is
a large literature on changelings, but it is not generally realized
that it was not only deformed children who were killed as

changelings but also those who, as St. Augustine puts it, "suffer from a demon . . . they are under the power of the Devil . . . some infants die in this vexation. . . ." Some church fathers declared that if a baby merely cried it was committing a sin.

The belief that infants were felt to be on the verge of turning into totally evil beings is one of the reasons why they were tied up, or swaddled, so long and so tightly. One feels the undertone in Bartholomaeus Anglicus (c. 1230): "And for tenderness the limbs of the child may easily and soon bow and bend and take diverse shapes. And therefore children's members and limbs are bound with lystes [bandages], and other covenable bonds, that they be not crooked nor evil shapen. . . ." It is the infant full of the parent's dangerous, evil projections that is swaddled. The reasons given for swaddling in the past are the same as those of present-day swaddlers in Eastern Europe: the baby has to be tied up or it will tear its ears off, scratch its eyes out, break its legs, or touch its genitals. As we shall see shortly in the section on swaddling and restraints, this often includes binding up children in all kinds of corsets, stays, backboards, and puppet strings, and even extends to tying them up in chairs to prevent them from crawling on the floor "like an animal."

The number of ghostlike figures used to frighten children throughout history is legion, and their regular use by adults was common until quite recently. The ancients had their Lamia and Striga, who, like their Hebrew prototype Lilith, ate children raw, and who, along with Mormo, Canida, Poine, Sybaris, Acco, Empusa, Gorgon, and Ephialtes, were "invented for a child's benefit to make it less rash and ungovernable," according to Dio Chrysostom. Most ancients agreed that it was good to have the images of these witches constantly before children, to let them feel the terror of waiting up at night for ghosts to steal them away, eat them, tear them to pieces, and suck their blood or their bone marrow. By medieval times, of course, witches and devils took front stage, with an occasional Jew thrown in as a cutter of babies' throats, along with hoards of other monsters and bogies "such as those [with] which nurses love to terrify them." After the Reformation, God himself, who "holds you over the pit of hell, much as one holds a spider, or some loathsome insect, over the fire," was the major bogeyman used to terrify children, and tracts were written in baby talk describing the tortures God had in store for children in Hell: "The little child is in this red-hot oven. Hear how it screams to come out. . . . It stamps its little feet on the floor. . . ."

This need to personify punitive figures was so powerful that adults actually dressed up Katchina-like dummies to use in frightening children. One English writer, in 1748, while explaining how terror originated with nurses who frightened infants with stories of "raw-head and bloody-bones," said:

> The nurse takes a fancy to quiet the peevish child, and with this intent, dresses up an uncouth figure, makes it come in, and roar and scream at the child in ugly disagreeable notes, which grate upon the tender organs of the ear, and at the same time, by its gesture and near approach, makes as if it would swallow the infant up.

These fearful figures were also the favorites of nurses who wanted to keep children in bed while they went off at night. Susan Sibbald remembered ghosts as a real part of her eighteenth-century childhood:

> Ghosts making their appearance were a very common occurrence. . . . I remember perfectly when both the nursery maids at Fowey wished to leave the nursery one evening . . . we were silenced by hearing the most dismal groanings and scratchings outside the partition next the stairs. The door was thrown open, and oh! horrors, there came in a figure, tall and dressed in white, with fire coming out of its eyes, nose and mouth it seemed. We were almost thrown into convulsions, and were not well for days, but dared not tell.

Another whole area of concretization of this need to terrorize children involves the use of corpses. Many are familiar with the scenes in Mrs. Sherwood's novel *History of the Fairchild Family*, in which the children are taken on visits to the gibbet to inspect rotting corpses hanging there, while being told moral stories. What is not often realized is that these scenes are taken from real life and formed an important part of childhood in the past. Classes used to be taken out of school to hangings, and parents would often take their children to hangings and then whip them when they returned home to make them remember what they had seen. Even a humanist educator such as Mafio Vegio, who wrote books to protest the beating of children, had to admit that "to let them witness a public execution is sometimes not at all a bad thing."

The effect on the children of this continuous corpse-viewing was of course massive. One little girl, after her mother showed her the fresh corpse of her nine-year-old friend as an example, went around saying, "They will put daughter in the deep hole, and what will mother do?" Another boy woke at night screaming after seeing hangings, and "practiced hanging his own cat."

Even such a simple act as empathizing with children who were beaten was difficult for adults in the past. Those few educators who, prior to modern times, advised that children should not be beaten generally argued that it would have bad consequences rather than that it would hurt the child. Yet, without this element of empathy the advice had no effect whatsoever, and children continued to be beaten as before. Mothers who sent their infants to wet nurses for three years were genuinely distressed that their children then didn't want to return to them, yet they had no capacity to locate the reason. A hundred generations of mothers tied up their infants in swaddling bands and impassively watched them scream in protest, because they lacked the psychic mechanism necessary to empathize with them. Only when the slow historical process of parent-child evolution finally established this faculty through successive generations of parent-child interaction did it become obvious that swaddling was totally unnecessary.

Infanticide and Death Wishes Toward Children

The history of infanticide in the West has yet to be written, and I shall not attempt it here. But enough is already known to establish that, contrary to the usual assumption that it is an Eastern rather than a Western problem, infanticide of both legitimate and illegitimate children was a regular practice of antiquity, that the killing of legitimate children was only slowly reduced during the Middle Ages, and that illegitimate children continued regularly to be killed right up into the nineteenth century.

Infanticide during antiquity has usually been played down despite literally hundreds of clear references by ancient writers that it was an accepted, everyday occurrence. Children were thrown into rivers, flung into dung heaps and cess trenches, "potted" in jars to starve to death, and exposed on every hill and roadside, "a prey for birds, food for wild beasts to rend" (Euripides, *Ion*, 504). To begin with, any child that was not perfect in shape and size, or cried too little or too much, or was otherwise than is described in the gynecological writings on "How to Recognize the Newborn That Is Worth Rearing," was generally killed. Beyond this, the first-born was usually allowed to live, especially if it was a boy. Girls were, of course, valued little, and the instructions of Hilarion to his wife Alis (1 B.C.) are typical of the open way these things were discussed: "If, as may well happen, you give birth to a child, if it is a boy let it live; if it is a girl, expose it." The result was a large imbalance of males over females, which was typical of the West until well into the Middle Ages, when the killing of legitimate children was probably much reduced. (The killing of illegitimate children does not affect the sex ratio, since both sexes are generally killed.) Available statistics for antiquity show large surpluses of boys over girls; for instance, out of seventy-nine families who gained Milesian citizenship about 228–220 B.C., there were 118 sons and twenty-eight daughters; thirty-two families had one child, thirty-one had two. As Jack Lindsay puts it:

Two sons are not uncommon, three occur now and then,
but more than one daughter was practically never reared.
Poseidippos stated, "even a rich man always exposes a
daughter." . . . Of 600 families from second-century in-
scriptions at Delphi, 1 per cent raised two daughters.

The killing of legitimate children even by wealthy parents was
so common that Polybius blamed it for the depopulation of
Greece.

Philo was the first person I have found who spoke out clearly
against the horrors of infanticide:

Some of them do the deed with their own hands; with
monstrous cruelty and barbarity they stifle and throttle the
first breath which the infants draw or throw them into a
river or into the depths of the sea, after attaching some
heavy substance to make them sink more quickly under its
weight. Others take them to be exposed in some desert
place, hoping, they themselves say, that they may be saved,
but leaving them in actual truth to suffer the most distress-
ing fate. For all the beasts that feed in human flesh visit
the spot and feast unhindered on the infants, a fine ban-
quet provided by their sole guardians, those who above all
others should keep them safe, their fathers and mothers.
Carnivorous birds, too, come flying down and gobble up
the fragments. . . .

Although, in the two centuries after Augustus, some attempts
were made to pay parents to keep children alive in order to
replenish the dwindling Roman population, it was not until the
fourth century that real change was apparent. The law began
to consider killing an infant murder only in A.D. 374. Yet even
the opposition to infanticide by the Church Fathers often
seemed to be based more on their concern for the parent's soul
than with the child's life.

After the Council of Vaison (A.D. 442), the finding of abandoned children was supposed to be announced in church, and
by A.D. 787, Dateo of Milan founded the first asylum solely for

abandoned infants. Other countries followed much the same pattern of evolution. Despite much literary evidence, however, the continued existence of widespread infanticide in the Middle Ages is usually denied by medievalists, since it is not evident in church records and other quantitative sources. But if sex ratios of 136 to 100 (c. A.D. 801) and 172 to 100 (A.D. 1391) are any indication of the extent of the killing of legitimate girls, and if illegitimates were usually killed regardless of sex, the real rate of infanticide could have been substantial in the Middle Ages. Certainly, when Innocent III began the hospital of the Santo Spirito in Rome at the end of the twelfth century he was fully aware of the number of women throwing their babies into the Tiber. As late as 1527, one priest admitted that "the latrines resound with the cries of children who have been plunged into them."

What is certain is that when our material becomes far fuller, by the eighteenth century, there is no question that there was high incidence of infanticide in every country in Europe. As more foundling homes were opened in each country, babies poured in from all over, and the homes quickly ran out of room. Even though Thomas Coram opened his Foundling Hospital in 1741 because he couldn't bear to see the dying babies lying in the gutters and rotting on the dung heaps of London, by the 1890s dead babies were still a common sight in London streets. Late in the nineteenth century Louis Adamic described being brought up in an Eastern European village of "killing nurses," where mothers sent their infants to be done away with "by exposing them to cold air after a hot bath; feeding them something that caused convulsions in their stomachs and intestines; mixing gypsum in their milk, which literally plastered up their insides; suddenly stuffing them with food after not giving them anything to eat for two days. . . ."

Urges to mutilate, burn, freeze, drown, shake, and throw the infant violently about were continuously acted out in the past. The Huns used to cut the cheeks of newborn males. Robert Pemell tells how in Italy and other countries during the Renaissance parents would "burn in the neck with a hot iron, or else drop a burning wax candle" on newborn babies to prevent "falling sickness." In early modern times, the string underneath the newborn's tongue was usually cut, often with the midwife's fingernail, a sort of miniature circumcision. The mutilation of children throughout the ages has excited pity and laughter in adults, and was the basis for the widespread practice in every age of mutilating children for begging.

Throwing the swaddled child about was sometimes practiced. A brother of Henri IV, while being passed for amusement from one window to another, was dropped and killed. The same thing happened to the little Comte de Marle: "One of the gentlemen-in-waiting and the nurse who was taking care of him amused themselves by tossing him back and forth across the sill of an open window. . . . Sometimes they would pretend not to catch him . . . the little Comte de Marle fell and hit a stone step below." Doctors complained of parents who break the bones of their children in the "customary" tossing of infants. Nurses often said that the stays children were encased in were necessary because otherwise they could not "be tossed about without them. And I remember an eminent surgeon say a child was brought to him with several of its ribs crushed inward by the hand of the person who had been tossing it about without its stays." Doctors also denounced the customary violent rocking of infants, "which puts the babe into a dazed condition, in order that he may not trouble those that have the care of him." This was the reason that cradles began to be attacked in the eighteenth century; Buchan said he was against cradles because of the common "ill-tempered nurse, who, instead of soothing the accidental uneasiness or indisposition to sleep of her baby, when laid down to rest, is often worked up to the highest pitch of rage; and, in the excess of her folly and brutality, endeavors, by loud, harsh threats, and the impetuous rattle of the cradle, to drown the infant's cries, and to force him into slumber."

Infants were also sometimes nearly frozen through a variety of customs, ranging from baptism by lengthy dipping in ice water and rolling in the snow, to the practice of the plunge bath, which involved regular plunging of the infant over and over again in ice-cold water over its head "with its mouth open and gasping for breath." Elizabeth Grant remembers in the early-nineteenth century that a "large, long tub stood in the kitchen court, the ice on the top of which often had to be broken before our horrid plunge into it. . . . How I screamed, begged, prayed, entreated to be saved. . . . Nearly senseless I have been taken to the housekeeper's room. . . ." Going back to the ancient custom of the Germans, Scythians, Celts, and Spartans (though not Athenians, who used other hardening methods), dipping in cold rivers used to be common, and cold-water dipping has since Roman times been considered therapeutic for children. Even the putting of children to bed wrapped in cold wet towels was sometimes used both to harden and as therapy. It is not surprising that the great eighteenth-century pediatrician William Buchan said, ". . . almost one half of the human species perish in infancy by improper management or neglect."

Abandonment, Nursing, and Swaddling

Although there were many exceptions to the general pattern, up to about the eighteenth century, the average child of wealthy parents spent his earliest years in the home of a wet nurse, returned home to the care of other servants, and was sent out to service, apprenticeship, or school by age seven, so that the amount of time parents of means actually spent raising their children was minimal.

It was the sending of children to wet-nurse which was the form of institutionalized abandonment most prevalent in the past. The wet nurse is a familiar figure in the Bible, the Code of Hammurabi, the Egyptian papyri, and Greek and Roman literature, and they have been well organized ever since Roman wet nurses gathered in the Colonna Lactaria to sell their services. Doctors and moralists since Galen and Plutarch have denounced mothers for sending their children out to be wet-nursed rather than nursing them themselves. Their advice had little effect, however, for until the eighteenth century most parents who could afford it, and many who couldn't, sent their children to wet-nurse immediately after birth. Even poor mothers who could not afford sending their children out to nurse often refused to breast-feed them, and gave them pap instead. Contrary to the assumptions of most historians, the custom of not breast-feeding infants at all reaches back in many areas of Europe at least as far as the fifteenth century. One mother, who had moved from an area in northern Germany where nursing infants was more common, was considered "swinish and filthy" by Bavarian women for nursing her child, and her husband threatened he would not eat if she did not give up this "disgusting habit."

As for the rich, who actually abandoned their children for a period of years, even those experts who thought the practice bad usually did not use empathic terms in their treatises, but rather thought wet-nursing bad because "the dignity of a newborn human being [is] corrupted by the foreign and degenerate nourishment of another's milk." That is, the blood of the lower-class wet nurse entered the body of the upper-class baby, milk being thought to be blood frothed white. Occasionally the moralists, all men of course, betrayed their own repressed resentment against their mothers for having sent them out to wet-nurse. Aulus Gellius complained: "When a child is given to another and removed from its mother's sight, the strength of maternal ardor is gradually and little by little extinguished . . . and it is almost as completely forgotten as if it had been lost by death." But usually repression won and the parent was praised. More important, repetition was assured. Though it was well known that infants died at a far higher rate while at wet nurse than at home, parents continued to mourn their children's death, and then helplessly handed over their next infant as though the wet nurse were a latter-day avenging goddess who required yet another sacrifice.

Except in those cases where the wet nurse was brought in to live, children who were given to the wet nurse were generally left there from two to five years. The conditions were similar in every country. Jacques Guillimeau described how the child at nurse might be "stifled, overlaid, be let fall, and so come to an untimely death; or else may be devoured, spoiled, or disfigured by some wild beast, wolf, or dog, and then the nurse, fearing to be punished for her negligence, may take another child into the place of it." Robert Pemell reported the rector in his parish told him it was, when he first came to it, "filled with suckling infants from London and yet, in the space of one year, he buried them all except two." Yet the practice continued inexorably until the eighteenth century in England and America, the nineteenth century in France, and into the twentieth century in Germany. England was, in fact, so far in advance of the continent in nursing matters that quite wealthy mothers were often nursing their children as early as the seventeenth century. Nor was it simply a matter of the amorality of the rich; Robert Pemell complained in 1653 of the practice of "both high and low ladies of farming out their babies to irresponsible women in the country," and as late as 1780 the police chief of Paris estimated that of the twenty-one thousand children born each year in his city, seventeen thousand were sent into the country to be wet-nursed, two thousand or three thousand were placed in nursery homes, seven hundred were wet-nursed at home, and only seven hundred were nursed by their mothers.

Tying the child up in various restraint devices was a near-universal practice. Swaddling was the central fact of the infant's earliest years. As we have noted, restraints were thought necessary because the child was so full of dangerous adult projections that if it were left free it would scratch its eyes out, tear its ears off, break its legs, distort its bones, be terrified by the sight of its own limbs, and even crawl about on all fours like an animal. Traditional swaddling is much the same in every country and age; it "consists in entirely depriving the child of the use of its limbs, by enveloping them in an endless length bandage, so as to not unaptly resemble billets of wood; and by which, the skin is sometimes excoriated; the flesh compressed, almost to gangrene; the circulation nearly arrested; and the child without the slightest power of motion. Its little waist is surrounded by stays. . . . Its head is compressed into the form the fancy of the midwife might suggest; and its shape maintained by properly adjusted pressure. . . ."

Swaddling was often so complicated it took up to two hours to dress an infant. Its convenience to adults was enormous—they rarely had to pay any attention to infants once they were tied up. As a recent medical study of swaddling has shown, swaddled infants are extremely passive, their hearts slow down, they cry less, they sleep far more, and in general they are so withdrawn and inert that the doctors who did the study wondered if swaddling shouldn't be tried again. The historical sources confirm this picture; doctors since antiquity agreed that "wakefulness does not happen to children naturally nor from habit, i.e., customarily, for they always sleep," and children were described as being laid for hours behind the hot oven, hung on pegs on the wall, placed in tubs, and in general, "left, like a parcel, in every convenient corner."

Toilet Training, Discipline, and Sex

Although chairs with chamber pots underneath have existed since antiquity, there is no evidence for toilet training in the earliest months of the infant's life prior to the eighteenth century. Although parents often complained, like Luther, of their children's "befouling the corners," and although doctors prescribed remedies, including whipping, for "pissing in the bed" (children generally slept with adults), the struggle between parent and child for control in infancy of urine and feces is an eighteenth-century invention, the product of a late psychogenic stage.

It was the enema and the purge, not the potty, which were the central devices for relating to the inside of the child's body prior to the eighteenth century. Children were given suppositories, enemas, and oral purges in sickness and in health. One seventeenth-century authority said infants should be purged before each nursing so the milk wouldn't get mixed up with the feces. Héroard's diary of Louis XIII is filled with minute descriptions of what went into and came out of Louis's body; he was given literally thousands of purges, suppositories, and enemas during his childhood.

It was not until the eighteenth century that the main focus moved from the enema to the potty. Not only was toilet training begun at an earlier age, partly as a result of diminished use of swaddling bands, but the whole process of having the child control its body products was invested with an emotional importance previously unknown. Wrestling with an infant's will in his first few months was a measure of the strength of involvement by parents with their children, and represented a psychological advance over the reign of the enema. By the nineteenth century, parents generally began toilet training in earnest in the earliest months of life, and their demands for cleanliness became so severe by the end of the century that the ideal child was described as one "who cannot bear to have any dirt on his body or dress or in his surrounding for even the briefest time." Even today, most English and German parents begin toilet training prior to six months; the average in America is more like nine months, and the range is greater.

The evidence which I have collected on methods of disciplining children leads me to believe that a very large percentage of the children born prior to the eighteenth century were what would today be termed "battered children." Of over two hundred statements of advice on child rearing prior to the eighteenth century which I have examined, most approved of beating children severely, and all allowed beating in varying circumstances except three, Plutarch, Palmieri, and Sadoleto, and these were addressed to fathers and teachers, and did not mention mothers. Of the seventy children prior to the eighteenth century whose lives I have found, all were beaten except one.

Beating instruments included whips of all kinds, including the cat-o'-nine-tails, shovels, canes, iron and wooden rods, bundles of sticks, the *discipline* (a whip made of small chains), and special school instruments like the flapper, which had a pear-shaped end and a round hole to raise blisters. Their comparative frequency of use may be indicated by the categories

of the German schoolmaster who reckoned he had given 911,-
527 strokes with the stick, 124,000 lashes with the whip, 136,715
slaps with the hand, and 1,115,800 boxes on the ear. The beat-
ings described in the sources were generally severe, involved
bruising and bloodying of the body, began early, and were a
regular part of the child's life.

Century after century of battered children grew up and in
turn battered their own children. Public protest was rare. Even
humanists and teachers who had a reputation for great gentle-
ness, like Petrarch, Ascham, Comenius, and Pestalozzi, approved of beating children. Milton's wife complained she hated
to hear the cries of his nephews when he was beating them,
and Beethoven whipped his pupils with a knitting needle and
sometimes bit them. Even royalty was not exempt from battering, as the childhood of Louis XIII confirms.

The beating of the smallest of infants out of swaddling
clothes occurred quite often, a sure sign of the "battering"
syndrome. Susannah Wesley said of her babies: "When turned
a year old (and some before), they were taught to fear the rod,
and to cry softly." Giovanni Dominici said to give babies "frequent, yet not severe whippings. . . ." Rousseau said that
babies in their earliest days were often beaten to keep them
quiet. One mother wrote of her first battle with her four-month-
old infant: "I whipped him til he was actually black and blue,
and until I *could not* whip him any more, and he never gave
up one single inch."

The child in antiquity lived his earliest years in an atmosphere of sexual abuse. Growing up in Greece and Rome often
included being used sexually by older men. The exact form and
frequency of the abuse varied by area and date. In Crete and
Boeotia, pederastic marriages and honeymoons were common.
Abuse was less frequent among aristocratic boys in Rome, but
sexual use of children was everywhere evident in some form.
Boy brothels flourished in every city, and one could even contract for the use of a rent-a-boy service in Athens. Even where
homosexuality with free boys was discouraged by law, men kept

slave boys to abuse, so that even freeborn children saw their fathers sleeping with boys. Children were sometimes sold into concubinage; Musonius Rufus wondered whether such a boy would be justified in resisting being abused.

The sexual abuse of boys was not limited to those over eleven or twelve years of age, as most scholars assume. Sexual abuse by pedagogues and teachers of smaller children may have been common throughout antiquity. Although all sorts of laws were passed to try to limit sexual attacks on school children by adults, the long, heavy sticks carried by pedagogues and teachers were often used to threaten them. Quintilian, after many years of teaching in Rome, warned parents against the frequency of sexual abuse by teachers, and made this the basis of his disapproval of beating in schools.

The evidence from literature and art confirms this picture of the sexual abuse of smaller children. Petronius loves depicting adults feeling the "immature little tool" of boys, and his description of the rape of a seven-year-old girl, with women clapping in a long line around the bed, suggests that women were not exempt from playing a role in the process. Aristotle said homosexuality often becomes habitual in "those who are abused from childhood." It has been assumed that the small nude children seen on vases waiting on adults in erotic scenes are servants, but in view of the usual role of noble children as waiters, we should consider the possibility that they may be children of the house. For, as Quintilian said about noble Roman children: "We rejoice if they say something over-free, and words which we should not tolerate from the lips even of an Alexandrian page are greeted with laughter and a kiss . . . they hear us use such words, they see our mistresses and minions; every dinner party is loud with foul songs, and things are presented to their eyes of which we should blush to speak." Suetonius condemned Tiberius because he "taught children of the most tender years, whom he called his *little fishes,* to play between his legs while he was in his bath. Those which had not yet been weaned, but were strong and hearty, he set at fellatio."

Giovanni Dominici, writing in 1405, said children after the age of three years shouldn't be allowed to see nude adults. For in a child "granted that there will not take place any thought or natural movement before the age of five, yet, without precaution, growing up in such acts he becomes accustomed to that act of which later he is not ashamed. . . ." That parents themselves are often doing the molesting can be seen in the language he used:

> He should sleep clothed with a night shirt reaching below the knee, taking care as much as possible that he may not remain uncovered. Let not the mother nor the father, much less any other person, touch him. Not to be tedious in writing so fully of this, I simply mention the history of the ancients who made full use of this doctrine to bring up children well, not slaves of the flesh.

The campaign against the sexual use of children continued through the seventeenth century, but in the eighteenth century it took an entirely new twist: punishing the little boy or girl for touching its own genitals. That this, like early toilet training, was a late psychogenic stage is suggested by the fact that prohibitions against childhood masturbation are found in none of the primitive societies surveyed by Whiting and Child. The attitude of most people toward childhood masturbation prior to the eighteenth century can be seen in Fallopius' counsel for parents to "be zealous in infancy to enlarge the penis of the boy." Although masturbation in adults was a minor sin, medieval penitentials rarely extended the prohibition to childhood; adult homosexuality, not masturbation, was the main obsession of premodern sexual regulation. As late as the fifteenth century, Gerson complains how adults tell him they never heard that masturbation was sinful, and he instructs confessors to ask adults directly: "Friend, do you touch or do you rub your rod *as children have the habit of doing?*"

But it was not until the beginning of the eighteenth century, as a climax of the effort to bring child abuse under control, that parents began severely punishing their children for masturbation and doctors began to spread the myth that it would cause insanity, epilepsy, blindness, and death. By the nineteenth century, this campaign reached an unbelievable frenzy. Doctors and parents sometimes appeared before the child armed with knives and scissors, threatening to cut off the child's genitals; circumcision, clitoridectomy, and infibulation were sometimes used as punishment; and all sorts of restraint devices, including plaster casts and cages with spikes, were prescribed.

Periodization of Modes of Parent-Child Relations

Since some people still kill, beat, and sexually abuse children, any attempt to periodize modes of child rearing must first admit that psychogenic evolution proceeds at different rates in different family lines, and that many parents appear to be "stuck" in earlier historical modes. There are also class and area differences which are important, especially since modern times, when the upper classes stopped sending their infants to wet nurses and began bringing them up themselves. The periodization below should be thought of as a designation of the modes of parent-child relations which were exhibited by the psychogenically most advanced part of the population in the most advanced countries, and the dates given are the first in which I found examples of that mode in the sources. The series of six modes represents a continuous sequence of closer approaches between parent and child as generation after generation of parents slowly overcame their anxieties and began to develop the capacity to identify and satisfy the needs of their children. I also believe the series provides a meaningful taxonomy of contemporary child-rearing modes.

1. *Infanticidal Mode* (*Antiquity to Fourth Century* A.D.): The image of Medea hovers over childhood in antiquity, for myth here only reflects reality. Some facts are more important than others, and when parents routinely resolved their anxieties about taking care of children by killing them, it affected the surviving children profoundly.

2. *Abandonment Mode (Fourth to Thirteenth Centuries)*:
Once parents began to accept the child as having a soul, the
only way they could escape the dangers of their own projections
was by abandonment, whether to the wet nurse, to the mon-
astery or nunnery, to foster families, to the homes of other no-
bles as servants or hostages, or by severe emotional abandonment at home. The symbol of this mode might be Griselda,
who so willingly abandoned her children to prove her love for
her husband. Or perhaps it would be any of those pictures so
popular up to the thirteenth century of a rigid Mary stiffly holding the infant Jesus.

3. *Ambivalent Mode (Fourteenth to Seventeenth Centuries)*: Because the child, when it was allowed to enter into
the parents' emotional life, was still a container for dangerous
projections, it was their task to mold it into shape. From
Dominici to Locke there was no image more popular than that
of the physical molding of children, who were seen as soft wax,
plaster, or clay to be beaten into shape. Enormous ambivalence
marks this mode. The beginning of the period is approximately
the fourteenth century, which shows an increase in the number
of child instruction manuals, the expansion of the cults of Mary
and the infant Jesus, and the proliferation in art of the "close-
mother image."

4. *Intrusive Mode (Eighteenth Century)*: A tremendous reduction in projection and the virtual disappearance of reversal
was the accomplishment of the great transition for parent-child
relations which appeared in the eighteenth century. The child
was no longer so full of dangerous projections, and rather than
just examine its insides with an enema, the parents approached
even closer and attempted to conquer its mind, in order to control its insides, its anger, its needs, its masturbation, its very
will. The child raised by intrusive parents was nursed by the
mother, not swaddled, not given regular enemas, toilet-trained
early, prayed with but not played with, hit but not regularly
whipped, punished for masturbation, and made to obey
promptly with threats and guilt as often as with other methods

of punishment. The child was so much less threatening that true empathy was possible, and pediatrics was born, which along with the general improvement in level of care by parents reduced infant mortality and provided the basis for the demographic transition of the eighteenth century.

5. *Socialization Mode (Nineteenth to Mid-twentieth Centuries)*: As projections continued to diminish, the raising of a child became less a process of conquering its will than of training it, guiding it into proper paths, teaching it to conform, socializing it. The socializing mode is still thought of by most people as the only model within which discussion of child care can proceed, and it has been the source of all twentieth-century psychological models, from Freud's "channeling of impulses" to Skinner's behaviorism. Also, in the nineteenth century, the father for the first time begins to take more than an occasional interest in the child, training it, and sometimes even relieving the mother of child-care chores.

6. *Helping Mode (Begins Mid-twentieth Century)*: The helping mode involves the proposition that the child knows better than the parent what it needs at each stage of its life, and fully involves both parents in the child's life as they work to empathize with and fulfill its expanding and particular needs. There is no attempt at all to discipline or form "habits." Children are neither struck nor scolded, and are apologized to if yelled at under stress. The helping mode involves an enormous amount of time, energy, and discussion on the part of both parents, especially in the first six years, for helping a young child reach its daily goals means continually responding to it, playing with it, tolerating its regressions, being its servant rather than the other way around, interpreting its emotional conflicts, and providing the objects specific to its evolving interests.

Each of these six modes of child rearing produced specific historical personality types, which in turn formed the basis for the historical periods of the past. Early Christianity, for example, directly acted out the infanticidal mode of the killing of a Son under orders of the Father. Believers were "buried with Christ" and were baptized and fed wine and bread as repetitions of the washing and feeding of those newborn babies who were allowed to live. Medieval adults defended against fears of abandonment through complicated "I won't abandon you" bonds of feudal loyalty. Renaissance ambivalent-mode parenting produced depressive personalities, Hamlet being the paradigm, who felt *proud* of their melancholy as a historical advance. The modern world's intrusive parenting gave us the standard compulsive personality—Freud's "anal personality," Fromm's "hoarding character"—more recently "socialized" into the various types of anxiety characters that form the "best and brightest" in our society today.

This new "psychogenic theory of history" views the evolution of parent-child relations as an independent source of historical change, producing a "generational pressure" for psychic change each time a parent faces a child and attempts to regress to the child's psychic age and work through the anxieties of that age in a better manner than they had experienced with their own parents. The process is similar to psychoanalysis, which also involves regression and a second chance to face childhood anxieties. The term "psychogenic" reflects the notion that the ultimate source of all new historical personalities is not economics but psychic interaction between generations, thereby putting *love* at the center of historical change and viewing man as less *homo economicus* than *homo relatens*. Each time a child challenges an adult to help it meet its needs, history is determined anew. When the adult cannot respond, it is called "discipline" and history is frozen at the parent's level; when the adult meets the child's need, it is called "psychogenesis" and a new historical personality is forged. Thus Love, not Reason, Id, not Ego, move history.

Here is a recent account of a child terribly abused, of adults who stepped in to try to help, and of the poignant results.

The mistreated child was returned by the state to his "rightful" parents.

They Tried to Help

BOB GREENE, Chicago *Sun-Times*

CHICAGO—This is what happens to a two-year-old boy who is beaten to the point of torture.

The story is told by two families who tried to help the little boy, and who found out that no one cares enough to do anything about it.

The story begins a little over two weeks ago. Mr. and Mrs. Gene Skoda were asked by Cheryl Nelson, a woman they had known since childhood, if they would take care of Mrs. Nelson's son Ryan—for "a while." The Skodas replied negatively; they have four children of their own, and on several other occasions had agreed to watch Ryan "for a few hours" that turned into several days.

When Mr. and Mrs. Skoda said no, they report that the mother telephoned them and said, "If you don't take this kid, I may kill him. I can't stand him, and I'm really going to hurt him."

Hearing that, the couple agreed to take the little boy. They say that the mother brought him to their apartment the next morning, put him on the floor, and said, "Here he is, but he's all beat up."

At that point, Mrs. Skoda had only time to notice the boy's face, which was bruised, and she asked the mother what had happened.

"Oh, you know how it is," the mother reportedly replied. "You just get mad and hit them." She said that that morning, she had finally "had enough of that kid," because he had eaten two pieces of chicken out of the refrigerator and had spilled some milk, trying to pour himself a glass while she slept.

She then turned and left, without leaving her address (the Skodas knew that she lived somewhere in the neighborhood, but not exactly where). Skoda picked up the little boy and began to examine him closely.

Skoda said he became physically ill when he looked at the child.

Ryan had large knots on each side of his forehead. He had an enormous bump on the back of his head. A patch of his hair had been pulled out. There was a bump on top of his head. His face was covered with scratches, bruises, and small cuts. His right ear was swollen and bruised. The area behind his ear was black and blue. There were actually fingerprints on his throat, which had turned purple where he evidently had been choked.

On the palm of one of the little boy's hands was a fresh cigarette burn. On his back were numerous bruises, along with two older cigarette burns. Ryan wet his pants, and when the Skodas tried to change him he went into hysterics. They discovered that his penis was black and blue.

His stomach was swollen, his ribs protruding. There were blisters on his feet and between the toes. His shoes were size 5. When the Skodas took him to get new shoes, they found that he needed size 7, and they could not believe that his feet had been jammed into the other pair.

The Skodas were shaken and uncertain about what to do. They drove to the home of Skoda's sister and brother-in-law, Mr. and Mrs. William Coleman. The Colemans were as deeply affected as the Skodas had been. The Skodas told the Colemans that the boy's mother had repeatedly said she did not want the child. The Colemans said that they would let Ryan live with them and their two children until the mother could be contacted.

"It was pity at first that moved us to take Ryan," Mrs. Coleman said Monday. "But it's amazing how quickly that pity turned to affection. He is one of the most loving and lovable children I have ever seen. The Skodas told us that Ryan's mother had said, 'He is a stranger, I can't stand him.' We thought that perhaps we could let him stay with us, and save him from being hurt any more. We had no idea of the nightmare that was about to happen."

Mrs. Coleman said her first concern was to restore Ryan

to health. "He's nothing more than a baby, really," she said. "I wanted to give him a little sense of security, even if it was only for a short time."

Ryan began to heal. The Colemans said that in the next two weeks, the child was happy; he laughed and played with their children. Then Cheryl Nelson, Ryan's mother, called the Skodas. She said she had been in the hospital to have another baby boy. She did not ask about Ryan.

The Skodas explained that the child was at the home of another family, who loved Ryan and wanted him permanently. The mother then reportedly said, "Gee, I'm not sure, I'll have to think about it."

Mrs. Nelson was supposed to telephone again the next day, but did not. Three days passed. Finally Cheryl Nelson's own mother called, and said that she would pick up the boy for Cheryl. Skoda explained about the condition Ryan had been in when he had been taken in. "Oh, my God," the grandmother said. She said she would talk to Mrs. Nelson.

The next morning, Mrs. Nelson appeared at the Skodas' home, accompanied by policemen. She demanded that Ryan be given back to her. The Skodas told their story; the officers were sympathetic. According to the Skodas, the policemen said that the law might not always be just, but that under the law a mother has a right to her child.

It was agreed that Ryan—who was still at the Colemans' house—should be brought to the Skodas' that night at 8 P.M., and that a decision would be made at that time about what would happen next.

When the Colemans were told that Mrs. Nelson was demanding Ryan back, they called the child-abuse hotline of the Illinois Department of Children and Family Services. The man at the bureau checked his files; he said that there was already a file on Ryan Nelson.

(A check by the Chicago *Sun-Times* Monday showed that Ryan and other children in the Nelson family have been the subject of investigations by the department.)

The man at the hotline gave Mrs. Coleman the telephone

number of a caseworker at the Department of Children and Family Services who had been assigned to Ryan. Mrs. Coleman called the number. She was told that the caseworker no longer worked there. She was told to wait until it could be determined who the new caseworker was. She was put on hold. She remained on hold from 4:35 until 5 P.M., at which time her call was disconnected.

Mrs. Coleman called the main hotline number again. The man on duty said that Mrs. Coleman should turn Ryan over to the police herself; he said that the police would take the child to a hospital, contact youth workers, and make sure that the mother did not gain immediate custody of him. Then, he said, the Colemans could work with the Department of Children and Family Services to try to have Ryan placed in their home.

"We were so concerned," Mrs. Coleman said Monday. "Ryan had undergone such wonderful emotional and physical improvements. He had gained eleven pounds, and many of the bruises and blisters were healing considerably. Where in the beginning he would only mumble, or sit perfectly still, now he laughed and talked in sentences and seemed to be so happy.

"I don't mean to imply that we did anything spectacular. All it took was the normal care that a normal person would give a two-year-old boy. Plus some love."

That night, the Colemans took Ryan to the Skodas' house, under the impression that if they signed papers testifying to the abuse, Ryan would not immediately be turned over to the mother. But Mrs. Nelson insisted on having Ryan back. So the child, along with his mother, the Colemans, and the Skodas, went to the Deering district police station.

"A policeman told us not to worry; he said that Ryan would not have to go back to his mother," Mrs. Coleman said Monday. "He made a call and said that the authorities had a file on Cheryl Nelson in connection with Ryan and her other children. He said that there was no way that, with that record, Ryan would have to go back to his home.

"We felt a little better. But then two policewomen arrived, from the youth division. They questioned us as if we were the offenders. They kept referring to the fact that we had no doctor's report to substantiate our 'claims.'

"We asked if seeing the bruises, marks, and scars that still remained wasn't enough. One of the policewomen replied, 'No. I'm no doctor.' So we asked if a doctor couldn't be called in to examine Ryan and determine how he was injured and how old the wounds were. They said no, because 'no doctor wants to get involved, and it really takes a lot before a doctor will sign child-abuse papers.' "

At 2 A.M., the policewoman said that Ryan was being given back to his mother.

"We were stunned," Mrs. Coleman said. "Up until then, the other policemen we had talked to made it clear that under no circumstances would Ryan be sent home to the mother—he'd either be turned over to family services, or to us. We began to cry. It wasn't that we were thinking how much we loved him and would hate losing him that made us cry—it was knowing what he was going back to, and that it could happen again."

The policewoman said that they had contacted the Department of Children and Family Services and that since Ryan's was a "borderline" case, he could be returned to his mother.

By that time, Ryan—and Cheryl Nelson—had left the police station.

"We were told that we could contact the family services department next morning, but that it would probably be futile," Mrs. Coleman said. "I guess they were right. We called three times, and never had the call returned. We tried again, but they were evidently closed, because there was no answer."

Now Mr. and Mrs. Coleman believe there is no way to help Ryan.

"We've called, we've begged, we've prayed," Mrs. Coleman said Monday. "Our own lawyer told us that there's nothing that can be done until Ryan is abused again. But then it may be too late!

"One of the policemen we talked to put it perfectly. He said that 'we keep taking the kids away from parents like that, but they always get them back!' So what can we do?

"Is there anything we can do?

"We pray that we can get Ryan back with us. But if we can't have that miracle—isn't there some way that we can shake people enough to keep that little boy safe?

"Doesn't anyone understand that Ryan is a little boy with feelings—who needs help desperately? It could happen to him again. He's not a piece of paperwork—he's a human being who might die soon if someone doesn't do something.

"Can't anyone do anything?"

Removed from her home because her mother was allegedly beating her, Deb was locked up for three months in the County Youth Home, where the rules were less humane than those for adults sentenced to a maximum-security prison. Punishment was meted out for looking out the window or going to the bathroom at night. All letters going out and coming in were screened and censored. Personal belongings were not permitted, not even a comb or a pencil and paper, and she was forced to sleep on a mattress on the floor. Sometimes it almost seemed like a contest between the home and the state to see who could do more damage.

In New York City in only one year, twenty-two thousand children were battered and abused by parents, and the courts handled it by sending many of them to such shelters, to live with criminals and the retarded.

Do You Want to Get Beat Up at Home or in Prison?
"DEB"

DETROIT, Mich. (FPS) The Wayne County Youth Home is generally used as a short-term jail for young people accused or convicted of having committed crimes. But not everyone in it is there for this reason. Children whose parents have mistreated them are also detained there.

A legal suit has now been filed in an attempt to stop this practice. The suit charges that the living conditions in the home are inhuman—it is greatly overcrowded; educational, recreational and eating facilities are bad; and there is little communication with the outside. In addition, the ward supervisor and other personnel severely punish anyone who breaks any of a myriad of rules—speaking without permission, looking out the windows of the ward, "slowness" in reacting to a supervisor's command, possessing personal belongings or reading material not approved and issued by the staff (all recent issues of magazines or newspapers are prohibited, so is watching the news on TV).

Punishments used on children who violate these rules, according to the suit, include the following:

1. "Isolation"—any child may be locked up in a small room with only the bare essentials (a bare mattress, no sheets or blankets, a toilet, a window) for periods of up to three days. This may be extended indefinitely "with permission" from higher personnel.

2. "Tracking"—a child is forced to stand on a square piece of the linoleum floor without moving, sometimes with her/his arms outstretched, for periods of up to eight hours.

3. "Clonking"—a child is hit severely on the head by the supervisor using her/his keys and/or key chain. This is done constantly, the suit charges, at the whim and fancy of the supervisor.

4. "Paddling"—a child (usually a boy) is spanked by the supervisor, using a wooden paddle, and with great force.

Below, we have reprinted an affidavit filed by one of the girls who was kept in the home. As you read it, keep in mind that she has committed *no crime*; she is being kept there only because her parents mistreated her.

Youth and the Law

THE AFFIDAVIT

DEB _____, being first duly sworn, deposes and says as follows:

1. I was held in the Wayne County Youth Home for approximately three months, from the beginning of February 1971 until the beginning of May 1971. I was held there not for anything I had done or been accused of, but because my parents had allegedly beaten me. Although I am only sixteen I am intelligent and I remember very well what the Youth Home was like and how I felt being there.

2. The girls in the Wayne County Youth Home are divided into units, one for each floor. I was in more than one unit while I was there. The girls in each unit mostly ate together and went to school together. I found out that some of the girls in the units I was in were there for the same reason I was, but others had committed crimes or had run away. One girl had stabbed and killed someone, and others had taken dope. I heard some girls planning break-ins for when they got out, but I tried not to listen. While I was in the Youth Home I tried not to become sneaky or hardened, like many of the girls, but it was difficult not to.

3. There were always more girls in the units I was in than there were beds in the rooms. Nearly all the time I was in the Youth Home I slept on a mattress on the floor in a hall. The light was always on and it was hard to sleep. We ate meals in our unit's common room; since everyone could not fit at the little tables, some of us ate sitting on the floor or on a bed.

We ate from metal plates that looked like dog dishes to me, and we had only spoons to eat with.

4. There were many things we couldn't do. They made me feel like I was in a prison because I had done something wrong. Some of the rules were that we were never allowed to look out a window and we weren't allowed to keep anything at all of our own—we couldn't even have a picture of our parents or a handkerchief. In some units I was in we couldn't have a comb and we were not allowed to come out of our room or leave our mattress at night even to go to the bathroom. We had to wear only the clothes supplied by the Youth Home. There were heavy screens on all the windows and we were always locked in. We never had any free time where we could decide what to do—we were always told what to do.

5. In the Wayne County Youth Home I felt very lonely. I had been cut off from all my family and friends without warning. In the Youth Home I was never permitted to use the phone. We were allowed to write letters only to our mother, father, or legal guardian. We could write only on Wednesdays and could not keep the pencils or paper for other times. My letters were always read by the women in charge before they were sent. Once, I wrote a letter to my father and the floor supervisor wouldn't send it. She told me the reason was that she disapproved of what I had written. I thought it was because I had written about the Youth Home. Whenever other girls I knew wrote about conditions in the Youth Home, their letters did not get sent. The mail we received sometimes had parts scratched out by the supervisors before we got it.

6. Most of the time I was in the Youth Home, the only visitor I was allowed to have was my mother. She was allowed to come only once a week. Finally, a few weeks before I got out, a nun who taught at my regular school, Sister Jolene, was allowed to see me once a week. Also, my parents' student attorneys visited me during the two weeks before they got me out.

7. Some of the time I was in the Wayne County Youth Home I went to school at the Home. I didn't start school until four weeks after I had been put in the Youth Home. I was

supposed to wait two weeks before starting school because everybody does, but I had to wait four weeks. They told me it was
because of overcrowding. I had nothing to do while I waited
to start school but sit around all day. When I finally went to
the Youth Home School, I went to class with all the girls in
my unit. They were ages eight to sixteen and we were all in
class together. I was in tenth grade before being put in the
Youth Home, but we used a book at the Youth Home school
that I had used in fifth grade in my regular school. I didn't
keep up at all with my regular school work. When I went back
to my regular school, I was very far behind and had to do extra
work every day to try to catch up. I don't know for sure yet,
but I might have failed some classes.

8. We were not allowed to see the nurse unless our supervisor
gave permission at the evening sick line. All the time I was
in the Youth Home I had a bad rash on my face and head
and was always itchy. Only after my parents' attorneys talked
to the supervisor, a few weeks before I got out, did the supervisor let me see the nurse about the rash. The nurse gave me
enough cream to put on once and said to come back every night
because the harsh soap was causing the rash, but the supervisor
never let me go back again. She said I just wanted to see my
friends in Unit Three, so I couldn't go. When I had bad cramps
and needed a pain pill, I had to show a soiled sanitary pad
first for proof before I could go to the nurse. This made me
feel embarrassed and like nobody trusted me.

9. In the three months I was in the Youth Home, I was allowed to go outside only twice. Once, we went out in gym class
for a few minutes. The other time, our unit went out to play
baseball. This was the day before I got out. We had no coats
to wear and only wore our Youth Home uniforms and sweaters.
When two girls, Robin and Barbara Durr, asked our supervisor
why we couldn't go outside more, she said it was too cold to
go without coats and we couldn't go out with coats on or we
could climb over the wall and escape. Outside the wall we
wouldn't be noticed so much with coats on over our Youth
Home uniforms, she said.

10. If we broke any rules we were disciplined by being put alone in one of the discipline rooms. There were four of these rooms on each floor—they were little rooms with only a bed and sink and toilet, and the doors could be kept locked. The supervisor said if we were really bad we would go to the Wayne County jail. I was put in a disciplinary room twice for a few hours. I was very scared at the thought of being put in the room. There was usually someone in a disciplinary room every day. Girls in discipline were kept from going to school. I saw girls kept there three or four days, and one girl, Joann, was there for a week. A girl named Wanda, who was ten years old, was locked in a room with no mattress and with the water turned off until she stopped acting wild. She stayed all day like that. She was locked up because she wouldn't go to sleep.

11. I think I cried every day that I was in the Youth Home. I usually cried myself to sleep, which I don't normally do. Most nights, I had nightmares and woke up crying. I don't usually do that in my own home.

12. I was assigned a probation officer named Mrs. Martin. She said to call her my "worker," but I knew she was a probation officer. I didn't like it. I kept wondering why I was being kept in the Youth Home, and if I hadn't done anything, why I needed a probation officer. I felt like I had committed a crime. Mrs. Martin kept trying to convince me of things—she kept saying, "You don't want to go home, do you?" She told me about other homes and schools I could go to, but I don't trust them any more now that I know what the Youth Home is like. There isn't anything I can think of that anyone could do to me that would ever make me want to go back to the Youth Home or to any other state school or home.

"Children have a right to grow up nurtured by affectionate parents," proclaimed the White House Conference on Children (1970). But in this case, reported by Sanford N. Katz of the

*Boston College Law School, the agency argued in court that
". . . because of the great love of the foster parents for the
child, Laura should be removed from their custody and placed
in a neutral environment." Despite a psychiatrist's testimony
that Laura needed the security of a sustained relationship with
her foster parents, the agency won.*

Who Looks After Laura?
SANFORD N. KATZ

The history of Laura, the five-and-a-half-year-old child whose
custody was at issue in the New York case of *In the matter
of Jewish Child Care Association,* is similar to that of many
other children who are similarly involved in the struggle of
foster parents to adopt children over the objections of placement agencies. When Laura was thirteen months old, she was
placed by the Jewish Child Care Association, a foster-care
agency, with Mr. and Mrs. Sanders, a childless couple in their
thirties. Laura's mother, eighteen years old and unwed, had
been unable to care for the baby at birth and had placed her
with the New York City Department of Welfare, which transferred the child's custody to the Jewish Child Care Association
(hereinafter referred to as the Agency).

At placement, the Sanderses were required to sign a document in which mutual promises were exchanged. Among other
things, the couple promised to accept Laura as a member of
their family and, as foster parents, to give her affection and care.
They promised to follow the Agency's regulations regarding the
boarding arrangement, notification of and care during the
child's illnesses, and changes in living conditions that would affect the child, such as modifications caused by vacations, job
changes, and other events. They also agreed to co-operate with
the Agency's plans for continuing a relationship with the child's
natural mother. Should the couple be unable to continue as
foster parents, they promised to work with the Agency in making an orderly transition to another placement. The Sanderses

acknowledged that they were accepting Laura for an indeterminate period and were aware that the "legal responsibility for the child" remained with the Agency.

During the first year after placement, the Sanderses spoke with the Agency about adopting Laura. They were told that adoption was not possible and were asked to help the child understand who her natural mother was. The child had seen her natural mother once during the first year of placement. During the second year of foster care, the Sanderses again mentioned their desire to adopt Laura. The Agency refused to consider the proposal and required the couple, as a condition for keeping the child, to sign a statement acknowledging that they had the child only on a foster-home basis. Despite the signed statement, the Sanderses persisted in their efforts to adopt Laura, unsuccessfully seeking approval from the child's natural mother, grandmother, and other relatives. When the Sanderses requested permission to take Laura with them on an out-of-state vacation, the Agency refused, asserting that the child should be returned to her natural mother during that time. Laura, then four, had lived with the Sanderses for three years and had seen her natural mother only twice. She was not to see her mother again until the litigation over her custody began.

The Sanderses' constant efforts to adopt Laura in contradiction of their statements, along with the Agency's belief that the couple had become too emotionally attached to the child, prompted the Agency to demand Laura's return. The couple refused, and the Agency brought a writ of habeas corpus to demand the child's release from the Sanderses' home. As seen from the perspective of the foster parents, the Agency's action was potentially beneficial for various reasons. It allowed the Sanderses to bypass administrative remedies and to obtain an immediate judicial review of the Agency's decision denying their adoptive suitability. Considering their strained relations with the Agency, the Sanderses' chances for administrative relief would probably have been slim. Furthermore, since a habeas corpus proceeding is a method by which a court may explore the child's welfare beyond the narrow issue of the legal right to custody, the fact that the Agency was the legal guardian of Laura did not place it in a significantly advantageous position vis-à-vis the Sanderses.

The Trial

In the trial-court proceedings to determine whether Laura's "best interests" would be served by a custodial change, much of the testimony was focused on the effect that the proposed change would have on the child's natural mother as well as on the child's own physical and emotional well-being. The line of questioning in which the trial judge and the attorneys engaged seemed to be based on the underlying assumption that the goal of the proceedings was to determine how Laura's needs could best be secured in light of the inability of the natural mother to raise the child.

The trial judge heard testimony from the foster parents, representatives of the Agency, the Department of Welfare, and a psychiatrist. The Agency acknowledged that the Sanderses had taken good care of the child and were providing her with a comfortable home environment. However, it claimed that, because of the great love of the foster parents for the child, Laura should be removed from their custody and placed in a "neutral environment," where foster parents would be called "aunt" and "uncle" instead of "mother" and "father" and where "there would not be this terrible pull on the child between her loyalty to her foster parents and her mother." In other words, the Agency did not claim that the foster parents were depriving the child of love but, rather, argued that they were indulging her with too much love. The effect of their indulgence on the child, the Agency urged, was a strain on her relationship with her natural mother.

A large part of the trial consisted of the interrogation of a psychiatrist called by the foster parents. In his testimony, he analyzed the effect of a custodial change on Laura's emotional development. In his opinion, the Sanderses' love for the child had positive rather than damaging emotional effects; indeed, Laura's removal from her foster parents would be detrimental to her emotional growth. He stated that latency was a critical period in a child's development and that, at Laura's age, she needed the security of a sustained relationship with her foster parents.

The trial judge apparently either was not sufficiently convinced by the psychiatric testimony or was persuaded by the Agency's argument that the child was becoming too attached to her foster parents, thus threatening her "relationship" with her natural mother. He decided to remove Laura from her foster parents and to allow the Agency to regain custody and place her in a "neutral environment." After the intermediate appellate court affirmed the decision of the trial court, the Sanderses appealed to the New York Court of Appeals, which held in favor of the Agency in a split (4–3) opinion.

The Appeal

In the New York Court of Appeals' report, there is a discernible and major shift in emphasis from that found in the lower court's opinion. The trial court viewed "the best interests of the child" doctrine in terms of securing Laura's health needs in light of her natural mother's condition. The New York Court of Appeals first concentrated on the legal status of the claimants and then interpreted "the best interests of the child" in terms of the continuity of family loyalty and the law.

To the majority of the Court of Appeals, the fact that the Sanderses were Laura's *foster*, rather than natural or future adoptive, parents was crucial. The court perceived foster parenthood as something less than full parenthood. By showing "extreme love," "affection," and "possessiveness," and by acting more like natural than like foster parents, the Sanderses, in the court's estimation, had gone beyond the limits of their role as set out in the placement agreement. In essence, what the ma-

jority took as conclusive in the case, namely the "vital fact
. . . that Mr. and Mrs. Sanders are not, and presumably will
never be, Laura's parents by adoption," was the very issue the
court was to decide.

The court stressed its concern for preserving the natural ties
between Laura and her mother. "In considering what is in
Laura's best interests," the court wrote, "it was not only proper,
but necessary . . . to consider the facts in terms of their significance to Laura's eventual return to her own mother." And
later the court stated:

> What is essentially at stake here is the parental custodial
> right. Although Child Care has the present legal right to
> custody . . . it stands, as against the Sanders, in a repre-
> sentative capacity as the protector of Laura's mother's in-
> choate custodial right and the parent-child relationship
> which is to become complete in the future.

Finally, in its concluding remarks, the court crystallized its main
preferences as follows:

> [T]he more important considerations of the child's best
> interests, the recognition and preservation of her mother's
> primary love and custodial interest, and the future life of
> the mother and child together are paramount.

Family loyalty. The parental right to custody, the doctrine
referred to by the court as both "paramount" and "fundamental," holds that any biological parent is entitled to the custody
of his child unless the parent is affirmatively shown to be unfit.
Many courts have claimed that the right is based on principles
of morality and natural affection. However, the common-law
history of the doctrine reveals that it may have been created
for considerations of wealth rather than the dictates of a moral
code. During the feudal period, custodial rights, which had commercial value, were subject to transfer and sale; a child was a
financial asset to his father. During this early period, therefore,
a custodial right was a property right. In time, as concern de-

veloped for the child's welfare and as the mother was legally considered a joint custodian together with the father, the emphasis shifted from the property theory of custody toward the personal-status theory. That is, the natural parents, because of their relationship to the child, were presumed to be the custodians best fitted to serve the child's needs.

At first glance, the parental right to custody may seem to be a doctrine competing with "the best interests of the child" approach. Indeed, the parental-right theory has been described as a secondary doctrine in child-custody matters. Perhaps, however, it is more appropriate to say that the parental-right doctrine is often treated as if it were an expression of "the best interests of the child." Most frequently courts, invoking the parental-right doctrine when they prefer to award custody to the child's natural parents rather than other claimants, assume that the disposition best serves the child's welfare. When custody is awarded to others, it is likely that courts will simply state that "the best interests of the child" demand such a disposition, or that "the superior rights" of parents, or the presumption in their favor, must yield to "the best interests of the child." It seems safe to say that when courts invoke the parental-right doctrine to award custody to the natural parents, they are merely articulating an archaic notion, based upon a preference for the continuity of blood ties or the preservation of kinship loyalty, in order to justify a decision. It is a significant aspect of *Child Care* that the majority was more concerned with the *symbol* of natural family loyalty than its *fact*. As indicated previously, Laura's natural mother had seen the child twice in four years, and Laura's loyalty to her would seem, at best, to be more imaginary than real.

Integrity of the law. In his final remark in his opinion for the Court of Appeals, Chief Judge Conway came to grips with what appeared to be his primary concern. While the interests of Laura and her natural mother (but apparently not those of the foster parents) were of significant importance, another factor was involved. The integrity of the law, as manifested in the child-placement contract and in the administrative decisions of a private agency, had been challenged. In order to maintain authority, these administrative policies had to be affirmed and the child-placement agreement enforced: "[T]he program of agencies such as Child Care . . . may not be subverted by foster parents who breach their trust."

The majority in *Child Care* was again concerned with symbols. Judge Conway seemed compelled to preserve the sanctity of legal doctrines and, indirectly, the reputation of a community institution. The Sanderses had been a threat both to the integrity and the stability of the placement contract and to the prestige of the Agency. To give Laura to her foster parents would have been to reward persons who had failed to fulfill their promises and who had undermined the Agency's decision. It seems that by protecting community institutions, the court shifted its focus from Laura's welfare to other matters: the continuity of legal doctrine and the prestige of a social-service agency.

Child-custody proceedings, more than other litigation, may be merely a cover for the real conflicts: a power struggle between individuals, institutions, or individuals and institutions, that culminates in a decision that indicates a preference for certain social values over others. It is sometimes said that, in child-custody disputes between divorced parents, the child may act as a tool of the parents and the court as an arena in which the parents can display their mutual hostilities. In *Child Care*, one was not witnessing an intrafamily conflict but, rather, a struggle between community institutions: welfare agency and foster family. The important question before the court was not necessarily who should be awarded custody of Laura, although this inevitably was resolved, but whose decision-making power was to be recognized, the welfare agency's or the foster parents'. In *Child Care*, the Agency prevailed, and the decision therefore may be described as one which furthered the best interests of the *Agency*. Whether it was in the best interests of the child is hard to say. The psychiatrist and a dissenting judge thought it was not.

*Perhaps Larry's foster homes would be called neutral by the
agency that took Laura away from her adoring foster parents,
but Larry didn't see them that way. Now a college senior, Larry
has become articulate enough to speak for the 350,000 children
in the United States.*

Foster Homes That Are Not "Too Loving"

JEAN DIETZ, *Globe* Staff

There are six thousand children now growing up in foster
homes in Massachusetts under the protection of the state.
Thousands more have outgrown their foster homes.

Larry, a twenty-three-year-old college senior, is one of them.
His life as a foster child, he thinks, was not the best and possibly
not the worst although it was more bad than good.

Larry, not his real name, would like to see more control over
the welfare of children who are sent to private homes where
foster parents are paid for the care of the children by the state.

He began his life in foster care at the age of three, soon after
the birth of his younger brother. That's when his mother was
taken to a state mental institution for keeps.

Seven children were left for his father, a construction laborer,
to care for, but working two jobs, sixteen hours a day, proved
too much. In five years his father was dead.

During that five years Larry was housed at Nazareth in Ja-
maica Plain, a child-care center staffed by Sisters of Charity for
the Archdiocese of Boston. All of the children of Larry's family
came home to their father on weekends.

"When my father died, something happened inside. I was
about eight years old then. They said I became unmanageable,"
he recalled.

The eight-year-old boy left Nazareth with a social worker to
be introduced in his first foster home, one of five he would live
in, in addition to two institutions, two private schools, and a
variety of summer camps.

Things started to go wrong immediately. Larry now thinks this was because he just wasn't ready to become a "stranger's child."

The couple was very nice, he said, upper-class childless people who also took one of his brothers and later adopted him.

"The whole thing came apart because they tried too hard to become my parents, and I knew inside I had parents or at least used to have," he said.

Another social worker took Larry to a home in Hopkinton, where there were twenty-five children, twenty boys and five girls ranging in age from about eight to fourteen.

He labeled this the worst foster home in his experience.

The foster mother demanded to be called "Mommy," and her second order was that Larry give up all of his clothes for community use by the other children.

Larry was assigned a bed with three other boys, one of whom was a bed wetter. For six months, Larry wore the same dungarees before they were washed for the first time, he said.

All of the children were too scared to talk when social workers came to check on conditions, he said, so after eighteen months he ran away.

Natick police then picked up the scrawny eleven-year-old and asked why he didn't want to go back.

"I told the truth about the woman and how the kids were treated, but the police said I had to go back. A reporter in the police station heard the story and printed it in the Natick paper," he added.

Larry said "Mommy" gave him the worst beating of his life and demanded he retract the story in the newspaper. He refused.

A few weeks later, a social worker took him away. Soon after that a law was passed to prevent so many foster children being housed in one home.

"I think that is why they always tried to place me in a nice home—one that I might like," he said.

He was placed in a home in Everett along with three other foster children, and from there he was moved to a Dorchester home where he slept with nine other boys in a third-floor room.

After six months there he got into trouble for telling jokes in school and was scheduled to be hit with a rattan.

"I can't accept a stranger hitting me; I ran," he said. He hid in the cellar of a friend's home in Everett but was picked up later by police, who transferred him to the Roslindale Detention Center of the former Youth Service Board.

"They didn't know what to do with me. Every month, they'd trot me into court but the judge would continue the case. Although I had not been charged with anything, I stayed there six months," he said.

He was sent to a summer camp in Brewster, "which was a real nice place," and then, as fall arrived, he made short-lived attempts to live with relatives that ended with two years at the Hillside School in Marlboro and two more years at Thompson's Academy, on an island in Boston Harbor.

Although Larry claims to have had close to one hundred social workers in his life, only one, he said, made any difference.

That was Joe Leavey, now head of the Division of Youth Service.

"He was the only one who asked me what I wanted and where I wanted to go," said Larry.

In three years, Larry graduated from Brookline high school and is about to finish college.

Despite the money spent by the state on providing "humane care" for Larry, he claims to have been half starved at times, has had to steal for food, has been beaten by foster mothers and now is blind in one eye from a condition which could have been readily corrected in childhood if medical care had been available.

After a young lifetime in foster care, his advice to others making decisions about foster children is simple. "If the children are old enough to talk, please ask them what they think. Listen. They will tell you the truth."

One rages within against parents who brutalize innocent and defenseless children. One readily concedes that in such cases the child's rights must supersede that of the abusive or "battering" parent. And one even has the impulse to confront such parents, to try to open their eyes to the damage they are doing. But the danger of doing that, as this extraordinary report by Thomas Cottle reveals, is that one discovers that the abusive parent, too, is a human being more sinned against than sinning. Shall such parents, having themselves suffered brutalization and abandonment, now become victims anew, this time of our self-righteousness? Theodore Solotaroff wrote of Cottle's book The Abandoners, *from which this is an excerpt, "He knows the difference between facing a problem and facing a face." His deep humanity reminds us that the abused child is not just a problem in social technics, but part of a human tragedy of awesome depth, in which all parties command compassion.*

The Child Is Father to the Man
THOMAS J. COTTLE

Eight o'clock at night and I'm walking into a darkened neighborhood where people live who have nothing whatsover in the world in common with me except for one troubled youth who cuts school and comes to see me, and talks poetry. Gerard Manley Hopkins!

Then the apartment building; walking up decaying wooden steps to a freshly painted front door; the inside hall; the names on the mailboxes; the inner door, which surely has not been locked in years, leading to the apartments; the worn rubber treads on the stairs, and the shabby halls. What's the use of describing these scenes any more?

"That you, Cottle?" It was *his* voice coming from the very top. That's his voice, eh? Jesus. Thunder had rumbled in the poorly lighted stairwell. That you, Cottle, huh? I felt myself whistling in that breathy way, whisper whistling or whatever it's called. At last I made it to the top, panting a trifle more than I really had to, just to make him believe I was older than I was; out of shape and all that.

"I'm glad to meet you, Mr. Holden," I said. "Fact, I'm just glad to make it up these stairs. You gotta be a young man to negotiate them." I smiled. He looked quizzical. I held out my hand. He said, "Yeah," and turned to go inside. We were both shaking our heads. But, no matter, for whatever happened I was taller than he was, and men know that that always matters. Moreover, I had been in this home before with Peter, and whether or not Mr. Holden knew this, the fact remained that I had something going with his son and knew my way around. Funny, I remember wondering at the time what it must be like to face the husband of a woman with whom one is having an affair.

"You've been here before, so you know where the living room is," he said without looking at me. "I'm going in the kitchen for a beer. You want one?"

"No. No, thanks. I just ate and I think I'm set."

"Don't be so polite. Around here you don't have to be so polite. We ain't Harvard here. I'll bring a beer in, maybe you'll change your mind."

Malcolm Holden was a man of average height with a sizable chest and belly, particularly his belly. It was large and taut under the long-sleeved, checkered sport shirt. He wore freshly cleaned beige trousers, shiny loafers, and white socks. His features were small, but his nose and lips were thick. Barely visible pockmarks lined the upper rim of his cheeks. I recall going through a list of his characteristics, attempting to match them with my expectations of him. The face was red enough, the arms and neck and belly big enough, the thinning silver hair and hairline just about right, and the quality of his features, actually, not that far off. But those pants! And the loafers and white socks! Indeed, the whole clean appearance. That I hadn't counted on. He had returned with two cans of beer. "You wanna glass?"

"No. Don't need one. This is perfect."

"Who you kidding? You never drink beer from a can unless

you wanna impress the old lady. Right?" He laughed the words almost as one reads them in a book. Hah, hah, hah, hah, hah.

"I gotta admit, you're right, Mr. Holden."

"Out of a can, eh?"

"Yeah, I'm sorry. I think I just wanted to make it easier for you."

"Huh?"

"You know, save you the trouble of getting glasses and all."

"Oh." There was a pause.

"I'm really very happy that we could get a chance, maybe, to speak a bit about Peter," I started. Another pause.

"Yeah?" Listen, you sonofabitch, I thought. Don't you just sit there with that gut of yours, giving out with "huh's" and "yeah's" and "oh's." I didn't come here for that. You won the first round with the beer cans and the glasses routine, but don't forget for a minute that you've lost the other fourteen rounds when it comes to your kids, and to your wife. Man, if this is the kind of shit you hand out to your family on a regular basis, if this is what those family therapist types are used to dealing with, then it's no wonder Peter is . . .

"I've been spending some time talking with him, you know, and I thought we should talk," I heard myself saying. "You and I, that is. Peter didn't suggest it, I want you to know that. I thought it might be a good idea, you know, and that's why I called you."

"You're the guy who did, . . . ah . . . with my son John, aren't you." It was not a question.

"Yessir."

"Sent him off to college and all that."

"He's a terrific kid."

"I wouldn't know."

"I don't understand," I said. We were sitting in the living room, I on an old couch facing a bricked-up fireplace painted green to match the wall, Mr. Holden on an easy chair at right angles to me. There was a silence as he sat erect and still, looking at me as though to say, so you're the guy I have to compete with for the *possession* of my sons. So you're the guy. A phony drinker, phony panting, overly polite, long-haired intruder who can't even handle an eleven-word question: "I'm going in the kitchen for a beer. You want one?" So you're the guy. You'll have to excuse me, but I can't believe it.

The even intensity of his staring was preventing me, suddenly, from getting in touch with the anger I was feeling for him. But it was there, along with plenty of other feelings: Hey, Mr. Holden, is this the room where you beat your wife? And is that the table your two little boys had to reset for dinner when you with your violence pulled the dishes off? Where's the bedroom where they had to drag her? And that reminds me, where do you hit Peter? In here, or do you take him into the kitchen or out back somewhere? Do you wear your clean after-work loafers and white socks when you beat him, or do you crack him while you still have on your mud-caked boots, which I saw out in the hall? Say, any traces of your wife's blood still on the floor? No, I suppose you can always move some of these throw rugs around to cover up the spots.

I smiled a faint smile, my cheeks feeling like iron weights. "Really, I don't understand. Don't you see Johnnie?"

"*John* and I never speak. That is, not since you and your little friends decided I wasn't doing a good job with him. I mean, not being a *real* father to him. Isn't that about it?"

"No, not really," I replied.

"Then, suppose you tell me just exactly what the truth *is*."

"Well, it's more our feeling that we like to work with kids, like Johnnie, and Peter—"

"Let's leave Peter out of this discussion for a moment, may we," he interrupted. "We'll get to *him* in a minute."

"Well, we feel that quite often schools fail children—" Why can't one tell these people right out what one believes. We hold back, saving it all for the parties and books and seminars. We make all sorts of pledges the night before our visits, but on their ground we're timid, compromising, and always compassionate, so we believe. Maybe in the end, that's the best way.

"They're not children, Doctor, ah, Cottle? Is it Cottle?"

"Yeah. Cottle. Please call me Tom. Yes. Anyway, so when

schools don't have the time to work with some of the kids we try to help out, too. A little bit. With their work and all."

"But you're a psychiatrist, aren't you?"

"No, not really. But I do work with some kids who are having psychological problems." My own words would have made me distrust me. Psychological problems. Disturbance. Trauma. Countertransference. Mr. Holden just sat there, immobile. Neither of us had taken a drink.

"You're not a psychiatrist, but you work with kids' problems. And who gives you the permission to do this?" he asked.

"Well, in this case, your wife."

"I see. I see. You mean what the father says doesn't matter any more. The world belongs to psychiatrists, mothers, and kids, eh?"

"Well, I don't really think . . ."

"You see what I'm saying? You follow me, Doctor?"

"Yessir."

"You don't have to yessir me, son. Save that for Harvard. I've been a welder's foreman three years here. Pretty young to have that job. I got now fifteen guys, damn good men, work for me. None of 'em calls me 'sir.' You don't have to call me 'sir.' It's not the words that matter, it's showing respect and appreciation day by day."

It was becoming a television show. Any minute, George C. Scott or one of those hip lawyers like Joseph Campanella or James Farentino would come out of the kitchen and take the whole thing over. It wasn't a *déjà vu*; we were playing out some cliché-ridden script. I could practically hear some swish director with a billowy-sleeved shirt and sleazy pants: Now, remember, Holden, you're an angry, bitter man who's lost faith in America and can't really admit it, if in fact he understands it. You gotta show that pressure, that never-explained tension. Know what I mean? You're a wife beater, a kid wrecker, you know the type, see 'em every day of your life, yet you believe deep down in your heart you're really doing the best you can and that guys like Cottle here, good or bad, right or wrong, have no right interfering in your life. For that matter, they got no business even being in your home. Okay. Good. Work on it. Now, Cottle, you've come in with anger to beat the band. So far so good. You know about this guy; you've gotten the word on him. From social workers, Upward Bound people. Right? You know him, you know his kind, you know the dangers he presents. Now, you also know his kid, who's the guy you really side with. So in you come with the anger and the knowledge, but also with a sense of, you know, principle. Ethics, whatever the hell you want to call it. You know you gotta hold your feelings in check, but you also gotta let *us* know that something's boiling inside. It's not working out well. From the beginning you know you're not going to make it. You're losing round after round; pretty soon you're going to lose the whole thing. It's not going to be like those other shows, you know, where justice wins out. The audience has got to see that you're definitely in the right but that you're not going to make it with this guy. Human nature is not gonna change with one confrontation this time. Okay? Got it? Now, show me the tension. No, no, no. Don't, don't grimace. Show the tension with your body. Move around on the couch. Just slightly. Change positions, like your back's hurting or something. Use your body. Good. Good. Very good. That's good. Just like that. Don't change a thing. Awright. Let's take it from that second stare. Holden, you're getting ready for the big speech and the revelations. Cottle, you're resigned, getting interested, changing, but still burning inside. Don't forget the body. Holden, you're only going to be effective if you stay real still. Body at right angles, turning the head. A little more. Hold it! Good. Good. Oh, one last thing. Remember, Holden, you're not a heavy. You're a victimized guy, profoundly unhappy, never had enough, and this punk psychologist, who doesn't look the part, wants to throw it all up to you. Okay. Let's try a take. And there was silence on the set.

"Yes, well, Mr. Holden, I want to talk if we might, a bit about Peter."

"No, we ain't going to talk about Peter because you and Peter are through! You're not seeing him any more."

"I don't understand."

"There's nothing *to* understand. If there's understanding, I'm going to be doing it from now on."

"Is something wrong?" I asked, and felt at once it was the worst question I could have asked.

"Is something wrong? Is that the question? Is something wrong? That's what you want to know? You come into my house when I'm not here and talk poetry with my kid Peter. You send John to a school I've never seen and the kid never writes. I don't know what you did to *him*. I haven't seen him in ten months. What's more, you got it arranged I don't have to pay for the boy. Everything's free. Everything's a scholarship. Money coming in to him from all over God's country, eh? And you expect me to be thankful for taking the burden off my back? Poor man, struggling to keep his family eatin', can't pay for his kid's education. A failure. You arrange for the money just like that, and I'm s'posed to be beholden. Yes? Is something wrong? I'm not your patient, Doctor. And don't you forget that while you're in my house. I'm not one of your boys or one of your freaky playmates in Harvard Square. I don't care how smart they are. I didn't go to college, if you want to know. You probably went to Harvard?"

"Yessir."

"Yeah, well, I wasn't as fortunate, shall we say. I'll tell you the truth, I didn't finish high school. I'm not ashamed to say it. Went second year and quit. Oh, don't get me wrong," he went on ironically, "we loved all the subjects and all the teachers. The teachers, especially, they were wonderful. They were so wonderful and understanding. Not like today. I mean they just said, like, 'Malcolm, you didn't do your little homework, so naughty, naughty. Try to do better tomorrow.'" I tried my best to smile, but the invisible weights on my cheeks were even heavier than before. His tone changed. "Would you like to know what they did in those days? They did exactly what my father did. They cracked you in the side of the head when you didn't shape up and told you to do the work or get the hell out. They screamed at you and embarrassed you before your friends in the class. My God, how they embarrassed us! You wouldn't know about that. You're too young. How old are you, anyway, that you're suddenly taking over for all the crummy fathers and schoolteachers in the world? What, about thirty maybe. Less? Huh?"

"Hmm. Yes. I do know something about the schools you're describing, though. Not everything's that different. You should visit some of—"

"What do you know? What are you talking about? The schools haven't changed? You ask your father what schools were like when he went. Your father living?"

"Yes."

"He work?"

"Yes."

"What does he do?"

"He's a doctor."

"A doctor? A doctor like you or a doctor?"

"A doctor. Surgeon."

"Some guy I'm asking about schools. Millionaire's son." He looked toward the hall as though he were speaking to someone.

"We're not exactly millionaires," I said.

"Your father's a millionaire all right," he responded abruptly. "He's a millionaire. Don't forget, son, some people call themselves by what they earn in a year. Like your father. Other guys have to call themselves by what they earn in a lifetime. I work just as hard as your father and will never make anywhere near as much as he does. I'll bet his house doesn't look like this. Huh? Tell me, does it?"

"Well, there are some similar—"

"Come off it."

"Well, no." Okay, you're right, but don't call me "son."

" 'Well no,' the man says. And you drink beer, do you, you and your father, out of a can every night?"

"No. We don't."

"And your father, this is great, your father, tell me, has psychiatrists or psychologists or cheap-looking college kids coming to his house in the evening or calling him five times a week to set up an appointment to talk with him about his son?"

"No. That's never happened." Jesus, God Almighty. His voice suddenly was beginning to crack and get so old-sounding. What if he started to cry, maybe drop dead right on the spot? Oh, my God. My few words were so soft.

"You follow me?" Mr. Holden asked.

"Yes, I do."

"You see, there's a big difference, isn't there?" he said.

"Yes," I obeyed, "there's a difference."

"Well, that's the reason you and Peter are finished. No more messing around or whatever you two do together. I may be the world's worst father, but I'm still a man and the boy's father, and I'm not about to turn him over to you. Not this time. You got one, okay, but I'm keeping this one. I don't care what happens to him. You don't have to stick your nose into it. You don't have to call me five times every week. Call someone else for a change." Then, for no reason, neither of us spoke for several minutes.

"I want you, Doctor, to put yourself into my shoes." At last, as a page somewhere turned and his tone softened, I felt a spell of relief. "Fact is, I'd like for you to spend a day or two with me. Huh? How 'bout it? Come down to the shop. Meet the boys. Eat where we eat. Go drinking a little, you know. You like it? Surely Harvard guys drink." He was excited by his own suggestion. Beer out of a can, I thought. Real cute. "You come with me. The whole day, like. Forget the youngsters for a while. Let 'em go one day. Look at the older generation just a little for a change. Take a little vacation. Peter says you do a little writing, eh?"

"A little," I responded.

"About people, like? About real life?"

"Yes, about people. Real life, I guess."

"Good. Hey, maybe you could write a little story about us. You know, at the shop, after work, at the bar. Human-interest stuff. What they call a slice of life. That'd be good, wouldn't it? It's a good thought, ain't it? You know what I mean? You don't see stuff about my kind very often.

"I want you to know *me*, not my sons," Malcolm Holden

was saying. "Anybody ever do research on guys like me? All you care about is the kids, probably 'cause they have a *future*. What the hell I got left anyway? August twenty-eighth I'm going to be forty-four years old. That seem old to you, Doctor? Forty-four?"

"No. Not really."

"No? I ain't no spring chicken, you know. Neither's the old lady. I got a little ways to go before retirement, although to hear these kids around here talk about it you'd think I was ready for a hospital or old lady's home already. My father died when he was twenty-four. He was one of those builders, you know, builds high buildings and bridges. Steelworker is what he was. Got crushed to death. I barely knew him. Fact is, I can't even remember him. The old lady didn't have a single picture of him. She just threw him out of her memory like you'd rip a page out of the phone book. You know what I mean?"

"Yes."

"Yup. One down and God only knows how many to go for her. We had more men coming in and out of our house as a boy. 'This is your Uncle This or Uncle That,' she'd say. Who the hell was she trying to kid? I wonder. Christ, we'd see 'em together in the room at night taking off their clothes and humpin' the shit out of each other. We had a place half this size then. Kids slept in the big room, five of us. I had a kid sister died right after she was born, too. Nobody knows to this day who *her* father was. Died so soon nobody even found a name for her. Never had a name. Think of *that*. Jesus. Anyway, we slept in this big room and she slept in the one bedroom. Didn't even bother to close the door most of the time. Then, when I was about six, she marries this guy Holden, and we all have to change our name and ways and everything. She had a lot of nerve, my mother. She comes in the house one night drunk as a goddamn lord and says, 'Now you listen to me for once. This is your new father,' she goes. 'I want everyone to love him as I do and respect him and do whatever he says in the house.' God, I will *never* forget that scene if I live to be a hundred years old. Love him and respect him, and the two of them there can barely stand up in front of us, laughin' and all. Just 'cause you're a kid, you know, doesn't mean you forget that kind of thing. You know what I mean?" I couldn't answer him. I sat there motionless, watching him intently, urging my senses to flush respect and compassion into my face. He was in a melancholy reverie, his being draped in the blankets of his childhood, his senses working to blow away the dust that clings to the surfaces of the events and people that constitute history.

"You know, I can still see them. And every time I think of that evening . . . it was a Tuesday. For some reason, I always remember it as a Tuesday. Like tonight. That's funny, ain't it? I still see them. The two of 'em. One minute I have no father and I'm Malcolm Henry Savanola. The next minute I got a father again and I'm Holden. I mean, just like that. My brother Henry, 'Henkie' we used to call him, God bless him, he passed away this time two years ago. Terrible. Forty he was. Just turning forty. They found a cancer, right here at City Hospital, and he was gone. Bingo." He snapped his fingers. "Just like that. God bless him. One minute he was with us, the next minute he was gone. Strangest damn thing I ever saw. Absolutely healthy, big and strong like an ox. Then, poof. He was gone." Mr. Holden halted momentarily for something to pass.

"Anyway, I remember 'Henkie' standing there holding Margaret's hand, that's my older sister. He says to my old lady: 'What should we call him? Still Uncle Robert?' That was his name. Robert. Can you beat that? 'Still uncle,' he goes. God strike me dead if that isn't exactly what he said. One minute that sonofabitch is a friend from business, or an uncle or somethin', and the next minute he's our father. I'll never forgive him that. He wasn't well a day in his life in that house. And we had to wait on him. Jesus, how I hated that. The girls didn't mind it that much. He just barely had the strength to get out of bed once or twice a day to take a crap or yell at us. Or beat the crap out of us more likely. And she let him, like we were his kids, not hers. Fact is, when he didn't have the energy, *she'd* take to beating us. I remember times, for no good reason she'd just come up to us where we'd be playin' or something, and *boom*." He pounded his right fist into the palm of his left hand. "We didn't know a moment of peace. Not in that house or at school. Nowhere. We were always talkin' about running away somewhere. There was always a fight or an argument. Jesus Christ, that unnamed sister, I told you, wasn't buried two hours we came home fighting about something or other. There was always someone being hit. Always. It was always the same. Every day." His voice trailed off.

"I never really told the story of my life to anyone." He looked at me, expecting something, asking something perhaps. I nodded. "I'm not sure what I want of you. I don't know what I'd like you to say. Maybe before I did. Lotta people have had it tough. Maybe what I'm doing is feelin' sorry for myself or making a whole lot of excuses. Who knows? Maybe that's what I'm doing. Maybe fathers are tough on their kids. Maybe especially on their sons. What do you think? Maybe I'm right, huh? But I just didn't know any other way. When a kid got out of line, you hit him. That's what I grew up on, like Pablum. That's what I learned, and that's what I passed on. Kid's got to show respect for his elders, particularly his father. That's the basis of the family. He doesn't have to love 'em. I didn't love my old man, I mean, you know, my stepfather. I never really knew what kind of a man my real father was. But this guy Holden, him I knew. I was glad when they both died. I mean it, even if God's listening to me right now. I hated them. I wanted them both dead, my mother and my stepfather. It was the only thing that coulda stopped them. Then, when my own Johnnie was born, I sort of went crazy you could almost say. In the beginning it was okay 'cause Mary, my wife, did 'most all the work. But when he got older and the other kids came along I'd lose my temper all the time and hit him or run out of the house or go find the boys and have a drink. The bills began piling up. You borrow up to here, if you can even get the credit. You can't take vacations like guys you hear about. You work two, maybe three jobs. Maybe you get one afternoon a week free, like Sunday maybe, and the kids are running around making noise. And the place is too small for everybody.

"What's the use?" He blew out a long breath. "What's the use any more?" I made a gesture to leave. It was an ambiguous motion, but he held his hand out to detain me. "Stay one minute. I want to tell you one more thing. Like a confession, you know what I mean, Doctor?" He laughed quietly.

"Yes, I do."

"I've fooled around a bit. You know what I mean? You know, a woman here and there. I can't say that I've been totally faithful. I'll be truthful. In the beginning I was. That's the God's truth. Then the kids came and, like I said, something happened. Like, especially when she'd be pregnant. I'd have a few drinks in a bar like at Carmen's or someplace, and meet someone, and, you know. But I swear to you, I was always discreet and proper. I never let on.

"You think maybe I tried to clear myself for what I did to John and Peter?" He was soft again.

"Maybe. I don't know."

"Yeah. Maybe. Maybe I did. I could have spent a helluva lot more time with them and been more patient probably. Not sent 'em out of the house when I did. But goddammit," his anger was on the rise, "no one ever gave *me* a second look. No one felt sorry for *me*. I was, like, doomed from the start. Nothing I did seemed to be any good to anyone. D'you know the feeling of being a failure?"

. . . when we get into the action, when the discussions blaze, just two generations appear before us, and we seem to side with one against the other, or just make believe generational transactions take place in one direction only. Still, it doesn't give the guy the right to ruin his sons. That right he doesn't possess.

What's really going on here? This is a guy who's had it rough and I'm seeing his kid, once, twice a week maybe. And this bitter, moody fourteen-year-old boy who gets his insides beaten out of him practically every month is reading Keats and Yeats and Pushkin and Kafka. And probably because of those fascists who torment him, or a father and a mother, and somehow his grandparents too, who have brutalized him, he's injecting himself with thirty (sic) bags of heroin a day. And I didn't even know about this until a few weeks ago, and nobody can get this boy to change, or to see someone who might be able to help him. So what happens? His mother finally realizes he is suddenly quiet and withdrawn. I talk to his father and we don't even mention the drug business. We don't even mention *the* problem. I don't even know if the father knows, or if he knows that I know. Or what his mother knows or senses. Or, for that matter, what the boy knows. And still, they all love one another and need one another desperately. It's absolutely unbelievable what's going on here.

The personal history of an abusive parent, familiar now from the story told by Thomas Cottle, is understandable if not forgivable. But here Justine Wise Polier reveals how some state agencies inflict even grosser inhumanities through bureaucratic means. Children are being literally banished from their home states, shipped clear across the country to places where they are forever inaccessible to their families and friends. Their crime: being diagnosed retarded, or judged "lacking in control," or abandoned by their parents.

Banished Children
JUSTINE WISE POLIER

Banishment has always been regarded as a harsh punishment. Generally, it has been imposed on adult criminals and political or religious dissidents. Today, in this country, it is increasingly being practiced against disabled children nobody wants.

Two years ago, a member of the American Friends Service Committee asked me to examine the proposed juvenile code for Rhodesia. I was shocked to find provisions that authorized the juvenile court to place juvenile delinquents thousands of miles away, in South Africa, if the court had "no appropriate facilities."

Recent travels have disclosed similar incidents in the United States. Not only delinquent but also incorrigible, neglected, and dependent children with physical, mental, or emotional disabilities are being shipped to remote states. Home states avoid the responsibility of creating appropriate facilities.

Thus, in Illinois, hundreds of children were exiled to proprietary institutions in Texas until their mistreatment was exposed following the death of a girl. In Kansas, at a Child Welfare League of America regional conference, I learned that Indian children were being sent from Florida to southwestern states.

In Massachusetts, constantly cited for its effective closing of remote, fortress-like institutions in favor of community-based facilities, children not acceptable to the new programs are sent to institutions in Maine, New York, and Pennsylvania.

In Anchorage, Alaska, when I visited the only mental-health facility for retarded and disturbed children, I learned that children in need of long-term treatment were sent to private institutions in Colorado and California.

There is shocking cruelty to children of members of the military sent to institutions for treatment in various states. One of the institutions was operated by a man who appeared as a witness before me in family court. He was then running a private school for adolescents though he had no qualifications. After his "school" was closed in New York following the death of a student, he moved South and received Pentagon referrals and funding.

Both the New York State Department of Mental Hygiene and voluntary agencies have been reluctant to accept or provide treatment for many seriously disabled children. Denied adequate resources, the New York City Department of Social Services has felt forced to "warehouse" hundreds of children in temporary shelters that cannot provide appropriate care and, it is reported, has sent over 150 children to institutions out of state. Such placements have only recently become public knowledge.

Figures are not yet available, but it seems almost certain that they will show that banishment of children is disproportionately used against poor and non-white children.

It has become necessary to challenge out-of-state banishment in the federal courts as violating both the constitutional protection against cruel and unusual punishment and the constitutional guarantee of equal protection of the law.

On September 3, 1974, the Children's Defense Fund joined Louisiana attorneys in filing a federal class action to challenge the banishment of hundreds of poor children from Louisiana for confinement in "commercial institutions" in Texas as a violation of the constitutional rights of both children and their families.

Banishment of children is only one more tragic symptom of the gap between our professions concerning the value of children and what we are ready to do for those who need assistance. Studies have documented the lack of services for children and the far from equal availability. Yet, no meaningful funds have been provided. In New York the naming of an inspector general for children has been proposed as a quick solution as though more facts instead of appropriate services would end the banishment of children.

What goes on in the mind of a youth worker when he sees what is happening to the youngsters on the streets, in the alleys, and in the police stations and the courts? Larry Cole provides an unforgettable answer in this searing evocation of the sounds and smells of the streets, the rats and the sirens, the curses and the chains. It's the summer in the city, where you have to cut yourself off from feelings and thoughts or go crazy —and if you are able to cut yourself off, you are and act "crazy."

Kill Each Other, Be Killed, Kill Yourself

LARRY COLE

Kids without food, without clothes, and without teeth. Sick kids, sick with rickets, brain tumors, ulcers, and forgottenness. Kids who have seen a doctor only during their brief moment of birth and don't remember their unteeveed coming-out party.

Kids who have come to expect adults to exploit them. Their pride, their defenses, and their bodies. Kids who couldn't learn to read because they couldn't see. And nobody knew. And they weren't telling.

Kids who knew that California was in Jersey. Kids in public school for eight years who couldn't tell time. Kids who never knew their birthdays. Kids who never had a present or a kiss. . . . Kids who didn't give a shit for you and all your lies.

Kids stoned on glue, on goofballs, Carbona, and wine. The glassy-eyed indifference of the graduate to heroin. Shit. H. Junk. Dope.

Tears. Fearful mothers intimidated and disgraced by welfare workers poking through dirty laundry bags. Welfare police in midnight raids catching little-girl mothers unsafe even in bed.

Kangaroo courts in public housing evicting families whose children break the law. The law. Unmarried mothers of breathing children being refused a place on the housing list. People with no place to live. People living where people shouldn't.

A street rumble out of nowhere. Kids with guns, chains, and knives slashing and shooting other kids who can't say, either, why it is happening. Kids who have been offered a choice. Kill each other. Be killed. Kill yourself.

See Frankie run. Run, Frankie, run. Run out the door of school when they've got you down as present. Beat it to the bag of glue and get away. Up high. You can't read the label that says glue can kill you. You are a disruptive child. You are disadvantaged. You are a non-intellectual. You are delinquent, or if you're not delinquent, you're predelinquent. Everyone has a label, a reason, and ready-made absolution for their failure to teach you what you will need to grow up. You don't know when September is. You don't know that the guy who discovered America sailed from Spain. You don't know how to read your own name.

Your teacher is the cheerleader of mockery. You are a fourteen-year-old failure.

That's no way for kids to grow up. What the hell they doing with my money building World's Fairs when these kids are hungry? What the hell they shooting off those big missile fireworks when one of my kids does without five-dollar medicine? What the hell they up to sending congressmen to Europe when my kid never been past the Bronx? What the hell they teaching in their social work schools sitting behind their half-partitioned foggy glass walls when this kid wants someone to pick him up and squeeze him? How many times you walk in and see a social worker holding a kid? A big ugly kid. Wrestling. It's okay, Mr. Socialworker. He won't think you're a faggot if you hug him.

Walk the streets at night. Nothing open for kids. All the big-mouthed people have gone home to the hills. Rap all day about poverty wars and then cut out at sundown, when the troops are on the street. Weekends? Forget it. When you're in trouble, kid, just run like hell and hide.

Kids in candy stores, on the streets, and in hallways. Kids sitting on stoops watching fixed channel action. Kids in basements with glue bags and in playgrounds with half-filled wine bottles. Goofing.

No place to go. "Hey man, got a nickel?" Move off the corner when the cop comes around. How come with all this poverty money in the neighborhood a kid has no place to go at night? When he's out. Like it or not, he's out. And no place to go. A strange absence of legitimate activities. Stoop sitting. The corner. The hallway. In and out of fast illegalities. Snatching handbags. Smoking pot. Sometimes just rapping to the chicks in

the projects. The kids from the housing projects. They have
no place to go either. You just mill around. Waiting. For
nothing.

You are in the constant sight of the law. Since you have no
place to go you stand out in the open. You and the law always
looking each other square in the face. When something happens near you, man, you're in it. Like it or not. You are a part
of the scene. You will get busted for just being. You are too
close to the action not to get pulled along. Almost everyone
has a record. If you don't have a record you're a freak. You
know the odds keep building up against you. You know you'll
get busted sooner or later. Like it or not, you are part of the
scene.

It is a scene of multilanguage music straining down from
fire escapes onto streets and sidewalks filled with dirt and the
smells of cooped-up animals walking on leashes trained to relieve themselves in the gutter or on the tires of parked cars.
Cats playing with the leashed dogs, taunting them from under
cars and behind garbage cans. The smell from the street rises
to meet the soot and noises descending. Crumpled newspapers,
beer cans, and bottles lie in the street, moved only by cars and
occasional winds. Kids darting in and out of the cars, dodging
moving traffic, broken bottles, and shit. Running in this field
as if it were a fairytale meadow. Playing.

They play without caution or reserve. Boxes become cars.
Garbage-can tops become shields. Truck tires become amuse-
ment-park rides. The street is made to work. It is thorough-
fare, playground, trading floor, theater, battlefield, ballroom,
boardwalk, garbage dump, parking lot, convention hall, game
preserve, mortuary, boxing arena, and circus. It is a world,
total, bounded by two avenues. It has its own candy store, market, barber, shoe repair, drug store, cop, pusher, and politician.
The block doesn't need the world at all. And its kids become
part of its self-containedness. Their chauvinism bounded by
two avenues.

A littered minefield nestled safely away from affluence. Subways don't come here. Taxis don't stop. Everyone knows all

that, and it's okay until you need a way in. Or out. The things that happen here stay here. No one sees the whole show without a reserved seat. Recommended for mature audiences only.

A fat lady comes out of nowhere wearing nothing but panties. On Avenue C at 10:00 P.M. wearing nothing but panties. Beating a bum with a piece of board. A small crowd gathers. Kids laugh, others walk past, not caring. Someone calls the cops. Too much noise.

On Avenue D, nearly at the same time, a guy jumps off the roof of the projects. Ten floors to the bottom. Swing-out open windows crash as his body falls on its way to the litter in the street.

Kid runs up and says "Hey, what's a suislide? Some guy did a suislide."

The cops come and join the crowd cheering the near-naked fat lady. She has stopped being a nuisance. She is the fat lady. It is a side show.

The guy on Avenue D died, doing his jump without a net.

Study kids' faces and eyes through all of this. Try to find some measure of reaction. Something to measure your own sense of reality by. Is this really happening? These are kids and they see it all. Is it happening to them?

Look and look hard. You see nothing. It is not happening to them. It is Channel 14 that comes on when it's ready. It's you that turns on and off.

The kids are turned off. They're turned off to death, disease, school, destruction, adults, politics, rent strikes, reading, jobs, promises, cleaner streets, junkies, air pollution, high prices and low rents, principals, cops, social workers, priests, guidance counselors, welfare workers, building inspectors, mayors, and Reform Democrats. They are, above all, turned off to themselves. They have nothing to lose.

Depression. Try to find words to put feelings in boxes. WHAT DO I DO WITH THIS? I see it all. Feel the sticky, dirty heat in the summer. Smell the same smells. But I am not of this place, and this confused outrage is my proof of birth.

I see a cop punch a fourteen-year-old kid in the mouth and

push him into a hallway to finish the job. I see a car drop a package of heroin to a local pusher in front of fifty people. I see someone breaking a car windshield with a garbage can. I see a judge read *The Daily News* while a trial is in session. I see a stabbing where people cheer. And all the time, I watch the kids' faces. It is not happening to them.

When funds are cut for the kids who most need help, we mortgage the present to the future. But it is hard to make public officials, and even the average person, understand this. Nat Hentoff, a brilliant journalist who has devoted his career to writing in the public interest, tried to bring the point home to a city on the brink of disaster.

Turning Kids into Waste
NAT HENTOFF

The youth worker and I were in front, half a dozen gang members behind us, and it was pitch black—the youth worker feeling the way along the walls of the cellar that would lead us to a gym in the basement of a church. We were taking this Stygian route because two of the wildcat warriors in our party had been banned by the elderly priest who had once lived his life secure in his infinite capacity for love of the poor, especially the children of the poor. In recent months, however, this priest was beginning to look as if he were going to end his sour nights in a Graham Greene novel. Anyway, we were burrowing into his church on the thesis that if the two kids he had kicked out did not come back through the front door, the priest would never know they were there again. "All Puerto Ricans," the gang members stoutly maintained, "look alike to that motherfucker."

"Hey," a soft, hoarse voice I knew all too well enlivened the

darkness. "Why don't we waste the reporter and the youth
worker?"

There was general laughter, the youth worker's being a bit
too hearty, I thought. I cackled softly to be polite; but knowing Carlos, the gang leader who had just made the enchanting
proposal, I was not all that sure I would see another morning.
Finally, though, we left the blackness for one of the most cheer-
ful sights I have ever seen—a sweaty, crummy basketball game
in a church basement.

"He could have done it, you know," I said to the youth
worker. "A sudden crack inside his head, a rush of 'Why the
hell not?' and we'd have been on page four of the *News*, head
down."

"But the thing is," the youth worker said, "he didn't do it.
He might have a year ago. In fact, he came very close with that
kid up the block. You know, the one he stabbed in the throat.
But he's changed. Or at least he's changing."

And so he was. Because of this youth worker and a couple
of other youth workers, Carlos finally had adults he could talk
to, call up in the middle of the night, lean on, learn from. I
don't mean to romanticize what was going on. He was still a
dangerous kid, but dimly, remotely, there might be some options for him other than a nasty, brutish, and probably short
life during which he would nastily shorten others' lives.

Although he had been labeled retarded in an elementary
school where no one on the staff, so far as I could find out,
spoke Spanish (this was in the early 1960s), Carlos was bright.
Not only street sharp but with a taste for abstract reasoning.
He was a fan of the Warren Court's rulings on the rights of
defendants—in part, of course, because he had a keen survival
interest in that branch of constitutional law but also because
he found it fascinating to juggle such concepts as "due process"
and "equal protection."

I told him he ought to think about going to law school.

"Shit, man," he said, "I ain't been to high school in a year
and a half."

I don't know what eventually happened to Carlos. The youth-worker program in his neighborhood shut down. A budget cut. For a few months, I heard stories about him, some of them monstrous. I suppose it's possible he finally got a steady gig and is now a vociferous member of the PTA where his kids go to school, but I do not think so. I think Carlos has been wasted. And who knows how many he's wasted.

I've known a lot of wasted kids like Carlos. Their families couldn't afford them. The schools professed not to know what to do with them. And that's true. The schools didn't know. They should have known, but nobody in this or other school systems gets fired for not knowing how to deal with kids who are "emotionally handicapped," as some of them are gracefully categorized. There are exceptions. Some teachers do know; and over long, patient months and years, they have been responsible for quite astonishing changes in such kids. But there have never been enough knowing teachers, because there has never been enough funding to begin to establish the large numbers of small classes and specially trained teachers that are needed for the continually growing number of kids on the edge of being wasted. And who then may waste you.

Our priorities are socially insane. A terrifying phenomenon of the seventies is kids, very young kids, who kill, more of them than ever before. Look at their school records. It is as if they were sent to school to ensure their being wasted. Kids already feel like mud, the schools make them feel like shit. Obviously not all of them go on to kill, but many of them, one way or another, wind up costing the rest of us much, much more than it would cost, in school, to enable them to find and hold onto their self-respect.

However, when, as now, budgets are gutted, services are first taken away from those with no political constituency. Especially from kids with no resources at all.

"The slashes may not be entirely disastrous," a source of mine at the Bureau of Child Guidance says, "but, at best, kids who need help desperately are going to lose an awful lot of clinical services, psychotherapy, and speech therapy. And I don't think we're going to be able to hold onto those classes in which there are no more than ten children. Our kids badly need to be that close to a teacher. How can City Hall possibly increase the size of those classes? Because, to them, those kids don't exist.

"When you recognize the consequences of ignoring these children," she continued, "it's crazy. I see young kids all the time who show the first signs of the kind of ego damage that can lead to psychotic behavior. Believe me, you can see it and do something about it now. You don't have to wait until they're fourteen and kill someone."

As this city's budget slashes move from rhetoric to what actually is going to be lost, it would be extremely useful if a skilled budget analyst were to publish the amounts and percentages of "savings" which are going to come out of the already squashed lives of the poor—particularly the children of the poor.

"Juveniles" can be jailed without charges, without a sentence, with no time off for good behavior. This can happen to them for being too noisy or rude in school, for being "ungovernable," for sexual experimentation, for stealing candy, or for being truant. Youngsters are regularly put away for up to ten years on the basis of several accusations of misbehavior, none proved, each "heard" by a judge in less than five minutes of court time.

Judge Lois G. Forer's book No One Will Lissen is written from the notes of such cases. "There are two separate and unequal justice systems in the United States," she concludes. "One process of law for the middle class and wealthy, and a second-class justice system for the poor."

That the word "justice" is used at all is an irony for most of the children (90 per cent black) processed by the juvenile courts and the youth houses. These are young people denied the right to counsel and even a chance to be heard. Since 70 per cent of male youths in many urban neighborhoods will be found delinquent at least once, this unquestionable bias against poor, non-white folk is personally experienced by so many, that one can only wonder how they can forgive us for our silent complicity.

"No One Will Lissen"
HON. LOIS G. FORER

Intake, in the juvenile justice system, is the step that precedes the actual court hearing. It is supposed to weed out the unimportant and frivolous charges against children, reserving only the important cases for the juvenile-court judge.

After a child is arrested, and if the charges are not dropped at the police station, intake is the next step in his delinquency processing. If the child has well-to-do parents who can be reached by phone and who will hurry over to the police station, the charge will be dropped unless it is a serious crime. If the child's family has no telephone, if he is ragged, if he is black—he will very likely be held in detention overnight. Even if he is released at the police station, the parent must sign a slip agreeing to present himself or herself and the child at the detention center the next morning for an intake interview.

What occurred at the intake interviews reported in this chapter is reconstructed from parents' accounts to me and from innumerable observations of other intake interviews. No transcript is made of intake interviews. No judge is ever present, and rarely an attorney or an observer. I do not know of any researcher in the annals of practices of the juvenile court who has observed intake interviews and analyzed their procedures and results.

Intake is not authorized by statute. It grew up as a convenient way of siphoning cases away from the overworked juvenile-court judges. It also provides an easy method of getting information on those cases that do go to court. This material later comes before the judge as the social worker's recommendation for disposition, that is, sentencing. Often the child's statements made at intake are used by the judge at the trial to test his credibility. If there is a discrepancy between the report of what the child said at intake and his testimony under oath in open court, the judge may conclude not that there was an error in the very casual report but that the child is a liar.

The intake interviewer is usually a social worker or probation officer. Like his counterpart in welfare agencies, the interviewer questions the child and other people and then decides what, in his opinion, is best for the child.

The critical importance of intake is recognized by students of the juvenile-court system. The Institute of State and Local Government (in its 1957 report, *The Philadelphia Juvenile Court*) found: "The juvenile's first contact with the Court is through intake interviews. This first meeting is crucial to the child, the community and the Court. In brief intensive interviews, delicate judgments must be made whether the case should be adjusted or held for formal court hearing, and whether the child should be held in detention pending hearing. Skilled staff, clear policy, and careful controls are essential." This analysis of "intake" is accurate.

There are three choices—"adjustment," "court out," and "court in." When a case is adjusted, no further action is taken. The child and his parents assume that the charges have been dropped and that the child is exonerated. But the court does not attach this significance to adjustment. It simply means that the intake interviewer has determined that it is in the best interest of the child, whether guilty or not, to take no further action. The charge remains on the child's record. "Court out" is a decision to release the child pending trial and to have a petition of delinquency placed against him. The child will be brought to trial weeks or months later. "Court in" is an order to hold the child in detention (jail) until he has a hearing before the juvenile court. This hearing may be a day or a month later. There is no statutory time in which the child must be brought to court, and few juvenile courts have any fixed rule as to the limit of pretrial detention.

In welfare agencies the intake interviewer screens persons

applying for some sort of grant, such as public assistance, medical care, orthopedic appliances, psychiatric help, or family counseling. What the applicant wants costs money, and the interviewer is the guardian of the purse strings who must determine eligibility and need. Often these two criteria merge in a generalized decision as to "worthiness." The interviewer must be wary of lies. If the applicant does not answer the questions or if his answers are unsatisfactory, his request will be denied.

Why should such a procedure be applied in the juvenile-justice system? The child at a juvenile intake interview is not asking for anything. He and his parents are compelled to submit to this interview, which may result in loss of freedom for the child.

Intake, like the juvenile court itself, has a crowded schedule. A single interviewer may be expected to process forty or more children in a day. These brief interviews fall far short of the intensive, delicate decision-making proceedings envisioned by the Institute of State and Local Government. Being trained in the social disciplines rather than the formalisms of the law, the interviewer puts aside questions of fact and law such as, Did the child do the act? and, Is it an offense? Instead he is supposed to establish a rapport with the child and, in less than ten minutes, arrive at a solution to the social problems presented by the whole child that will be conducive to his rehabilitation.

Every day, in every city and county in the United States, intake interviewers are making decisions affecting the liberty of children. In some communities the interviews are longer; in others they are shorter. The structure is the same. An individual who is not a judge makes a decision whether to deprive a child of his liberty on the basis of a hearing at which none of the safeguards of the law is observed. The so-called evidence read from a paper is pure hearsay. The person who gathered the information is not there to be cross-examined. The eyewitnesses from whom the reporter obtained his information are not present to be examined or cross-examined. The facts as reported often indicate that no crime was committed, and yet the child is held for trial. The child does not have a lawyer and is not informed of his right to have counsel or his privilege against self-incrimination. He is not permitted to confront his accuser. Neither the protections of the law nor the supportive aids of social work are possible at such a mongrelized proceeding.

The standard by which the intake officer is guided is whether the best interests of the child *and* the public will be served by detaining or prosecuting the child. Such a standard if applied by a court would be held void for vagueness. Its two criteria present conflicting interests. The probation officer may believe that it is in the best interests of society to lock up a child who has not committed any crime but whose home conditions are such that he *may* get into trouble. If he thinks that the child's home is unsuitable or that the child is lying or unrepentant, he can order him to be held in custody.

Many social workers and judges believe that freeing a child is not fair treatment even when there is insufficient evidence to sustain a conviction. They are concerned that acquittal of a possibly guilty child will lead him to think that crime does pay. The role of the juvenile court, they believe, is to change the attitudes of these children. A child who admits his misconduct and promises to sin no more will often be released, while one who firmly insists upon his innocence will be held for the discipline that will break his unruly spirit and reform his evil heart. For this reason, many children admit offenses that they never committed. Some are released. Others are held in jail until trial. At the court hearing these confessions are often introduced in evidence.

On the other hand, the intake officer may believe that it is in the best interests of a child who has a good home to release him even though he has committed an offense. The ghetto child runs a high risk of incarceration, while the middle-class white child is seldom deprived of his liberty regardless of the offense. Substitute for the word "poor" the word "black" and for the word "middle-class" the word "white": This is what the children and their parents see at intake. They do not know that they are not in court. The intake interviewer is frequently called judge and rarely disclaims the title.

No one knows how long or short a time a child will remain in the center. It is impossible to plan a program of any sort. Many of the children are emotionally disturbed and can't function in a classroom. They become upset. They scream; they cry; they throw things, anything that comes to hand.

Chemistry makes things easier for the administrators of these juvenile warehouses. Thorazine calms children; it also depresses their spirits. But it is cheap and convenient. It may dull the mind after prolonged use. But in many institutions it is commonly and indiscriminately given to children.

The problems and needs of children in detention are extremely varied. There were six boys in the center awaiting trial for murder. Some are there because they ran away from home. Many have been there more than a year. Some will remain only a week or a month. Many of these children sit in idleness. In the adult jails, where the older children are placed, there is little schooling. Most of them wash dishes or do other menial tasks.

The percentage of arrested girls who are committed to institutions is higher than that of the boys. In a sample examination of the records of 103 children, seventy-nine were released immediately to their parents. Although only sixteen girls were included, five of them were held in custody before trial. Four of these girls remained in custody a total of sixty-one days. The fifth girl was held in "temporary" detention for 150 days. Detention-center statistics reveal that 40 per cent of the girls arrested are held in custody pending trial.

The girls are usually charged with incorrigibility, truancy, and runaway, none of which is a crime. They often run away from home to avoid sexual molestation by roomers or by members of the household. In such a situation, the girl is confined in the center while her attacker—an adult, entitled to release on bail, jury trial, and the panoply of constitutional protection— is free. The girl may remain in detention until the man is tried.

Girls who for any reason are held in custody are subjected to peculiarly repulsive indignities. It was from Mary Ann S. that I first learned that every girl in the Youth Study Center is required to submit to an internal vaginal examination. Many other girls later complained of these examinations. Denise M., a thirteen-year-old black girl, was examined internally, and she also complained that a middle-aged white matron went into the shower with her and patted her breasts. Denise cried and shuddered while she told me these things.

A girl named Patricia was also examined internally while she was in the center for four days awaiting trial. The doctor reported that Patricia O. was not a virgin and that she was promiscuous. She did not have venereal disease. This report was sent to Patricia's parochial school.

Patricia came back to see me several weeks after I had obtained her discharge from the court. She told me about the report of the medical examination at the Youth Study Center. She had objected to the examination but was told that she had to submit. She was not told of the results or that this report would be transmitted to anyone. Patricia was in anguish. "I'm a virgin. I've never had anything to do with boys—anything like that. You do believe me. Now the nuns want me to leave school before graduation. Can't you help me?"

Again I had to call on a friend. All of us in the office were shameless. When one of "our children" needed help, we would plead with any friend or acquaintance and beg for free services. A gynecologist agreed to see Patricia without fee. He reported that there was no evidence that she was not a virgin. Fortified with this information, I called Judge Frank J. Montemuro, who was most sympathetic. He ordered Patricia's "record" expunged. I also wrote to the school. Patricia graduated with her class.

Mary Ann was the only girl among our clients who resisted the internal examination. She had been arrested for throwing a snowball at an elderly neighbor, and was taken to the Youth Study Center. There a check of her school record was made, and the charge of truancy was added to assault and battery with a snowball. She adamantly refused to submit to the examination. The Youth Study Center just as adamantly refused to release Mary Ann until she permitted the examination. After days of tears and defiance, Mary Ann's mother came to the office to see if the law would protect the privacy of a thirteen-year-old girl's body.

For two weeks, Mary Ann was kept locked alone in a room. The authorities insisted that this was not solitary confinement. She was deprived of her clothing, permitted only a pair of pajamas, while she defied the power of the state to thrust its hands into the private parts of her body. I visited this frantic, hysterical child between trips to the court. Petitions were presented and denied. Some courts refused to docket them. Others received the petition but refused to act. No court would grant a protective order. No court would issue an order of mandamus to compel another judge who was considering the question to act upon the matter.

I argued in vain that the right of privacy extends to the integrity of one's own body. In 1890 Samuel D. Warren and Louis D. Brandeis found tucked away in the Bill of Rights an additional right never mentioned by Jefferson, Madison, or Hamilton: the right of privacy. The succeeding half century has seen the blossoming of this concept. It protects a man's papers from government law-enforcement agencies. It protects the marital relationship from the enforcement of laws banning artificial contraceptives; it protects the middle-class man who indulges his taste for pornography in his own home. It protects the man accused of illegal use of drugs from having his stomach pumped to obtain the evidence of his crime. It may even protect the middle-class college student from prosecution for the use of marijuana and LSD. (The American Civil Liberties Union believes that the right of privacy of the mind prohibits the state from interfering with these experiments, pleasures, and experiences.) But the right of privacy did not protect Mary Ann and thousands of other girls from forcible vaginal examination by the state. The merry-go-round of legal process was played to an inconclusive end. While the lawyers argued and the judges delayed, Mary Ann's strength gave out. The matrons held her legs and the doctor made the examination.

The boys in temporary detention also have a miserable time. Most of them do not belong in a jail. We discovered by check-

ing the records that fifteen of the thirty-three boys in custody
more than one hundred days in March 1967 were not even
charged with any criminal offense. They were listed as runaway,
incorrigible, medical examination, unsatisfactory probation, or
"report on adjustment."

Alvin B., like John R., was in the center awaiting placement.
His offense also was incorrigibility. This is not a crime for which
an adult could be jailed. Incorrigibility is a legally useful phrase
that permits parents to relieve themselves of a child and the
state to take control over his destinies. Upon the continued
supply of youngsters such as John R. and Alvin B. an enormous
bureaucracy depends. When I last checked the records, Alvin
had been in the center 628 days. He was then only twelve years
old. He had been before three different judges, fifteen times.
Each time, he was brought into court for not more than five
minutes and then returned to the center. He has been studied
and evaluated again and again. At each hearing, he was ordered
held in custody awaiting a plan to be submitted by the Department of Public Welfare.

On November 22, 1965, the court ordered that the boy might
be placed in a foster home pending placement arrangements.
No foster home was found. The record stated as of March 18,
1966: "Copy of summary [from psychiatric evaluation] received. Admission to a state school and hospital where boy can
receive psychotherapy, appropriate schooling, and help with pre-
pubertal phase of development, which is in his immediate future, was recommended." A year later, Alvin B. was still in the
Youth Study Center. He had not been before the court for
eleven months. The judges have forgotten him. The department
has no plan. The hospital to which he was referred has no room.

No one knows what thoughts come to him in his dark cell
in the basement of the courthouse, or as he lies on the floor
in the detention center, wearily waiting, waiting for the inscru-
table, unknowable order that will release him.

No one judge is responsible for any specific child. The ever-
growing files move from courtroom to courtroom while the
child waits for someone to help him. The consequences of this

system of irresponsibility are often tragic. The New York *Times* reported the case of Roxanne Felumero, a three-year-old girl, who was killed, allegedly by her stepfather. The case of this child was before the Family Court of New York many times. It came before several judges. According to the *Times*, "the Citizens Committee for Children believes that if Roxanne's case had been handled by the same judge each time, that judge would have realized that it was dangerous to leave her in her stepfather's home."

These children are forgotten in detention centers or left in dangerous homes because there is no place for them. Miss M. MacNeely, director of New York City's public adoption agency, considers a two-year-old child too old for adoption. There are few institutions for non-criminal children who are homeless. Society vainly hopes that citizens will "open their hearts and their homes to children other than their own." This is the plea of the Foster Home Educational Program, a United Fund agency that publishes attractive and expensive brochures advertising the need for foster homes. Because foster parents, unlike social workers in agencies, are not paid for a twenty-four-hour-a-day 365-days-a-year job caring for an unwanted and often difficult child, the shortage of foster parents is understandable.

On March 3, 1970, the Appellate Division of the New York State Supreme Court revoked the order of the Family Court committing a fifteen-year-old boy to a state training school (correctional institution) simply because his home was unsuitable. Justice Aron Steuer, writing for the court, said, "The court obviously cannot provide a facility where none exists." The boy was sent to another institution to await another hearing.

Children in all parts of the country sit behind bars because there is no other place provided for them.

Two little brothers aged eight and ten were placed in the Youth Study Center charged with "arson, assault with intent to kill and conspiracy." More than thirty months later I saw them. Aubrey H., the elder, had a large purple lump in the center of his forehead. His brother, Anthony, explained that Aubrey banged his head against the wall at night before he went to sleep. Aubrey did not speak much. He had forgotten how to read, although when he was placed in the center he was doing well in school.

The true facts of the heinous crime for which these children have been deprived of their liberty will never be known. There was never a trial on the factual question of whether the boys were guilty of arson. The court records show that the new "husband" of the boys' mother made a complaint to the court. There was a fire in the house when neither of the adults was home. It would appear that the criminally negligent person was the mother who left these little children alone. She, of course, was not prosecuted. She is free.

Was the fire an accident—or a deliberate attempt by the boys to burn down the house and kill their baby sister, Clarissa, as Mr. L. contended? The court never made a finding on this crucial question. Mrs. H. was at the hearing. So were the boys. The only attorney present was the assistant district attorney. He presented a report from the fire department. No witness appeared. There was no defense attorney for the boys to demand that a witness be produced and be cross-examined about the evidence of the origin of the fire. There was no evidence as to the intentions of the boys, their intelligence, or their understanding of the dangers of fire. Clarissa was, in fact, unharmed. A neighbor carried her out of the burning apartment. She also led the boys out. This neighbor was not called as a witness. The "husband" was never produced in court for examination. Did he like the boys? Were they a nuisance? Was this episode a convenient excuse to rid himself of these two children who were not his own and who were an expense and a nuisance? There was no one to ask these questions on behalf of the boys. The judge, as a wise, kindly father of the boys, did not make such inquiries.

I visited the boys at the center. Aubrey said he didn't want to talk about the fire. Anthony said Aubrey tried to iron Clarissa's dress and the iron caught fire. It happened so long ago that Anthony had forgotten almost everything. It was then thirty months since Aubrey and Anthony had been in the center. Aubrey asked me if he could see Clarissa. But it is against the rules for children to visit the center. Aubrey did not know whether Clarissa was dead or alive. He did not trust his mother, who told him Clarissa was fine. He did not trust me, a strange lawyer. His fears grew and tormented him. Aubrey had been tested, examined, and evaluated many times during these two and one half years. The reports do not indicate this obsessive anxiety, which is revealed so quickly in a short conversation, and which would be so easy to allay simply by bringing Clarissa to the center so Aubrey could look out a window and see her. The psychiatrists' recommendation for Aubrey was a mental hospital and separation from his brother, his only friend.

And what did Aubrey do all day in the center? He did not go to classes; he was too disturbed.

After some urging, Aubrey went to his quarters and brought back a neatly painted picture of Jesus. The colors were brilliant. Jesus had bright yellow hair and a gleaming halo. It was a canvas with the outlines drawn and numbered for the colors to be painted in. Aubrey had spent weeks painstakingly filling in the spaces. This was his only activity, day after day, as the tedious months of his childhood were counted out behind walls and bars.

The Office for Juveniles filed petitions on behalf of these two boys and of other boys and girls who had been waiting months and years for "suitable placement." The juvenile court rejected the argument that a child has a "right to treatment." The court also acted to cut off these embarrassing and time-consuming actions brought on behalf of the children. Orders were given that the monthly population records of the center were not to be given to the Office for Juveniles; no attorney was to be admitted except upon written authorization of the natural parent.

Efforts to get these unfortunate children out of "temporary detention" and to give them treatment or simply return them to life by the judicial process were halted. Those children who obtained release from the center succeeded in getting their freedom only after petitions were filed with the juvenile court by counsel acting on behalf of each child. Once a judge orders

a child placed—even temporarily—the matter may never be
brought to his attention again. There are more cases every day.
Who will speak for this helpless child walled off from life and
family? Certainly he cannot speak for himself. The wise, kindly
father figure of the juvenile-court judge cannot remember all
of these children.

Despite a study by the Fels Institute of the University of
Pennsylvania recommending against enlarging the center, several million dollars have been allocated for this purpose. No
new facility or addition has been constructed. None is even on
the drawing boards. The citizens who see this place are appalled
by the conditions and urge that more jail space be provided
so that each unfortunate child will have his own cot. A bed
of one's own in jail is certainly not the best answer society can
provide.

The overcrowded dockets of the courts list the same cases
month after month. January 25, 1968, was, if anything, a light
day in juvenile court. Of the thirty-two cases listed for one of
three courtrooms, twenty-five had previously been before the
court and were continued for one reason or another; many had
been continued more than three times. As the children in
detention grow older, one by one they are slowly siphoned out
of the center into overcrowded mental institutions. For a child
who has endured twenty or thirty months in the center, a mental institution may well be society's last refuge. It is chilling
to recall that the psychiatric evaluation of John R. at age nine
was that "psychiatric intervention would not curtail delinquency pattern." What is a suitable placement for these juvenile delinquents who have never committed a crime, these
emotionally disturbed children whom psychiatry rejects?

Many of the children held in temporary detention are neither
dangerously psychotic nor seriously criminal. Some are not even
charged with a crime. On July 8, 1969, I sat in juvenile court
waiting for the case to be called of a child whom I was representing. In less than ten minutes, five detention hearings were
held. Lee D. had been in temporary detention for two weeks
on a charge of stealing a TV set. Not only did he admit having

stolen the set, but he and his parents had returned it to the owner. The court ordered him back in temporary detention pending trial. Angela Y. is thirteen years old and very pretty. Her parents, middle-European immigrants, asked that she be held in detention because she does not keep her room clean. She was continued in custody pending a trial. A little black girl was held in custody on a charge of shoplifting—she had taken a blouse that probably was not worth five dollars. Daniel S. and Ronald H., both sixteen, were held in custody because the defender was not aware of their cases. Calvin J. is a dirty, ragged little black boy eleven years old. He had been in temporary detention for five weeks while the court issued bench warrants for his family, who had evidently disappeared. There was no return of service, and so Calvin remained in jail. His crime? Missing parents. This was the third time he had been brought before the court. Prosecuting Attorney Louis Mitrano was so dismayed by this child's appearance that he asked the court to take cognizance of the boy's clothing. The judge lifted his eyes from the file, looked at Calvin, and said, "You are the worst-looking child that's come before me."

More than a year after the *Gault* decision, these children were temporarily in jail, without meaningful counsel, without notice of the charges, without ever seeing an accuser, and without access to appeal of an order of temporary detention.

The National Council of Juvenile Court Judges held a summer college in 1967 to train judges appointed or elected to the bench since 1965 (reported by Judge Orman W. Ketcham, "Summer College for Juvenile Court Judges," *Judicature, The Journal of the American Judicature Society*, April 1968, p. 330). The cost of this program was covered by a grant from the National Institute of Mental Health. The judges met for four weeks in the idyllic setting of Boulder, Colorado. The fourth and final week of the program considered such issues as the proper use of detention, probation, institutional programs, and alternatives to commitment. The problem is nationwide. Every judge of every juvenile court has encountered a John, an Au-

brey, an Alvin, a Calvin. What instructions did they receive
at the college to enable them to order a "suitable placement"
for these children?

As the judges confer, the reporters expose, and the children
remain in custody, I think of a poem by James Dickey, *The
Eye-Beaters*. It is accompanied by this explanation: "A man
visits a Home for Children in Indiana, some of whom have gone
blind there. . . . A therapist explains why the children strike
their eyes."

Although more than 85 per cent of juvenile offenses are committed by boys, there is a sizable number of girls who are arrested and incarcerated. They are treated with exceptional
harshness. Although girls very rarely commit crimes of violence,
40 per cent of the girls arrested are held in detention pending
trial. And many of them are sent to correctional institutions,
not because they are dangerous but because society wants to
keep down the birth rate among poor black girls. Although no
judge ever articulated this reason for an order of commitment,
we learned in many cases that this was the only possible ground
for imprisoning young girls and women.

Lorraine D. came into the office with her mother and her
sister Cora. Lorraine was dressed in a skintight black gown that
clearly was not bought for her. She wore bright vermilion lipstick. Two front teeth were missing. She was at least forty
pounds overweight. Despite her dull gray skin, she was pretty.
She was also very nervous. Her large eyes widened as she looked
about the strange office in obvious fear.

Lorraine was twenty-four years old. This was the first time
Lorraine had visited her family in ten years. She did not know
how to behave. She was barely articulate. When I saw her, I
explained that the Office for Juveniles was limited to representing children, and Lorraine was an adult under the law.

Cora was the spokesman. She is slim and stylish. Her husband is a truck driver in the Sanitation Department. Mrs. D.
looks young and attractive. She has been employed in the same
blouse factory for seventeen years. Her husband has been dead
for many years. Her youngest son is in the military service. The

other children are married. Lorraine has no money at all. When Mrs. D. looked at Lorraine, her lips quivered.

Cora told me that ten years ago Lorraine was sent to Laurelton State Village by the juvenile court. Laurelton is described by statute as an institution for feeble-minded women of child-bearing age. Lorraine was out on a pass. It was a Friday afternoon. On Sunday a matron would come and take her back. Couldn't something be done? Cora asked.

The jurisdiction of the juvenile court terminates when a child reaches the age of twenty-one. By what authority was she being held? This was a question that I wanted answered. Clearly there was no legal right to keep this girl locked up on an order of the juvenile court.

Immediately, I placed a call for Judge Hazel Brown. It is difficult to claim one's constitutional rights over the weekend. Judges do not like to be disturbed. The clerk's office is closed. While a justice of the United States Supreme Court will enter an order of the court over the telephone, most lower-court judges will not even read a petition that has not been filed and docketed. Unless some court order were obtained, Cora and her mother would meekly and regretfully deliver Lorraine back to the institution. I was continually amazed by the essentially law-abiding nature of the poor. It would not have occurred to these people to hide Lorraine and place the burden on the institution to get a court order for Lorraine's return.

The story was slowly pieced together over a period of hours. In 1957, Lorraine D. was an overweight, sluggish, black fourteen-year-old. It was her first year in junior high school and it was a disaster. In elementary school, the teacher usually put Lorraine in the front row, where she could be watched. Whenever Lorraine would begin to doze off or just stare into space, the teacher called out, "Lorraine, no daydreaming!" Lorraine reluctantly turned to her book and the day was not a total loss.

There were twenty-three hundred children in junior high. The bell rang at the end of a forty-two-minute period. This signaled bedlam as the children dashed through the corridors, went to the lavatories, looked for their books, rushed to the candy machines, made dates for after school, sneaked out on the fire escape for a smoke. Five minutes later another bell rang. The children were supposed to have arrived at the next class, be seated at the proper desks with the right books, and be ready to start another period. Lorraine could never quite get to the right class at the right time with the right books.

A guidance counselor called Mrs. D., who gave up a day of work and went to school. She knew Lorraine was having trouble and that something was wrong. Lorraine's brothers and sisters managed to get through junior high. Cora was going to graduate from senior high school and become a nurse.

The counselor told Mrs. D. they just couldn't keep Lorraine in school, that she needed special help. There was a wonderful school for slow girls like Lorraine. The juvenile court would send her there and the state would pay for it. All that was required was that Mrs. D. sign a paper. She did so, believing what the school counselor told her. Also Mrs. D. did not know what she would do with Lorraine when she was put out of school. She couldn't leave a fourteen-year-old girl alone all day.

She pleaded with the counselor. Then she was referred to the school psychiatrist, who told Mrs. D. that the school could not "contain" Lorraine. There was no alternative. At the hearing, the juvenile-court judge assured Mrs. D. that this was a lovely boarding school and that Lorraine would be taught by special teachers. Reluctantly, Mrs. D. kissed Lorraine good-by. Cora, sixteen, told Lorraine to study hard and come home soon.

Cora did not see her sister again for ten years, not until Lorraine came home that morning on her first visiting pass. She did not want to go back to Laurelton State Village.

"Lorraine, tell the lawyer what you do all day at the village," Cora encouraged her.

"I works in the fields—dig potatoes."

"What happens when it rains or snows?"

"We works every day. Matron, she sit in car, smoke cigarettes. I digs."

Her hands are rough and scarred; her feet, squeezed into high-heeled shoes, are splayed.

I took over the questioning.

"Lorraine, do they have a TV set at the village?"

"Yup, for matrons. We not 'lowed to look."

"Can you remember, when you first went to the village, did you go to school?"

"Never go to school. Just work in fields."

Cora explained that when Lorraine was sent to the village she knew how to read and write but that she has forgotten now. After the first two years, she stopped writing letters. She was no longer able to write. Mrs. D. visited once or twice a year. Several times she was not permitted to see Lorraine because Lorraine had misbehaved.

"What did you do?"

"I run away three times. They came after me in jeep with dogs."

"Were you punished?"

"Tie me to bed springs with wet sheets."

"Where was the mattress?"

"No mattress."

Cora says that the sheets were dipped in the toilet bowl. Lorraine nods her head.

"Did anyone else try to run away?"

"Billy Mae run away, Clorina run away." She remembers several other names.

"Who works in the fields? Everybody?"

"No. Work in kitchen, scrub floors. Some old ladies, white hair in fields. Little girls, tiny kids."

Cora explained that Lorraine is so fat because she never gets meat or fruit, seldom any green vegetables.

"What do you do in the evenings?"

"Go to bed. Sunday night movie, if good."

"Did they ever take you to church?"

"No."

Mrs. D. explained that she had been to the court many times asking that Lorraine come home. She had never seen the judge again. The lady at the court told her that Lorraine is very bad. The village can't release her. If she continues to misbehave she

will be sent to another place. A year ago, Mrs. D. saw Lorraine
and pleaded with her not to run away, to behave so she could
come home. And now at last she was released on a four-day
pass.

I checked the court records and found that Lorraine was committed by the juvenile court in 1957 on a petition signed by
Mrs. D. The petition, which is a printed form, has typed in
the averment that Lorraine is habitually wayward and incorrigible. It is the practice of the probation officer to type up the
petitions *after* they are signed. The file shows fourteen visits
by Mrs. D. to the court. Each time, she pleaded with a court
employee to get Lorraine released. Mrs. D. never saw a judge.
No one suggested that she get an attorney. The court itself
never reviewed the file. Laurelton never asked that Lorraine be
released or that her case be reconsidered.

Lorraine's public school records list an IQ of 93 in fourth
grade, 94 in fifth grade, 90 in sixth grade, and 88 in seventh
grade. A score of 90 is considered the cutoff for normal intelligence. There is no record of a psychological or psychiatric evaluation. In seventh grade, Lorraine read at fifth-grade level.

Judge Brown returned the call. She was sympathetic and explained that the commitment was only for Lorraine's protection. After all, if she were at home she might become pregnant.

I volunteered to take Lorraine to Planned Parenthood and
also suggested that we might petition for a writ of habeas corpus
if the commitment were not terminated. Judge Brown suggested
that she call the probation officer and extend the pass for thirty
days. This would save Lorraine from returning to the institution. In the meantime, a proper hearing could be held to determine Lorraine's rights and what care would be appropriate for
her. I readily agreed. All month, I attempted to get a hearing
for Lorraine. The judge who had signed the original commitment could not remember Lorraine. He was not astonished that
she was still at Laurelton. After all, she would be of childbear-
ing age for many more years. The pass was extended again. Finally, without a hearing, the court ordered that Lorraine be
discharged.

Lorraine is working as a countergirl in a hamburger place. She has a social security number. She is self-supporting.

Cora took Lorraine to a public-health clinic, where she was diagnosed as hypothyroid. She was given medication and has lost more than twenty pounds. Lorraine is learning to read again. Her skin is now a warm brown and she smiles gaily. Mrs. D. says she still screams in her sleep, dreaming that she is in the village. But Lorraine has a boyfriend and Mrs. D. is planning a wedding.

Juvenile detention centers brutalize inmates. To survive, they must become more like hardened criminals. Dr. Susan Fisher of Harvard takes us on an unforgettable vicarious visit to such a place. From her account it becomes clear why they breed further rage and violence.

The Smell of Waste
SUSAN M. FISHER, M.D.

The children come out of vans, handcuffed to policemen. Their belongings are taken, except a comb. They wait in the lobby from ten minutes to half a day. No one looks at them. From the start, no one wants to know them. They are there awaiting trial. Some for ten days, some for three hundred, they never know when they will go to court, when they will see their probation officer, when they will be visited. If convicted, the time spent waiting does not count in their sentence; time in the detention center is not related to time before or time that will come. A twelve-year-old waits from October to June to be screened. He has been forgotten. The children are issued clothes, stripped, and searched for drugs. Sometimes drugs are

This is a revised version of a paper presented at the International Congress of Child Psychiatry, Jerusalem, Israel, August 1970.

in balloons, swallowed, to be vomited up later. No rules are explained to them. They are put onto the units without introductions. Girls are separated. The boys are grouped by age, except the armed offenders, and a special unit for homosexuals, transvestites, and the rare white boy. Segregation by race, poverty, education, capacity to adapt, has occurred already. One counselor watches thirty children in space meant for fifteen. Eight hours. Brick walls, naked light bulbs, loud music; no solitude is permitted voluntarily. They must stay together in the main room of the unit, yet for any alleged infraction—smoking outside the allotted smoking period, cursing back a counselor— or for no specific violation at all, they can be put into isolation. Officially all isolation detentions are to be reported; reports are often not made, and any child can be locked up within the eight hours of a shift, and no one will know. And with other such institutions, it shares: one hundred degrees in summer, smells of urine and unwashed bodies. Twenty-three beds in a sleeping room; some isolation rooms have only a toilet bowl, and the counselor can turn off the water supply. To fight roaches, the rooms are heavily sprayed. Physical abuse with no redress; the word of a child is never accepted against that of a staff member.

These children are innocent before the law. Some are accused of major crimes—assaults, armed robbery, rape, murder. Others are not held for crimes at all but for being unmanageable and intractable in homes and schools where rebellion may be a measure of vigorous health; such children are designated "beyond control." Some are detained because mental hospitals refuse them and they are caught in a circuit between detention center, foster home, and hospital. They have the same needs for "rules of the game" as any incarcerated person, the same needs to create an internal social structure in which to participate, but it is hard to establish one when the formal roles and relationships of the institution are undefined, illusive, even contradictory. They are innocent but treated as guilty. Counselors are to maintain safety, watch, and protect them but often abuse and threaten them. Held within a legal system designed to insulate them from depersonalized adult bureaucracies, they have no civil rights and are isolated from the world of their origins. The atmosphere within the detention center is chaotic for the children and the staff. The chaos mirrors the inner state of the children and the social existence they came from.

The children are almost all black, between seven and eighteen. White children are not so quickly picked up for similar offenses. Frequently, black parents are not called from the station house and their children are detained before the parents know where they are, whereas white parents are usually located and the children released into their custody.

Some common perceptions of the world unite these children before they reach the detention center. They have learned to view social authorities as persecutory and punishing, coming at them with prejudged expectations of their responses and performances—guilty, stubborn, irresponsible, unlovable. They have been faceless objects to be manipulated, as others are to them; and manipulation is effected through behavior, not language. The establishment figures of their world—teachers, police, welfare workers, storekeepers, bus drivers—are to them arbitrary and rejecting; while their sources of food and shelter, the intimate associates to count on, are precarious. Psychiatrists might call these children paranoid, except that their perceptions are accurate most of the time; and the model for dealing with outer danger and uncertainty perpetuates a style of projection of internal distress.

On the units they are passive. They lie on the floor, near or on each other, sometimes playing games. Occasionally they riot, fight, or gang bang. Sudden swings from immobility to violence are part of accepted and expected behavior, for staff and children alike. They pass in lines from unit to school to meals to recreation. Unexplained shifts in schedule for work, school, and play occur almost daily; rules vary according to the counselor on duty.

One's fate is sealed on arrival day. Each new boy is physically challenged. If he doesn't defend himself, he will be beaten up or threatened sexually. If he fights but loses he will still be accepted. He must not back off or cry. Group homosexual assaults are common among the older boys. Younger boys are simply taken sexually; sometimes they offer themselves. A shrewd newcomer can ally himself with tougher kids by being a good "cracker," a style of speech to be discussed later. The genuinely innocent kid—the eight- or nine-year old who is not street-wise and is physically weak—gets it in every way and learns fast.

Throughout the system, anger is vented on weaker members, and weakness is defined in physical struggles. A tough counselor can alter the threats of violence on a unit by being the strong man himself. Often a less punitive counselor will ally himself with the toughest boy to maintain order and survive. A rare counselor interrupts this pecking order by engaging children in group activities and loyalties and presenting different values of strength. Such counselors, though respected by the children, usually do not last long.

Once a child has entered the unit, what are his strategies for survival? The only method with positive rewards is to con the system. This means being deliberately friendly with counselors and administrators, thereby getting jobs in the kitchen, the offices, school, and laundry. This gives extra privileges—more food, smoking, new contacts, and, most important, movement off the unit. All conning activities are safe as long as they are perceived by the other kids as tongue-in-cheek, as long as a child is not thought a "patsy" or a "ratter."

The second major tack to survive, by far the most prevalent, is to disappear into the woodwork, to be utterly passive, faceless, non-existent. Even bizarre behavior is not seen. I learned from one therapy group of a sixteen-year-old boy drinking his own urine, burning his forehead with cigarettes, and calling himself "black Jesus." He was not noticed by the staff. From another, I met a group member who used different names each time he came to the detention center without anyone ever recognizing it was the same child.

Only rarely will a child beat down the system. These are big kids who are good "crackers" and physically overbearing. They are the brightest boys, who supersede whatever alliance a counselor makes with other tough kids and become a kind of spokesman. They are feared by the staff because of their cunning, their power to disrupt. The hostility toward them is intense, but they are left alone. The system often expels them and, for some, the penalty is high. Sammy was a master at this, and intimidated the staff to its limit. Having traveled between hospital and detention center, he was released to his home, where he was stabbed to death by his father.

Closely tied to survival is the informer system. The administration corrals, bribes, and frightens certain children into informing on their peers. The rules are strict. If discovered, informing is tolerated by the other children if suffering would have been the penalty for silence—if you would have gotten more time, or been severely punished. But one can never inform to gain something. The penalty for this is physical abuse, rape, or ostracism.

An important aspect of survival is called "cracking." It is a mocking, jeering, joking use of language that establishes with words the same pecking order as physical strength does initially. You crack *on* someone, you don't crack *with* him. "Ass-kissers," boys who con about going straight when they get out, are particular targets. This is vicious humor, and in therapy groups it is important to cut through it but not threaten its effectiveness on the units. It is the major non-physical cohesive force that allies them. Cracking represents an implied ability to fight and to withstand and dish out verbal abuse. You put people down, put feelings down, always mocking tenderness and sentiment. Feelings are hidden. Language is not a neutral vehicle for contact or communication. When not cracking, the boys sit silently on the floor. It is the only conversation.

When is there tenderness? When is there protection? Only under extreme circumstances. Most of the time, extreme physical helplessness is protected. A severe stutterer on a very tough unit cannot be teased. I learned of a boy in isolation for twenty-four hours in severe drug withdrawal. The administration had refused to send him and several others to the hospital, accusing them of malingering; some were, but some weren't. He lay with his head on a roll of toilet paper, his face in his vomitus, shaking under blankets. Outside the door, keeping check, was a boy from the unit who had watched him throughout the day, keeping him warm.

Psychological helplessness is not so protected, and the disturbed are good subjects for cracking. Out of fear, the extremely bizarre are left alone; sometimes boys will point out to a mental-health consultant sick kids ignored by the staff. Vince had been in isolation for six days and had not been visited except for food put in his room. He was locked up to finish an isolation punishment meted out a year before in a previous period at the detention center, unfinished because he had gone to court and been released. When I saw him, he was incoherent, babbling, drooling, terrified; his ravings soon became comprehensible to me. He wanted a particular doctor every day—a man who had been kind to him four years before. He had held the gun during an armed robbery because he wanted "those guys" to like him and he couldn't say no. He was afraid to go back to the unit because he would be raped.

The primary defense mechanisms operating on every level in the detention center are projection, denial, and dissociation. One's internal wretchedness, when experienced at all, is "because of them." Children are tormented by counselors, counselors are threatened by administrators, administrators are endangered by "downtown," and "downtown" is harassed by the legislators. Too often, they are right; the concrete realities of these people's lives makes interruption and examination of these defenses almost impossible. Few people within the detention center distinguish external and internal sources of misery or notice any personal difficulty in tolerating painful feelings.

Who are the counselors and administrators, and how do they function? Like the children, they have no options. Their supervisors and senior administrators offer them no intimacy, no range of techniques to handle problems; only authoritarian strength or deflection of responsibility to a vague "other." As the counselors fail the children, so the senior administrators

permit no identifications or sharing, acknowledge no conflic-
tual feelings. Like the children, counselors receive no positive
rewards, only negative reinforcement. If they fly through a window to prevent an escape, that is expected behavior. If they
are five minutes late, it is written into their record. They are
frequently spied upon and lied to.

Like the children, they wait—for promotions, commenda-
tions, course certificates that don't ever come or are delayed
without explanation. They too have no privacy. Personnel files
lie open, rumors abound and threaten everyone. Counselors
rarely protect each other, and children are pawns in staff rival-
ries. Three boys were left naked in one isolation room in a
struggle over which counselor would get them clothes.

The relationship between counselors and children is a deadly
game, and the main rule is "beat them or they'll beat you." A
drug user is caught by a counselor. In the morning statistical
report, without intended irony, is printed, "Congratulations,
Mr. X. You are the biggest drug catcher of them all." Counselors try to outguess and outfox the children, as in a ruthless
sport. Understanding, empathizing, helping is emasculating.
Fundamentally, the children must never be seen as like themselves; they cannot imagine their own children in such a setting.

Respectful intimacy is non-existent in the detention center,
and the counselors use the children in different ways. Like objects of pornography, they are erotically used. Some stimulate
the kids by teasing them and egging them on. One counselor
has the boys talk about homosexual exploits into a tape re-
corder. Some female counselors are visibly titillated by illegitimate pregnancies and stories of prostitution. Occasionally, a
counselor rapes a child, with or without consent. One senses
that the children are discharging the forbidden aggressive and
sexual impulses of the staff, who re-establish their self-image,
distance, and self-control by massively suppressing the children.

Most counselors cannot tolerate any physical and verbal
show of aggression in the children, and some hit and even beat
them at the first sign. Once, a counselor called a psychologist
for himself because he was putting a child into isolation for
no apparent reason, yet he knew he was going to hit him unless

he got rid of him. That amount of self-observation is rare. Encouraging and watching violence is irresistible for some, and their fascination is not acknowledged. A female counselor stood and impassively watched a girl bite out a piece of another girl's cheek and told me later, "Nice girls don't fight."

Always there is the reality of actual danger working with severe overcrowding. This too is used, and counselors often flirt with danger, provoking avoidable situations that excite them, and provide an opportunity to watch, experience unacceptable behavior, and then divorce themselves from it entirely. When overcrowding occasionally diminishes, there is no change in staff behavior.

The counselors use language as the children do—bitter cracking with each other; they rarely have shared, matter-of-fact exchanges. With their senior authorities, they retreat into sullen silence. Meetings between them reveal similarities with the children on the units. Counselors are impassive, talked at, immobile, and then break into fits of temper, screaming, physically threatening, banging chairs. These outbursts by counselors are dealt with by their bosses as tangentially and immaterially as the fires and riots of the children. I once dared a senior administrator to risk telling the counselors at such a meeting that he was sometimes depressed working there. They fell into an astonished calm.

Occasionally, more flexible persons are hired. Senior administrators don't want to hear their complaints and suggestions, and will harass them until they quit. Often such men cannot tolerate the frustration and depression. A powerful clique of authoritarian counselors makes life miserable for a more flexible person, and very few remain. The detention center is a place to get out of—for everyone who can. What remains is a group of people who feed on the chaos within the center to avoid facing their own doubts and fears, and issues of their own competence. Tactics to improve working conditions are never gripped and applied vigorously; they hide behind the system's inadequacies and extrude more effective people. What is rewarded is security, passivity, immobility, no overt conflict. And the staff lives with a sense of impending destruction—each television interview, meeting, call from a judge is potentially the loss of safety, job, promotion, status, perhaps reflecting deep projected guilts.

Although of different backgrounds, staff, like the children, are locked within constricted character structures with little internal mobility. Almost all black, with some higher education, the staff struggles to maintain a middle-class identity in jobs that have little social status. Significantly, a large number come from the rural South, farms or small towns, where angry outbursts were often forcibly suppressed, and the need for control was related to the dangers of white society "out there." Rarely, a counselor will admit his outrage at seeing these urban boys doing what he never could; sometimes senior administrators, who spend far less time with the children, connect their dislike of the new music, new haircuts, new freedoms to the compromises they made to "make it" in a white bureaucracy. Their hatred of the children, which is felt after a few hours in the detention center, is a necessary piece of the delicate equilibrium required to maintain their self-esteem.

Cracking, the only language effective on every hierarchical level of the detention center, is also a metaphor for the cracks, the split, the dissociation that mark this institution. Everywhere, one meets the illusion of infinite distance and difference. These children are a different species, not human. Top administrators are unreachable, unknowable bosses. Distance between castes is experienced as a non-crossable space. Yet each level is partially identified with and living through the other, dependent on the other; the illusion of infinite separation masks an unconscious fusion between the groups based on mutual projection—a partial symbiosis. Fusion versus infinity —on every level the same image is reflected, like facing mirrors.

No one trusts here, and everyone is hungry. In therapy groups, in consultations with senior administrators, in talks with counselors, the imagery is oral. Beneath the hatred, the backbiting, the projections, the chaos, lie enormous reservoirs of depression. Ultimately, the maintenance of the chaos may itself be defending against the hopelessness and lack of mobility in their lives, which gets perpetuated throughout the institution.

At the core of several decisions by the United States Supreme Court has been its recognition that the juvenile court system, established to protect the special interests of children before the law, has not only violated their civil rights under the Constitution but has perpetrated those very abuses of human growth the special systems were created to avoid.

This detention center represents the failure of all structures in urban society—family life, schools, courts, welfare systems, organized medicine, hospitals. It is a final common pathway to wretchedness. Occasionally, a scandal in the newspaper, an outraged lawyer, an interested humanitarian judge makes a ripple. The surface smooths rapidly over again, because, locked away in a distant part of town, society forgets the children it does not want or need.

It is shocking to learn that millions of our children who should be in school are not. And many of them have been forced out by the school authorities. "It is as if many school officials have decided that certain groups of children are beyond their responsibility and expendable," concluded the Children's Defense Fund, which exposed this situation. "Not only do they exclude these children, they often do so arbitrarily, discriminatorily, and with impunity."

We Are Failing the Children
MARIAN WRIGHT EDELMAN

A friend relates the story of visiting Iran when an earthquake occurred. The shah sent out the equivalent of the American Red Cross, ordered them to gather up all children left homeless by the catastrophe, and to make arrangements for their care. Agency members went out but reported back to the shah that no children had been found; they had simply been absorbed into the larger community.

This is in such contrast to America, where thousands upon thousands of children are left homeless, without schooling and hidden away in institutions without adequate provision for their minimal needs. Children still go hungry in America.[1] We are the richest nation in the world, yet an estimated 10 million of our children slip through the cracks of our health-care system.[2] Currently nearly 35 per cent of our children are not adequately immunized against polio, diphtheria, tetanus, and pertussis, diseases we know how to control.[3] Thousands upon thousands of children muddle along in custodial and even damaging day-care arrangements for lack of quality, publicly supported child-development services. Some young children are even left alone because their parents have to work and have no

[1] According to January 1974 U. S. Department of Agriculture figures, only 14,470,000 of the approximately 37 million people who are eligible for food assistance receive it. An unknown but high proportion of these are children (Community Nutrition Institute Weekly Report, May 16, 1974). The low rate of participation in food programs aimed specifically at pregnant mothers and young children underscores their needs. The Citizen's Board of Inquiry into Hunger and Malnutrition in the United States found that in 1972 only 20–34 per cent of children eligible for the school breakfast program received breakfast through the program (Hunger USA —Revisited, 1972). In 1974 funds were available to serve only 11 per cent of the pregnant women and children under age four eligible for supplemental foods (estimates by the Children's Foundation based on 1970 Census figures for numbers in need and 1974 official USDA figures for participation in the Commodity Supplemental Food Program and the authorized caseload in the Special Supplemental Food Program for Women, Infants and Children). For a good discussion of the politics of hunger see Nick Kotz, *Let Them Eat Promises* (New York, 1971).

[2] Charles Lowe and Duane Alexander, "Health Care for Poor Children," in Alvin Schorr, ed., *Children and Decent People* (New York, 1974).

[3] 1974 U. S. Immunization Survey, cited in a report by the Center for Disease Control (April 1975), p. 4.

one else to take care of them.[4] Tens of thousands of children
are detained annually in adult jails,[5] some in the same cells
with adult criminals,[6] because we have failed to help their families deal with them or to provide alternative community or
youth-placement services for them. Children's Defense Fund
staff have found children in jail simply because they had nowhere else to go. Millions of children languish in schools that
teach them neither to read, write, add, or substract.[7] At least
2 million children are excluded from all schooling.[8] Our juvenile justice system is so woefully underfunded, overworked,
and lacking in services that it breeds as much crime as it prevents.[9] Our infant mortality rates—we rate thirteenth in the
world—are those of an underdeveloped nation.

[4] Mary Keyserling, *Windows on Day Care* (New York, 1972).

[5] CDF published a report on the detention of children in
adult jails. But see also Sarri, *Under Lock and Key: Juveniles in
Jails and Detention* (Ann Arbor, 1974); Mattick, *Illinois Jails:
Challenge and Opportunity for the 1970's* (Chicago, 1969; *LEAA
Survey of Inmates in Local Jails in 1972* (Washington, D.C.,
1974); *National Jail Census, 1970: a Report on the Nation's Local Jails and Types of Inmates* (Washington, D.C., 1970).

[6] *Larry W. v. Leeke*, Civil Action No. 74-986, is a CDF suit
against law-enforcement officials in the state of South Carolina who
detained children in the same cell with adult prisoners. As a result, the children, five young boys in two different South Carolina
counties, were brutally raped and beaten.

[7] Herbert Kohl, *36 Children* (New York, 1967); Jonathan Kozol,
Death at an Early Age (Boston, 1967); Dentler and Worshaver,
Big City Dropouts and Illiterates (New York, 1965).

[8] See *Children Out of School in America*, a report of the Children's Defense Fund of the Washington Research Project, Inc.
(Cambridge, 1974), for analysis of 1970 U. S. Census data on non-
enrolled children (hereafter referred to as *Children Out of School
in America*).

[9] Justine Wise Polier, "Myths and Realities in the Search for
Juvenile Justice," in *Harvard Educational Review* edition *The
Rights of Children* (Cambridge, 1974). This volume is the best
recent compilation of articles on a variety of children's-rights
topics.

Why is this? Jane Addams asked in 1909 why it is that this country, technologically advanced and democratically oriented, could not service the needs of all its children. In 1975, seven White House conferences on children later, and after sixty-six years of effort by many, including Miss Addams, this question remains unanswered. For we have not yet accepted national responsibility for all of our children.

Americans are not a child-oriented people. Many of us love our own children or individual other children in our neighborhoods with whom we identify. But frequently we have not been able to translate this individual, selfish love into a broader love of the nation's children as a whole. Idolizing youth or loving individual children is not the same as placing societal priority on ensuring that all children get enough food, clothing, health care, education, and other services that will enable them to develop and function fully in American society.

Why a Children's Defense Fund

To speed up the achievement of rights and services for children, the Children's Defense Fund (hereafter CDF) was created in 1973. It is a national, non-profit organization that seeks to provide long-range and systematic advocacy on behalf of the nation's children. CDF is funded by a number of private foundations and is staffed with federal-policy monitors, researchers, community-liaison people, and lawyers who are dedicated to identifying, publicizing, and correcting selected serious problems faced by large numbers of American children.

We believe that children as a group have been ignored and unrepresented and that certain groups of children especially have been denied basic services and chances for minimally decent lives: poor children, racial- and language-minority children, "handicapped" children, and others with a range of special needs. This denial is not only immoral, it is unnecessary and foolhardy in terms of American self-interest now and in the future. Ignoring the needs of children now means we will pay later in dependency, illiteracy, alienation, juvenile delinquency, and crime. The cost in services is and will be enormous.

Children Out of School

To illustrate how fundamental the problems of American children are, our first report, *Children Out of School in America*, attempted to dispel the prevailing American notion that all children who ought to go to school in fact go to school.

At least 2 million children of school age were not in school. We found that if a child is not white, is white but not middle class, does not speak English, is poor, needs special help with seeing, hearing, walking, reading, learning, adjusting, growing up, is pregnant or married at age fifteen, is not smart enough, or is too smart, then, in too many places, school officials decide school is not the place for that child to be. The out-of-school children we found shared a common characteristic of differentness.

Poor and minority children are particularly singled out. This shows up graphically in our survey's suspension figures, in which almost 13 per cent of all black secondary students were suspended—three times the rate of white students suspended. The rate of black secondary school suspensions in some districts in our survey exceeded 30 per cent.

We found that 63.4 per cent of all the suspensions were for non-dangerous offenses; 25 per cent were for truancy and tardiness. Not only do schools suspend far too many children, they often do so unilaterally and without fair procedures.

Why We Should Care

Why should anybody care? We should care because we cannot teach our children justice if adults act unjustly.[10] It is indecent that some children are robbed of such minimum tools as

[10] *Children Out of School in America*, p. 126. See pp. 117–50 for discussion of school discipline and its exclusionary impact on students. See also a recent report of the Children's Defense Fund, *School Suspensions: Are They Helping Children?* (Cambridge, 1975).

schooling, which they need to survive in American society. As
the Fifth Circuit recently pointed out in a school suspension
case:

> In our increasingly technological society, getting at least
> a high school education is almost necessary for survival.
> Stripping a child of access to educational opportunity is
> a life sentence to second-rate citizenship.[11]

School exclusion is a major problem which reflects major institutional failure—most notably public-school failure. But it reflects the broader uncaringness of society which permits schools
to exclude children this way. Sadly, we will document this same
kind of institutional failure and societal unresponsiveness in
area after area, affecting millions of American children.

It has become clear to me that until all of us who say we
care about children begin to act on those concerns, our children
will get the leftovers of our national, local, and personal priorities and resources. As individual parents, we try to see that
our own children get first pickings, not scraps. As professionals,
it is time we extended that stance to include all children.

[11] *Lee* v. *Macon County*, 490 F. 2nd 458 at 460.

*Exploitation is relative, and the very constraints of child labor
laws and separation from adult society that critics now see as
damaging the youth of the seventies were heartily sought in the
late eighteen hundreds to save children from moral and physical
abuse. Socialist John Spargo wrote in 1906 of many problems
still with us, among them the high infant mortality rates and
malnutrition of the poor, and the need for public allowances
and child-care facilities for children of poor working mothers.
Most adults and children no longer face the totally unregulated
working conditions adults and children faced, sixteen hours a
day, six days a week, all of their short lives. Most children no
longer face this, but some still do.*

The Bitter Cry of Children
JOHN SPARGO

Not till they were forced by sheer hunger and misery, through the reduction of wages to the level of starvation, could the respectable workers be induced to send their children into the factories. In the meantime they made war upon the "iron men," as the machines were called, but of course in vain. To such a conflict there could be only one end—human beings of flesh and blood could not prevail against the iron monsters, their competitors.

But the manufacturers wanted children, and they got them from the workhouses.

[There were those who] made a profitable business of supplying children to the manufacturers. They deposited their victims in dark, dank cellars, where the sales to the manufacturers or their agents were made. "The mill owners, by the light of lanterns being able to examine the children, their limbs and stature having undergone the necessary scrutiny, the bargain was struck, and these poor innocents were conveyed to the mills." Their plight was appalling. They received no wages, and they were so cheap, their places so easily filled, that the mill owners did not even take the trouble to give them decent food or clothing. "In stench, in heated rooms, amid the whirling of a thousand wheels, little fingers and little feet were kept in ceaseless action, forced into unnatural activity by blows from the heavy hands and feet of the merciless overlooker, and the infliction of bodily pain by instruments of punishment invented by the sharpened ingenuity of insatiable selfishness."

The children were worked sixteen hours at a stretch, by day and by night. They slept by turns and relays in beds that were never allowed to cool, one set being sent to bed as soon as the others had gone to their toil. Children of both sexes and all ages, from five years upward, were indiscriminately herded together, with the result that vice and disease flourished. Sometimes the unfortunate victims would try to run away, and to prevent this all who were suspected of such a tendency had irons riveted on their ankles with long links reaching up to their hips. In these chains they were compelled to work and sleep, young women and girls as well as boys. Many children contrived to commit suicide, some were unquestionably beaten to death; the death rate became so great that it became the custom to bury the bodies at night, secretly, lest a popular uprising be provoked.

Worse still, the cupidity of British Bumbledom was aroused, and it became the custom for overseers of the poor to insist that one imbecile child at least should be taken by the mill owner, or the trafficker, with every batch of twenty children. In this manner the parish got rid of the expense of maintaining its idiot children. What became of these unhappy idiots will probably never be known, but from the cruel fate of the children who were sane, we may judge how awful that of the poor imbeciles must have been.

One immediate effect of the act of 1802 was the practical breakup of the pauper apprentice system. The reason for this is not difficult to determine. Wages had been forced down to the starvation level through the competition of the pauper apprentices with free, adult labor, with the result that poverty abounded. Parents were ready now to send their children into the mills. Hunger had conquered their prejudices—the iron man had triumphed over human flesh and blood.

"Provided a child should be drowsy (there were plenty working at six years of age), the overlooker walks around the room with a stick in his hand, and he touches the child on the shoulder, and says, 'Come here!' In the corner of the room is an iron cistern; it is filled with water; he takes this boy, and holding him up by his legs, dips him overhead in the cistern, and sends him to his task for the remainder of the day; and that boy is to stand dripping as he is at his work—he has no chance of drying himself."

If it were only possible to take the consumptive cough of one child textile worker with lint-clogged lungs, and to multiply its volume by tens of thousands; to gather into one single compass the fevers that burn in thousands of child toilers' bodies, so that we might visualize the Great White Plague's relation to child labor; the nation would surely rise as one man and put an end to the destruction of children for profit. If all the people of this great republic could see little Anetta Fachini, four years old, working with her mother making artificial flowers, as I saw her in her squalid tenement home at eleven o'clock at night, I think the impression upon their hearts and minds would be far deeper and more lasting than any that whole pages of figures could make. The frail little thing was winding green paper around wires to make stems for artificial flowers to decorate ladies' hats. Every few minutes her head would droop and her weary eyelids close, but her little fingers still kept moving— uselessly, helplessly, mechanically moving. Then the mother would shake her gently, saying: *"Non dormire, Anetta! Solamente pochi altri—solamente pochi altri."* ("Sleep not, Anetta! Only a few more—only a few more.")

And the little eyes would open slowly and the tired fingers once more move with intelligent direction and purpose.

The children who work in the dye rooms and print-shops of textile factories, and the color rooms of factories where the materials for making artificial flowers are manufactured, are subject to contact with poisonous dyes, and the results are often terrible. Very frequently they are dyed in parts of their bodies as literally as the fabrics are dyed. One little fellow opened his shirt one day and showed me his chest and stomach dyed a deep, rich crimson. I mentioned the incident to a local physician and was told that such cases were common. "They are simply saturated with the dye," he said. "The results are extremely severe, though very often slow and, for a long time, almost imperceptible. If they should cut or scratch themselves where they are so thoroughly dyed, it might mean death."

Child labor is now forbidden by law. But that law does not cover all children and all work. Many of the children who work are invisible to the mass of Americans. They work in fields and travel frequently, so we do not see them. If today's working children do not stand out like those John Spargo saw because of the bright red dye that covered their chests and poisoned their blood, they still are being destroyed by the months of breathing in and handling some of the most deadly poisons known to man. And they still work long, painful hours and suffer from malnutrition, lack of doctoring, lack of sanitation, and lack of hope. Robert Coles has gone into the fields and lived with the migrants, recording their words and their lives, and thanks to him we now know how their pain persists.

"God Save Them, Those Children; and for Allowing Such a State of Affairs to Continue, God Save Us, Too"

ROBERT COLES

The many young migrant children I have observed and described to myself as agile, curious, and inventive are, by seven or eight, far too composed, restrained, stiff, and sullen. They know even then exactly where they must go, exactly what they must do. They no longer like to wander in the woods or poke about near swamps. When other children are just beginning to come into their own, just beginning to explore and search and take over a little of the earth, migrant children begin to lose interest in the world outside them. They stop noticing animals or plants or trees or flowers. They don't seem to hear the world's noises. To an outside observer they might seem inward, morose, drawn, and tired. Certainly some of those qualities of mind and appearance have to do with the poor food migrant children have had, with the accumulation of diseases that day after day cause migrant children pain and weakness.

Yet, in addition, there is a speed, a real swiftness to migrant living that cannot be overlooked, and among migrant children particularly the whole business of growing up goes fast, surprisingly fast, awfully fast, grimly and decisively fast. At two or three, migrant children see their parents hurry, work against time, step on it, get a move on. At three or four those same children can often be impulsive, boisterous, eager, impatient in fact, and constantly ready—miraculously so, an observer like me feels—to lose no time, to make short work of what is and turn to the next task, the next ride.

However, at six or eight or ten something else has begun to happen; children formerly willing to make haste and take on things energetically, if not enthusiastically, now seem harried as they hurry, breathless and abrupt as they press on. I do not think I am becoming dramatic when I say that for a few first feverish years migrant children are hard-pressed but still and obviously quick, animated; tenacious of life is perhaps a way to say it. Between five and ten, though, those same children experience an ebb of life, even a drain of life. They move along all right; they pick themselves up again and again, as indeed they were brought up to do, as their parents continue to do, as they will soon, all too soon, be doing with their own children. They get where they're going, and to a casual eye they seem active enough, strenuous workers in the field, on their toes when asked something or called to do something. Still, their mothers know different; their mothers know that a change is taking place, has taken place, has to take place; their mothers know that life is short and brutish, that one is lucky to live and have the privilege of becoming a parent, that on the road the days merge terribly, that it is a matter of rolling on, always rolling on. So they do that, the mothers, go headlong into the days and nights, obey the commands of the seasons and pursue the crops; and meanwhile, somewhere inside themselves, they make their observations and their analyses, they take note of what happens to themselves and their children: "My little ones, they'll be spry and smart, yes they will be; but when they're older—I guess you'd say school age, but they're not all the time

in school, I'll have to admit—then they're different, that's what
I'd say. They'll be drowsy, or they won't be running around
much. They'll take their time and they'll slouch, you know.
They'll loaf around and do only what they think they've got
to do. I guess, well, actually, I suppose, they're just getting
grown, that's what it is. My boy, he's the one just nine this
season; he used to be up and doing things before I even knew
what he was aiming to do; but now he'll let no one push him,
except if he's afraid, and even then he'll be pulling back all
he can, just doing enough to get by. The crewleader, he said
the boy will be 'another lazy picker' and I stood up and spoke
back. I said we gets them in, the beans, don't we and what
more can he want, for all he pays us? I'll ask you. I guess he
wants our blood. That's what I think it is he wants, and if he
sees my children trying to keep some of their blood to themselves, then he gets spiteful about them and calls them all
his names like that; and there isn't anything you can do but
listen and try to go on and forget."

She tries to go on and forget. So do her children, the older
they get. Once wide awake, even enterprising, they slowly become dilatory, leaden, slow, laggard, and lumpish. Necessarily
on the move a lot, they yet appear motionless. Put to work in
the fields, they seem curiously unoccupied. The work gets done,
and by them, yet they do not seem to work. I suppose I am
saying that older migrant children begin to labor, to do what
they must do if they are not to be without a little money, a
little food; but at the same time the work is not done in a
diligent, painstaking and spirited way. It is done, all that hard,
demanding work; the crops get taken in. What one fails to see,
however, is a sense of real purpose and conviction in the older
children, who, like their parents, have learned that their fate
is of no real concern to others. The point is survival: mere survival at best, survival against great odds, survival that never is
assured and that quite apparently exacts its costs. If I had to
sum up those costs in a few words, I would probably say care
is lost: the child stops caring, hardens himself or herself to the
coming battle, as it is gradually but definitely comprehended,

and tries to hold on, persist, make it through the next trip, the next day, the next row of crops.

So, all year round, all day long, hour after hour, migrants stoop or reach for vegetables and fruit, which they pull and pick and cut; and at the same time those migrants settle into one place or prepare the move to another; and at the same time those migrants try to be parents, try stubbornly to do what has to be done—feed the children and get them to listen and respond and do this rather than that, and now rather than later. I have described the determination that goes into such a life of travel and fear and impoverishment and uncertainty. I have described the first and desperate intimacy many migrant children experience with their mothers. I have described the migrant child's developing sense of his particular world with its occasional pleasures, its severe restrictions, its constant flux, its essential sameness. To do so I have drawn upon what can actually be considered the best, the most intact, of the people I have seen and heard. After all, when parents and children together live the kind of life most migrants do, it seems a little miraculous that they even halfway escape the misery and wretchedness—that is, manage to continue and remain and last, last over the generations, last long enough to work and be observed by me or anyone else.

There is, though, the misery; and it cannot be denied its importance, because not only bodies but minds suffer out of hunger and untreated illness; and that kind of psychological suffering also needs to be documented. Nor can an observer like me allow his shame and guilt and horror and outrage and sympathy and pity and compassion to turn exhausted, careworn, worried, suffering people into brave and honorable and courageous fighters, into heroes of sorts, who, though badly down on their luck, nevertheless manage to win out, at least spiritually and psychologically. I fear that rather another kind of applause is in order, the kind that celebrates the struggle that a doomed man nevertheless at least tries to make. I fear that migrant parents and even migrant children do indeed become what some of their harshest and least forgiving critics call them: listless, apathetic,

hard to understand, disorderly, subject to outbursts of self-injury
and destructive violence toward others, and on and on. I fear
that it is no small thing, a disaster almost beyond repair, when
children grow up, literally, adrift the land, when they learn as
a birthright the disorder and early sorrow that go with virtual
peonage, with an unsettled, vagabond life. In other words, I
fear I am talking about millions of psychological catastrophes,
the nature of which has also been spelled out to me by migrant
parents and migrant children.

It is bad enough that thousands of us, thousands of American
children, still go hungry and sick and are ignored and spurned—
every day and constantly and just about from birth to death.
It is quite another thing, another order, as it were, of human
degradation, that we also have thousands of boys and girls who
live utterly uprooted lives, who wander the American earth, who
enable us to eat by harvesting our crops—yes, as children they
do—but who never, never think of any place as home, of themselves as anything but homeless. There are moments, and I believe this is one of them, when even doctors or social scientists
or observers or whoever, justly have to throw up their hands
in heaviness of heart and dismay and disgust and say, in desperation: God save them, those children; and for allowing such a
state of affairs to continue, God save us, too.

2.
The Oppression of the Young

Having surveyed the physical destruction of children that goes on pervasively but invisibly in American society, we turn to more subtle forms of abuse.

Oppression is the exercise of authority or power in a burdensome, cruel, or unjust way. There could be no better description of the condition in which children and young people often find themselves.

This is a perennial problem, though one that has been well suppressed by most cultures. As Mark Gerzon has pointed out, ". . . human childhood inevitably provides a potential basis for exploitation. . . . there will always be children. And children will always be dependent on the society of adults, not only economically but also psychologically and biologically. It is true that the activity of labor divided men into two major classes, one of which exploited the other. But it is also true that the activity of human development divided men into two generations, one of which is in position to control the other."

This section explores the forms this perennial exploitation and oppression take in America today. We have let the institution of the family disintegrate for lack of financial, social, and moral support. We have failed to provide a decent and promising world for young people to grow up into. We have pressed on our children both material goods and symbolic pressures that they don't need. And we have used our power over young people thoughtlessly and sometimes perversely. In the family, in schools, in the hands of the professionals who purport to be helping them, children find all too often that their real needs are ignored, that alien values are forced upon them, and that their legitimate claims to self-respect are violated.

In this statement by Youth Liberation of Ann Arbor, one group of young people speak for themselves about the conditions under which they live in their families and in their schools, and what they want to do about it.

"We Do Not Recognize Their Right to Control Us"
YOUTH LIBERATION OF ANN ARBOR

When I was six years old I ran away.

But I didn't go very far. My father followed me down the street with a movie camera, laughing at me. When I was thirteen I ran away again. The reason wasn't clear, but whatever it was I must have been feeling it pretty strongly. I stayed out in below-freezing weather and slept in an old bus. I was not free. I couldn't leave, because they have horrible, mind-shrinking places to put you in. I was lucky. My parents never called the police. But how many young people are not so lucky? Everyone needs Youth Liberation, not just young people, but also old people, new people, any people. At night I have this habit of running in the woods. Past curfew, past the houses, watching the dark.—*Laura, 16*

Ever since I was very small I had trouble with school. I was impatient and I had teachers that wouldn't tolerate this. I remember one year I went less than half the school year because

I became so hurt and upset. Going to high school, I came across many people telling me what "life's all about." Hell, it's been school that's been stifling my own self and keeping me from finding out what life's all about. School is a very clear symbol of how young people are treated. Living as a "minor," "juvenile," or any other label placed on young people, I rapidly became aware of our carefully drawn "limits."—*Cathi, 16*

I was raised in the movement. I was always taught that all people were equal and I would be too—when I grew up. I guess I sort of accepted it and did what I was expected to do. At least until fifth grade. Growing up in New York, and going to school in a black neighborhood of Brooklyn, the revolutionary and black separatist movements had great effect on all the people in my school. In fifth grade there was this racist, mean teacher who refused to let us use the class for black education classes. So we rebelled. We wore stickers to assemblies saying "Fuck Fisher," who was our assistant principal. We sat down in assemblies. We threw chairs out the windows and got suspended for refusing to come into the school until they started black history classes. All this went very well until the next year, when I was tracked away from all my black friends and they became black separatists. Things got on edge and it ended up where I kicked my ex-best friend's ass, had a bunch of people ready to kick mine, and was generally tired of the whole thing. So I split home. Moved in with some friends on the Lower East Side and stayed there for two days. I was caught and then I split again. The last time I split I went and stayed with two friends from Yippie! They gave me a bus ticket to Ann Arbor, fifty dollars, and a place to stay when I got there. So I went to Ann Arbor and stayed for three weeks. Went home and talked some things out with my parents. After that they sent me down to Florida to stay with some friends of mine. While I was there I got into a lot of death-culture drugs and ended up in the hospital from an overdose of ups and downs. The rest of the year was just as bad. I came back to Ann Arbor twice and went out to the West Coast. Finally my father got a job in Detroit and we moved to Ann Arbor. I've been living in a collective (with my parents, too) and been working on Youth Liberation ever since.—*Dave, 13*

I ran away three times last spring and my mother was thinking of putting me in a mental hospital because that's what her minister recommended. I came home and compromises were worked out. After a short period of time my mother had broken most of the promises she had made. When I brought up the subject she usually wormed out of it. Sometimes I used to wish I'd gone into the mental hospital; Jon was there and he said it wasn't bad. Anything to get out. I know my mother is wrong, horribly wrong, but she fools people well enough so they don't realize the frustration and bullshit I have to deal with every day. I can't even explain how awful it is. Sometimes I think of the butcher knife in the kitchen drawer and what I could do with it. When I'm in the same room as my mother I ignore her as much as possible because I dislike her. I'm scared of being like her. I'm moving out for the last six weeks of the summer to a house with three other sisters. I never want to come back to my mother's lifestyle. It's fucked up and I'll fight it til I die.—*Alice, 14*

Schools and families are the places where we begin to feel that we have to struggle for our freedom.

We want to learn what we need to make a good life on this earth, so we went to school. In school we found out that what was worth learning had been decided before we got there. It was laid out in neat chunks called grades, for twelve years in a row, and broken down into pieces, called subjects. But we wanted to know what the real world was like, and what does it mean to live a good life?

Questions like these got lousy answers. Just more subjects and tests and grades. We learned to stand in lines, to sit still and shut up, and to obey adults with authority. We learned to be bored and we hated school.

But we couldn't get out. Laws say that we have to take our bodies into those schools and police are hired to enforce them. Some of us tried to change things but we had no power. If we tried harder, like by calling a demonstration or by publishing an independent newspaper, we quickly learned that we did not have the right to free thinking, or freedom of speech, or freedom of the press, or freedom of assembly or anything else.

In our families we hoped for love and care and friendship and co-operation. Some of us had a happier time than others, but we all ended up in another system of absolute authority, with the young people at the bottom. We could only be as free as our parents allowed us to be. They punished us for refusing to obey. And, just like school, the police would come after us if we tried to get away. Our lives are considered the property of various adults. *We do not recognize their right to control us.* We call this control *adult chauvinism,* and we will fight it.

We quickly begin to learn that these schools and families are part of a whole system that is sick. Racism is bitterly damaging the lives of black and brown and red and yellow and white people. Sexism forces women into competition for men, into boring roles as the servants of men, and into objects for the sexual use of men. We know that free and open sexual relationships, homosexual as well as heterosexual, are beautiful, but we are taught that most are immoral. Society is divided into classes— the upper classes get the wealth and privileges while most of us spend our lives as exploited workers. American imperialism is attempting to milk the wealth of the whole world at gunpoint, and will destroy a country rather than "lose" it. We are fed an idiot culture through the TV tube, and our own new culture, from music and marijuana to free clinics and food co-operatives, is endlessly harassed. And now we learn that this whole system is being run so badly that the earth and its people are heading toward disaster. There are more possibilities of ecological disaster than we can keep track of. It is oppressive to think that you have a very small chance of dying a natural death, yet studies have shown that *most American young people believe they will die before their time.* And what kind of country is this, where the second-largest cause of death among young people is suicide? We formed Youth Liberation because we refuse to despair or give up.

Through our platform we try to look at the whole range of problems that face us. If we don't have a clear picture of our over-all situation and strategy, small defeats can take on too much significance. Our basic goal can be stated in a few words —*We want the power to control our destiny*—we want self-determination over our lives. This is not only our right; youth self-determination is necessary if human beings are going to survive on this planet.

The simple fact is that our generation is different from any other generation in history. We have lived our whole lives with the possibility of species suicide. We are the first products of a truly mass-based educational system. For the first time in history efficient contraception enables us to separate sex from having babies. We are the first generation to live in a time of instant global communications. We are the first generation to take basic material needs almost for granted, and thus be able to seek the real meaning and potential of our existence. We understand this world as the old people who created it and control it never can.

In this time, when great change happens at such rapid speed, it would seem reasonable that young people should be sincerely communicated with by older people. Cultural changes and adaptations made by young people should be respected. Since the outlook of young people has been completely shaped by the new world we live in, our perceptions and experience should be seriously considered as a guide and a path into the future.

Youths struggling for our liberation will succeed only through unity. But this will be difficult for many reasons. We don't have free access to communication or information, since we spend all our time in institutions run and controlled by adults. Racism, tracking, and other forms of manipulation are used to divide different races, sexes, and classes of youth so that they hate each other instead of the people in power. And even though most young people are beginning to realize how wrong things are, many of us see no hope. Many young people go for such short-term rewards as a boring but steady job. And many of us just want to forget what's happening—so we dose-up on dope, Jesus, TV, and booze, or we just give up and forget about trying to be free.

Youth Liberation believes that the hopeless can be organized to become fighters. We believe that when the youth mass begins to recognize that our political and physical survival is at stake, the differences between us will prove to be less important than our common goals. Large numbers of very young people can be recruited to the struggle if we treat children with dignity, respect, and full equality. We place our hope in children.

The goal of our organization is to unfold a whole new dimension of human liberation. There are seventy million human beings in the United States under the age of eighteen—that's one third of its population. Fifty million of these people are imprisoned in public school. But very few young people have been actually organized. On the Left, adult chauvinism still permeates. Too few radicals relate to adult chauvinism as an important aspect of human oppression. At present we are our only hope. Through hard work, and joy, we plan to educate and mobilize our people. Our ultimate goal is to join forces with all the people in the world in order to transform the earth.

Ann Arbor Youth Liberation has existed now for about two years. The first time most of us were together was at the Constitutional Convention in Washington, November 1970. We started talking about high school organizing and family hassles. We recognized that no political platform or group existed anywhere that spoke to our own basic needs and desires. One Sunday afternoon, a month or so after returning home, two of us sat down for five hours and drew up the first draft of the Youth Liberation Platform. We made a lot of copies but ended up throwing them away because the program continually had to be changed after discussions with new people. Twelve of us went out to a farm one weekend and went over each point, sentence by sentence. As soon as we released the platform it started getting printed in underground papers all over the country.

Some of our activities center on trying to end laws that discriminate against young people. In the spring of 1971 we convinced the Ann Arbor city council to drop its curfew laws. We presently have a case in court challenging adult-chauvinist election laws.

We went into the 1971–72 school year with big ambitions. We wanted to start a student union in all schools, which were to be local units of a city-wide Ann Arbor Student Union. Demonstrations were organized against the suspension policy. A committee was set up to investigate tracking. We had mixed results. In schools where we had strong organizers, we formed unions with large membership. We demanded and won the right to have meetings during school hours. Representatives from all the schools met and formulated city-wide demands for union recognition, teacher-student equality, and an end to tracking. But these unions were not able to sustain themselves.

Ann Arbor Youth Liberation still believes that student unions must be built, but we know that we were too naïve about it the first time around. During the 1972–73 school year most efforts will go into *Youth Rising*, our city-wide school underground paper. We will organize unions again after we have used the paper to build up the communication channels and the general consciousness of oppression necessary to make unions work.

In the spring of '72 we added electoral politics to our strategies. The local Human Rights Party, supporters of the youth liberation movement, nominated fifteen-year-old comrade Sonia Yaco to run on their slate for school board. "I'm running to prove a political point," said Sonia. "The Board of Education controls the lives of students, and therefore students should have a voice on the board." Her name was kept off the ballot by adult-chauvinist election laws. Still, in the write-in campaign, she received over thirteen hundred votes (8 per cent of the total), dramatizing the issue of adult chauvinism to the Ann Arbor community. (What if young people had been able to vote?!)

Youth Liberation has now incorporated CHIPS (Cooperative High School Independent Press Service—a newspaper exchange service) and FPS (the news service). Most of the articles contained in this pamphlet came from FPS. John Schaller, the founder of CHIPS/FPS, wrote a piece for this article explaining why he got started and how he joined up with Youth Liberation:

> In the end of 1968 my family had just moved to an all-white suburb of Chicago, and I was amazed at the racism displayed by many of the students. Here were attitudes which I hadn't known existed in that part of the country. Worse yet, almost no one was doing anything about this or the other problems that were crying for discussion, least of all the school newspapers. So a group of us decided to start putting out our own paper. It was fun at times, but we often felt isolated and alone. There we were, in a little suburb surrounded by cornfields, and we didn't know anyone else involved in anything like this.
>
> It was to relieve that feeling of isolation that I started CHIPS, which then stood for Chicago-area Highschool Independent Press Syndicate. It was a small group at first —even by late 1969 the members numbered barely a dozen —and its main function was to allow various papers to see what each other printed. At that point, letters from around the country were making it clear that high school papers everywhere were having the same isolation problems. So CHIPS became nationwide, and the name changed to Cooperative Highschool Independent Press Syndicate. It grew quickly from there, and soon had members in nearly twenty states—all of us exchanging our papers and trying to keep up with what was going on.
>
> Many of the people suggested that CHIPS could be even

more helpful by distributing short news stories to members in addition to helping them see each other's papers. From that grew the idea of a news service that would be directed at underground and independent high school newspapers, giving them news, feature stories, and graphics to reprint.

During the summer of 1970, after talking to students from various areas, I became convinced that such a service was needed and that it could be sent to people doing all types of work around high school and youth-related issues, not just those publishing papers. That September, the first issue of this news service, christened FPS, was published. It came out infrequently at first, but within a few months was meeting the goal of coming out biweekly.

About that time, I first heard about Youth Liberation, which was getting started in Ann Arbor. It was clear that we had similar goals, and we corresponded considerably. When the Youth Liberation program was printed in FPS, many readers showed an interest in it and wrote about some of the ways they had experienced age discrimination. The following summer, in 1971, I moved to Ann Arbor, where CHIPS and FPS became a part of Youth Liberation.

Young people are tricked and lied to from the first. Truth is confused, mystified, turned inside out, and then crammed down our throats. When we revolt as individuals we are isolated.

We of Youth Liberation believe that the time is soon coming when we will revolt together—then we can no longer be crushed. We will destroy all the myths that are fed to young people to keep us powerless. We will stamp out the false idea that the adults in power really do know what is going on and are somehow acting in our best interests.

We will tell the truth because we believe in our young sisters and brothers. The masses of young people will rise up when we begin to understand the truth. We will break down the barriers between us so that our strength can multiply. We will be living examples of a new kind of people living a life that has purpose.

The struggle for Youth Liberation is just beginning. We are like a newborn baby—we have no power, but unlimited potential. Like a baby, we will develop and become strong. The system of schools and families today holds total control over us, and many of us will not dare to fight. But in reality this system has long passed its time of usefulness and we all know it.

This culture that exploits and degrades us is in fact hanging on desperately trying to stop the advance of history. It won't fall by itself—we will have to push it over. Once we taste victory we can never be stopped. Soon the Youth Liberation struggle will surge forward to join all other liberation movements of oppressed people in the fight for a whole new civilization. The darkness will then pass from the sky and the sun will break through. Our enemy is nearing extinction while we are approaching victory. We are young. We want to live. We are the future.

The pressure on young people to conform has been criticized by such social reformers as Edgar Z. Friedenberg and Ted Clark. They score the suppression of young people's natural impulses to seek a fulfilling personal life and a just social order. Paul Goodman considered the lack of "man's work" for young people as seriously impeding full and healthful growth. The roots of the oppression of "adolescents" are traced to the "invention of childhood," which Philippe Ariès first described.

According to Ariès' study of the family, children for hundreds of years were accorded responsibilities and respect as full members of the adult community. People of different classes mixed freely too, and in work and play children, adults, rich, and poor interacted easily and unself-consciously.

But in the seventeenth century, claims Ariès, there evolved a new insular, private family concerned with the moral and physical development of children. It brought with it increasingly severe discipline for children and an "insistence on uniformity."

A Prison of Love
PHILIPPE ARIÈS

In the Middle Ages, at the beginning of modern times, and for a long time after that in the lower classes, children were mixed with adults as soon as they were considered capable of doing without their mothers or nannies, not long after a tardy weaning (in other words, at about the age of seven). They immediately went straight into the great community of men, sharing in the work and play of their companions, old and young alike. The movement of collective life carried along in a single torrent all ages and classes, leaving nobody any time for solitude and privacy. In these crowded, collective existences there was no room for a private sector. The family fulfilled a function; it ensured the transmission of life, property, and names; but it did not penetrate very far into human sensibility. Myths such as courtly and precious love denigrated marriage, while realities such as the apprenticeship of children loosened the emotional bond between parents and children. Medieval civilization had forgotten the *paideia* of the ancients and knew nothing as yet of modern education. That is the main point: it had no idea of education. Nowadays our society depends, and knows that it depends, on the success of its educational system. It has a system of education, a concept of education, an awareness of its importance. New sciences such as psychoanalysis, pediatrics, and psychology devote themselves to the problems of childhood, and their findings are transmitted to parents by way of a mass of popular literature. Our world is obsessed by the physical, moral, and sexual problems of childhood.

This preoccupation was unknown to medieval civilization, because there was no problem for the Middle Ages: as soon as he had been weaned, or soon after, the child became the natural companion of the adult. The age groups of Neolithic times, the Hellenistic *paideia*, presupposed a difference and a transition between the world of children and that of adults, a transition made by means of an initiation or an education. Medieval civilization failed to perceive this difference and therefore lacked this concept of transition.

The great event was therefore the revival, at the beginning of modern times, of an interest in education. This affected a certain number of churchmen, lawyers, and scholars, few in number in the fifteenth century but increasingly numerous and influential in the sixteenth and seventeenth centuries, when they merged with the advocates of religious reform. For they were primarily moralists rather than humanists: the humanists remained attached to the idea of a general culture spread over the whole of life and showed scant interest in an education confined to children. These reformers, these moralists, whose influence on school and family we have observed in this study, fought passionately against the anarchy (or what thenceforth struck them as the anarchy) of medieval society, in which the Church, despite its repugnance, had long before resigned itself to it and urged the faithful to seek salvation far from this pagan world, in some monastic retreat. A positive moralization of society was taking place: the moral aspect of religion was gradually triumphing in practice over the sacred or eschatological aspect. This was how these champions of a moral order were led to recognize the importance of education. We have noted their influence on the history of the school and the transformation of the free school into the strictly disciplined college. Their writings extended from Gerson to Port-Royal, becoming increasingly frequent in the sixteenth and seventeenth centuries. The religious orders founded at that time, such as the Jesuits and the Oratorians, became teaching orders, and their teaching was no longer addressed to adults, like that of the preachers or mendicants of the Middle Ages, but was essentially meant for children and young people. This literature, this propaganda, taught parents that they were spiritual guardians, that they were responsible before God for the souls, and indeed the bodies too, of their children.

Henceforth it was recognized that the child was not ready for life, and that he had to be subjected to a special treatment, a sort of quarantine, before he was allowed to join the adults.

This new concern about education would gradually install itself in the heart of society and transform it from top to bottom. The family ceased to be simply an institution for the transmission of a name and an estate—it assumed a moral and spiritual function, it molded bodies and souls. The care expended on children inspired new feelings, a new emotional attitude, to which the iconography of the seventeenth century gave brilliant and insistent expression: the modern concept of the family. Parents were no longer content with setting up only a few of their children and neglecting the others. The ethics of the time ordered them to give all their children, and not just the eldest—and in the late-seventeenth century even the girls—a training for life. It was understood that this training would be provided by the school. Traditional apprenticeship was replaced by the school, an utterly transformed school, an instrument of strict discipline protected by the law courts and the police courts. The extraordinary development of the school in the seventeenth century was a consequence of the new interest taken by parents in their children's education. The moralists taught them that it was their duty to send their children to school very early in life: "Those parents," states a text of 1602, "who take an interest in their children's education [*liberos erudiendos*] are more worthy of respect than those who just bring them into the world. They give them not only life but a good and holy life. That is why those parents are right to send their children at the tenderest age to the market of true wisdom [in other words to college] where they will become the architects of their own fortune, the ornaments of their native land, their family, and their friends."

Family and school together removed the child from adult society. The school shut up a childhood that had hitherto been free within an increasingly severe disciplinary system, which culminated in the eighteenth and nineteenth centuries in the total claustration of the boarding school. The solicitude of family, Church, moralists, and administrators deprived the child of the freedom he had hitherto enjoyed among adults. It in-

flicted on him the birch, the prison cell—in a word, the punishments usually reserved for convicts from the lowest strata of
society. But this severity was the expression of a very different
feeling from the old indifference: an obsessive love which was
to dominate society from the eighteenth century on. It is easy
to see why this invasion of the public's sensibility by childhood
should have resulted in the now better-known phenomenon of
Malthusianism or birth control. The latter made its appearance
in the eighteenth century, just when the family had finished
organizing itself around the child, and raised the wall of private
life between the family and society.

The modern family satisfied a desire for privacy and also a
craving for identity: the members of the family were united by
feeling, habit, and their way of life. They shrank from the
promiscuity imposed by the old sociability. It is easy to understand why this moral ascendancy of the family was originally a
middle-class phenomenon: the nobility and the lower class, at
the two extremities of the social ladder, retained the old idea
of etiquette much longer and remained more indifferent to
outside pressures. The lower classes retained almost down to
the present day the liking for crowds. There is therefore a connection between the concept of the family and the concept of
class. Several times in the course of this study we have seen
them intersect. For centuries the same games were common to
the different classes; but at the beginning of modern times a
choice was made among them: some were reserved for people
of quality, the others were abandoned to the children and the
lower classes. The seventeenth-century charity schools, founded
for the poor, attracted the children of the well-to-do just as
much; but after the eighteenth century the middle-class
families ceased to accept this mixing and withdrew their
children from what was to become a primary-school system, to
place them in the *pensions* and the lower classes of the colleges,
over which they established a monopoly. Games and schools,
originally common to the whole of society, thenceforth formed
part of a class system. It was all as if a rigid, polymorphous

social body had broken up and had been replaced by a host of little societies, the families, and by a few massive groups, the classes; families and classes brought together individuals related to one another by their moral resemblance and by the identity of their way of life, whereas the old, unique social body embraced the greatest possible variety of ages and classes. For these classes were all the more clearly distinguished and graded for being close together in space. Moral distances took the place of physical distances. The strictness of external signs of respect and of differences in dress counterbalanced the familiarity of communal life. The valet never left his master, whose friend and accomplice he was, in accordance with an emotional code to which we have lost the key today, once we have left adolescence behind; the haughtiness of the master matched the insolence of the servant and restored, for better or for worse, a hierarchy that excessive familiarity was perpetually calling in question.

People lived in a state of contrast; high birth or great wealth rubbed shoulders with poverty, vice with virtue, scandal with devotion. Despite its shrill contrasts, this medley of colors caused no surprise. A man or woman of quality felt no embarrassment at visiting in rich clothes the poor wretches in the prisons, the hospitals, or the streets, nearly naked in their rags. The juxtaposition of these extremes no more embarrassed the rich than it humiliated the poor. Something of this moral atmosphere still exists today in southern Italy. But there came a time when the middle class could no longer bear the pressure of the multitude or the contact of the lower class. It seceded: it withdrew from the vast polymorphous society to organize itself separately, in a homogeneous environment, among its families, in homes designed for privacy, in new districts kept free from all lower-class contamination. The juxtaposition of inequalities, hitherto something perfectly natural, became intolerable to it: the revulsion of the rich preceded the shame of the poor. The quest for privacy and the new desires for comfort that it aroused (for there is a close connection between comfort and privacy) emphasized even further the contrast between the material ways of life of the lower and the middle classes. The old society concentrated the maximum number of ways of life into the minimum of space and accepted, if it did not impose, the bizarre juxtaposition of the most widely different classes. The new society, on the contrary, provided each way of life with a confined space in which it was understood that the dominant features should be respected, and that each person had to resemble a conventional model, an ideal type, and never depart from it under pain of excommunication.

The concept of the family, the concept of class, and perhaps elsewhere the concept of race, appear as manifestations of the same intolerance toward variety, the same insistence on uniformity.

Among the first strong voices to say that the problems of growing up in American society derived from the nature of the society, rather than from the "deviance" of young people, was Paul Goodman. "I assume that the young really need a more worth-while world in order to grow up at all," he wrote in Growing Up Absurd, *in 1960. "And I confront this real need with the world that they have been getting. This is the source of their problems. Our problem is to remedy the disproportion."*

By 1970 the movement for children's rights had caused Goodman to reassess his position. His final feelings on the subject, the distillation of a lifetime's reflection, are summarized here.

Reflections on Children's Rights
PAUL GOODMAN

Children are an awkward subject for politics. Essays "toward the liberation of the child" always take contradictory tacks. Children should have "rights as full human beings," no different from those of adults: they should be able to vote, make contracts, and presumably commit felonies, just as adults do. On the contrary, runs another argument, they should have very special rights and immunities, because they are children; their rights should fit their "stage of growth." Similarly, one school says that the oppressive society of adults has so damaged the children that we must now provide them with remedial attention; on the contrary, say others, the best thing we adults can do is to get off their backs. And so on.

Even under good conditions, this confusion is deeply rooted in the nature of things. Human beings do pass through distinctive and well-marked stages of life—childhood and adolescence, middle age, old age—and yet we all, at every age, interact, must use and enjoy one another, and are likely to abuse and injure one another. This situation is not something to cope with polemically or to understand in terms of "freedom," "democracy," "rights," and "power," like bringing lawyers into a family quarrel. It has to be solved by wise traditions in organic communities with considerable stability, with equity instead of law, and with love and compassion more than either. But in modern times there are no such traditions, communities, or stability, and there *are* injustice, unnecessary suffering, and, worst of all, plain waste of young life. So there has to be polemical politics.

It has become common in liberation literature to say that Childhood is an invention of the past few hundred years in Western Europe, a means of rationalizing, controlling, and exploiting children. In more "normal" societies, it is claimed, children are just people, with the usual rights, immunities, and privileges, who take part in the community work according to their capacities. ("Adolescence" is an even more recent invention, a definition extended because of the trend toward earlier sexual maturation and longer exclusion from employment.) There is some truth in this thesis, but some liberators at once draw the polemical conclusion that children are identical to adults, must set up their own governments, and must have power to protect their interests. A recent publication of the radical caucus of the American Summerhill Society quotes

Huey Newton of the Black Panthers: "An unarmed people are slaves," and goes on to say, "We are asking for a 'human' standard to arm kids with, within which we as adults can deal with our own problems and uptightedness while kids are free to determine their own lives." That is, adults give power to the kids by disarming themselves. This is not a very authentic proposition. As an adult I am not at all willing to inhibit myself from doing my thing, I hope with temperance, justice, and compassion. The natural power that children have over me is not something I give them but stems from how they are and how I am.

Historically, treating children like little adults meant bringing a six-year-old to court for petty theft and hanging him and having nine-year-olds pick straw in the factory, not because their labor was useful but "to teach them good work habits." Presumably these children knew all about property rights and could contract their labor. Since the liberators of children do not mean this, they must think that in some respects children *are* special cases and must be protected from doing themselves harm. But even excellent progressive educators have fallen into the same equal-rights rhetoric. When Maria Montessori provided little chairs and tables in her classroom, she deprived the child of childhood, which more properly uses chairs and tables to crawl under and drape for tents. When A. S. Neill's kids are encouraged to "govern" themselves, one man one vote, in their court and parliament, he is taking the social contract and political democracy much too seriously; he is imposing adult ideas. This is *not* the form in which kids spontaneously choose up sides in a game, settle their disputes, and change the rules. Kids are far too shrewd to be democratic. They have more respect for strength, skill, and experience at the same time as they protect one another from being stepped on, humiliated, or left out. (They can also be as callous as the devil!)

There is an opposite interpretation of the concept of Childhood. It is a fairly recent idea, but it can be regarded as a discovery of gradually refining civilization rather than a device of malevolent exploitation, just as Greek tragedy, romantic love, and Nature also sprang from definite historical socioeconomic conditions but thereafter became permanent parts of how man has fashioned himself. This view makes children into a special class, not to control or mold them but to conserve them as natural resource or natural wonder. The key terms are not children's "rights" or "democracy" but their spontaneity, fantasy, animality, creativity, innocence. The British and North Americans especially have developed this notion in a vast juvenile literature that is sometimes cloying and whimsical but often beautiful. It was, of course, a chief theme of Wordsworth: the child trails clouds of glory and his experience abounds in intimations of immortality, until the shades of the prison house begin to close about the growing youngster.

Needless to say, the idea of Childhood can be stiflingly sentimental and can be used to keep children out of practical life, so that they are ignorant and retarded. It has been used as a basis for emotional exploitation of children, to serve the fantasies of regressed adults—perhaps even especially by way-out educators who run "free" schools. And there is always plain hypocrisy—with sentimentality goes cruelty—just as our quite genuine advance in humanitarianism goes nicely with napalm and so forth. Nevertheless, childhood *is* a special stage. Neoteny is an important factor in human biology. Psychoanalytically, we assign the highest importance to maintaining as distinct processes the living through of child life and that of adult life, so that we may draw on child powers without inhibition.

And, in the climate of modern times, overurbanized, over-technologized, too tightly organized, the chief present purpose of primary schooling—the only valid purpose, in my opinion— is to delay the socialization of children, to give their wildness a chance to express itself; for, at home, in the street, and in front of the TV set, children are swamped by social signals. As I have put it elsewhere, when the Irish monks invented academic schooling in the sixth century, there was some point to licking a few likely wild shepherds into social shape in order to take on the culture of Rome; now, when everything is too cultured, it is necessary to protect the wildness of the shepherds. I think that it is by implicitly performing this function that Summerhill is relevant in our generation. Neill's explicit purpose of making emotionally balanced individuals and co-operative citizens is far less important.

A gloomier version of our situation is that what we owe to children is therapy. A good school is best regarded as a half-way house for recuperation, rescuing the children from the insane homes and cities in which they have already been socialized and deranged. Summerhill, as described, usually sounds like a therapeutic community; the wounded child broods by himself in a secure and loving setting that imposes on him no pressure or compulsion, while nature heals.

When he was principal of a Harlem school, Elliot Shapiro tried out a curriculum consisting mostly of expressing hostility —the children gave talks, wrote compositions, and acted out why and how they hated their parents, their siblings, the police, the neighborhood, the school, the school's principal. The procedure raised their I.Q.'s, for stupidity is a character defense of turned-in hostility. There were also fewer windows broken from *outside*. Obviously, this technique is Frantz Fanon's prescription for colonized peoples; they must turn to hate and violence against the imperialist, in order to recover their own identities.

In my opinion, the only justification for high schools is as therapeutic halfway houses for the deranged. Normal adolescents can find themselves and grow further only by coping with the jobs, sex, and chances of the real world—it is useless to feed them curricular imitations. I would simply abolish the high schools, substituting apprenticeships and other alternatives and protecting the young from gross exploitation by putting the school money directly in their pockets. The very few who have authentic scholarly interests will gravitate to their own libraries, teachers, and academies, as they always did in the past, when they could afford it. In organic communities, adolescents cluster together in their own youth houses, for their fun and games and loud music, without bothering sober folk. I see no reason whatsoever for adults to set up or direct such nests or to be there at all unless invited.

Yet it is certainly the case at present that very many adolescents are so befuddled and discouraged that they cannot be thrown into society to cope, either to adjust or to be constructively revolutionary. They need "free" schools in order to get their heads together. The danger of such schools is that they take themselves too seriously, as counterculture rather than as hospitals. But the youth subculture is an obstacle to growing up; the young are right to cling to it, for it is theirs; but there is no excuse for adults to pander to it. In the best cases, free high schools are convenient administrative gimmicks to get around the compulsory-education law—and officials do well to encourage them and save on the expense of truant officers. For the young, they provide a safe home base to return to when they are anxious or in need of medical or legal aid.

Philosophically, the right relationship among children, adolescents, and adults—groups that are so unlike and yet like and that make up one community—should be a pluralism; in some areas they should leave one another severely alone; in other areas they need, use, and enjoy one another, can make demands, and have obligations. The really interesting facts of life have to do with the opportunities, dangers, and limits of how grown-ups and children can get something from one another. Yet it is rare that this *prima facie* and commonsense point of view is taken by our present liberators and school reformers.

When A. S. Neill says that his pupils don't know his religion, drug attitudes, or politics, I am simply baffled. He can't be taking his pupils very seriously, or he can't be taking his religion very seriously. If the young don't hear opinions about such things from a knowledgeable and trusted adult, from whom should they hear them? I too don't believe in "teaching" children unless they reach out and ask; it is folly to moralize or to try to coerce them into "learning" something. But why should children be protected from *my* reality? My religion, art, animality, and politics *are* my reality. I once had an argument in print with John Holt about Neill's proposition that at Summerhill rock and roll is equivalent to Bach, Beethoven, and Debussy. But it is *not* equivalent. More *happens* in two bars of the great music than in two minutes of the rock band, and this can be shown objectively—as John well knows, for he is a cellist and a fanatical discophile. There is potentially more musical experience in better music, and my behavior will say this. Naturally, kids can listen to what they like without lectures from me—unless, as sometimes happens, a kid bugs me with *his* nonsense about his music; and then I may take him by the scruff of the neck and make him listen to *my* music, plus an analysis of it.

It's a tough problem. I don't know any academic means of passing on the humanities; the schools do more harm than good, for they turn the young off. If the humanities do seem to survive, poorly, it is by contagion; some of us take them with surprising earnestness, some young people catch on.

Many, perhaps most, craftsmen, professionals, scholars, and savants need young apprentices, to see the tasks afresh through young eyes, to pass on the art as it was earlier passed on to them. But, in the relation of master and apprentice, the key is certainly not the freedom and rights of the young, nor the theory of the young, but the often harsh discipline of the craft and the objective nature of things. It is these that give identity and dignity and, finally, freedom. Yet from the talk of most free-school people, one would not guess that there are crafts, professions, and a nature of things; rather, one would think that the world consists only of interpersonal relations and put-downs by irrational authority.

I don't know what to make of the claim that "student power" should determine the content and method of courses. Why would I agree to teach what is not important and not relevant in *my* eyes? And how would I know what to teach in such a case? Of course, the students are free to stay away from my classes—I give them their A's anyway.

So there are areas of mutual need, demand, and giving. On the other hand, in many areas of experience it is best if children, adolescents, and adults have little to do with one another at all. There are entirely too many schoolteachers around who are eager to teach everything, including freedom and democracy and interpersonal relations. One of the beautiful experiments of the Peckham Health Center showed that, when small children were freely permitted to use the apparatus of a fully equipped gymnasium: (1) if there were older children present, there were many accidents, probably because of showing off and emulation; (2) if there was an adult teacher present, there were fewer accidents, but some children did not participate and some did not learn the apparatus; and (3) if the small children were left to themselves, all learned and there were no accidents.

A sign of the confusion of modern times is that we all pay too much attention to children, either depriving them of rights and freedom or trying to give them rights and freedom. This includes books of mine. I would suggest, as a program for the coming decade, that the best thing we adults could do for children and adolescents would be to renovate our own institutions and give the young a livable world to grow up in.

*A family's affluence no longer assures that its young are not
being neglected. The reasons are sharply probed by William
Shannon of the New York Times editorial board.*

Our Lost Children
WILLIAM V. SHANNON

Although Americans in recent decades have grown richer, our
children have grown poorer. Many families no longer adequately perform the nurturing and supporting function that
children need, emotionally and intellectually.

The evil consequences for children are not in dispute. The
rate of suicide among children aged ten to fourteen is twice
as high as it was twenty years ago. For children aged fifteen to
nineteen, the rate has tripled.

Since 1963, crimes by children have been rising at a faster
rate than the juvenile population. About half of such crimes
involve the traditional youthful offenses of theft, breaking and
entry, and vandalism; but serious, violent crimes—though still
involving a relatively small proportion of children—are going up
at a startling rate. The rate of armed robbery, rape, and murder
by juveniles has doubled in a decade.

The Senate Juvenile Delinquency Subcommittee surveyed
750 school districts and reported these changes between 1970
and 1973:

Dropouts increased by 11 per cent, drug and alcohol offenses
on school property were up 37 per cent, burglaries of school
buildings up 11 per cent and assaults on teachers up 77 per
cent.

Among those who are thought of as normal children, lower
reading scores and scholastic aptitude scores reveal intellectual
impoverishment. Beyond all this loom the apathy and waste of
the counterculture. Its existence is no longer news, but its ranks
are still swelled each year by thousands of pathetic runaways
and dropouts.

What forces are producing the increasingly severe stresses on today's children?

The phenomenon is complex and baffling, but several developments seem to be interacting. Urbanization is a factor. Children who might have made it on a farm or in a village—despite adverse family circumstances such as extreme poverty or a father's desertion—encounter disaster in a big city with its anonymity and diverse temptations.

Births by unwed mothers and divorce, two trends that are both rising steadily, result in depriving children of the stable, two-parent support that they need in their growing years. One out of every six children under eighteen today is living in a single-parent family. This is almost double the proportion in 1950.

Many divorced or widowed parents obviously succeed with their children. But, ideally, rearing a child is a two-person job. When one parent is missing, the risks of failure increase. Indeed, it is best if a child has grandparents or other supportive relatives on the scene as well.

Instead, what has happened is the near disappearance of the extended family and the substitution of television, the hopelessly inadequate electronic babysitter. One study, for example, revealed that fifty years ago half of the households in Massachusetts included at least one adult besides the parents; today the figure is only 4 per cent. In a small child's life, "Captain Kangaroo" is no substitute for a devoted grandmother.

If grandmothers are gone, mothers are going fast. As would be expected, the majority of mothers who lack husbands go to work, usually full time. What is astonishing and depressing is that in families in which the husband is present, 30 per cent of the mothers with infants work and more than one third of those with children under six do so.

These proportions are two or three times higher than they were in 1950. Financial necessity cannot account for this trend. There was inflation twenty-five years ago and family budgets were crimped then, too. In real terms, husbands are earning more money now than then. What has changed for the worse is not the family's income but the younger woman's attitude. She no longer regards staying home to care for small children as her overriding responsibility.

Mothers go to work for various reasons, and an outsider cannot judge a family's specific circumstances. But it can be said that a young child needs a one-to-one emotional relationship with a loving adult if the child is to grow into a stable, self-confident person. A full-time mother best provides that relationship.

Middle-class white families may assume complacently that disorganization and delinquency are the fate only of blacks or of the very poor. But as Urie Bronfenbrenner, professor of family studies at Cornell University, has observed: "In terms of such characteristics as the proportion of working mothers, number of adults in the home, single-parent families, or children born out of wedlock, the middle-class family of today increasingly resembles the low-income family of the early nineteen-sixties."

In short, family disorganization is spreading. Money alone is not a sufficient barrier.

The harm currently being done to children in our society has a history. Margaret Mead explores that background, which haunts our present efforts to deal more humanely with the young. And she suggests what we must do to overcome a tradition of isolating and mistreating them.

The Heritage of Our Children
MARGARET MEAD

Americans have long been accused by Europeans of being a child-centered culture. I have encountered Asians who add to this accusation the statement that Americans are too concerned with the past, that is with patterns of childhood which they see as the past, that are discarded in actively changing societies. At the same time, our society is coming under vigorous condemnation for its attitudes toward and treatment of the elderly. The young, the poor, and the elderly form a disadvantaged trio.

Meanwhile we have become increasingly aware of how grievously we have failed our children during the past fifty years, as many earnest reformers have tried sedulously to remove children from those of our social institutions which are deemed too terrible for the toleration of their presence. So we took children out of the regular court process and set up juvenile courts; we took children out of prisons and founded juvenile detention homes; we took children out of our great, impersonal high schools and invented the junior high school. And the state of the children within these new institutions designed to protect them from the otherwise uncorrected evils of our society has worsened; more and more children become homeless, grievously neglected, and abused. There would seem to be an extraordinary paradox in the fact that a child-centered society, a society so anxious to found special institutions for the protection of children, should be a society in which children seem to fare worse and worse. We may well ask, was the characterization wrong? were we really a child-centered society? what happened?

One explanation may lie in the discontinuity that we have all experienced and expected our children to experience between the traditional ways of the parental generation and the expected deviations of the child generation. This expectation was built into American culture from the arrival of Europeans and Africans to these shores. The experience of adults in the new world was necessarily more dependent upon the cultures within which they had been reared than was that of their children, born and bred in the new environment. The new environment not only contained forests to clear, vast fields to plough and mountains to mine, but also the special sets of expectations, fears, and bitternesses of the first generation of parents, whether they came as adventurers, religious or political exiles,

152 MARGARET MEAD

debtors, slaves, indentured servants, fugitives from justice, or simply hard-working, enterprising people hoping for a better life for their children.

Some break between parents and children was inevitable, and gradually it became so built into American cultural expectation that it was expressed within families who had themselves descended from immigrants who arrived many generations ago. Parents became spectators of their children's success, which in going beyond their parents' status in the world became the most important thing that children owed their parents, replacing the deference and support in old age that had been children's debt to parents in Europe.

Within this context, wherever the expectation failed there was trouble. It took many forms. In slums, urban gangs of youngsters formed where migrant parents failed to find a place worthy of their children's respect, and the teen-agers, anxious for some applause, turned instead for admiration of their anti-social activities to younger boys. Men who failed to make a living drifted away from home, and boys who would in turn fail to make a living were temporarily leaned on too heavily by their mothers. Large sections of the population ceased to believe in the possibility of mobility and reared their children with low expectations and little hope. This was true in families of Appalachia and among American blacks who made tremendous sacrifices to educate their children, only to find no opening for students with higher degrees except for such jobs as postman or housemaid. Farmers who lost their land in the Depression constituted another despairing group. With each wave of migration there was a fraction who failed, who stayed on, stuck at the bottom of society, in neighborhoods that had been Little Italies, ghettos, Spanish Harlems, or Chicano communities. Where some escaped poverty, those who remained were the more embittered. This was particularly well demonstrated by the Detroit riots of the summer of 1970. Many commentators on the race question had believed that there was less danger in Detroit, because a higher proportion of black Americans had prospered there.

These hopeless parents who did not believe in their children's future raised young people who, although having adequate intelligence to succeed in higher education, dropped out of high school and joined an unskilled and underemployed labor pool. Characteristically, instead of shouldering the responsibility for our failure to give them the kind of support they would have needed to continue in school, we accused them of "dropping out." In the mid 1950s it became clear that the old American expectation of children surpassing their parents was being shared by a smaller and smaller proportion of the American people, that a larger proportion was settling into a life of fatalistic desperation in which the price of crops, the vagaries of employment, the business cycle, the half-dug subways, the inflammable buildings, the weather, the corruption in high places, and the ethical inconsistencies of undeclared wars all blended together as a kind of inescapable fate.

These shifts in expectation have to be taken into account when we consider what has happened to our children since 1918, when my high school principal, himself an American-born son of Italian immigrants, read us a speech that began: "Boys and girls of America, you are the hope of the world." What is behind the disquieting statistics on how poor our children's health is, how badly they compare with European children in physical capacities, how poorly we stand on infant mortality, how severe the malnutrition is among 30 to 40 per cent of the population, and how an increasing proportion of slum-dwelling children are not learning to read.

We have been shifting away from a belief that the children in the next generation would have a better chance than their parents, would rise higher than their parents and reward their parents' hard labor with success. Among the affluent, this shift has been aggravated by the disaffection of middle-class young people from the suburban standard of living for which their parents paid so much in money, time, and effort to obtain for them. And in the colleges, during the troubles of the 1960s, it was the good, devoted teachers who were most hurt when a student generation repaid their years of devotion to earlier

student generations with insults. Urie Bronfenbrenner has
made a startling analysis of the extent to which we manage to
make our school-age youngsters allies of mischievous disruption,
while in the USSR their loyalty is successfully enlisted by the
state. The reciprocal of imprisoned teen-agers, kept in a school
that fails to hold their interest or give them any sort of promise,
is the increasing fear by adults, especially the elderly, of the
disaffected, idle, mischievous young, so that a cluster of teen-
agers on a street corner arouses a shudder in those for whom
they should be representing a future worth working for.
Examples can be multiplied. A college will count a library as an
educational expense but a nursery school as a liability.

There is a proliferation of zoned, closed communities in
which families with large numbers of children are excluded in
various ways because, owing to the way in which school taxes
are collected, poor families with children represent a burden
to the childless affluent. The very necessary campaign in favor
of zero population growth has carried with it—in many contexts—a rejection of parenthood and a rejection of children
themselves; unwanted children have been classified as a kind of
pollution. The number of doorstep children multiplies into
millions, as do the children with preventable handicaps that
come from malnutrition and neglect. Child abuse, a sign of
frantic and despairing parenthood, has increased in salience if
not in proportionate numbers.

We have become a society of people who neglect our children, are afraid of our children, find children surplus instead of
the *raison d'être* of living. Why? The conditions that have
brought this about are complex and poorly understood, but it
is possible to identify a few. In an increasingly urban society,
children no longer represent useful supplementary labor in
childhood and security for their parents' old age. The rate of
rapid change has meant that the traditional generation gap between parents and children everywhere has been intensified
until no children can expect to be the kind of persons their
parents were, and parents in their turn have no successors to
whom they look forward with certain pride. At the same time,

as a shared modern culture stretches around the world, the members of the post-World War II generation communicate better with each other, but through emotion-laden song and manners rather than through learning the content of one another's language. Earlier maturation by some four months a decade has meant that children are physically more mature at an earlier age, so that failure to give teen-agers responsibility becomes more conspicuous.

We have continued to misuse children as instruments of pride and power, instead of recognizing them as human beings with needs of their own. We are not, of course, the first society to do this; the world of subsistence agriculture sees children as a form of social security, and very often parenthood is the only route to social esteem. But in our urban society, as children ceased to be necessary to earning a living, they became increasingly instrumental for parental pleasure. Parents who expected children to remain a heavy expense and make no repayment, did expect to get their money's worth in joy, self-satisfaction, and self-congratulation. Being a joy to one's parents, whom one did not choose, is a heavier burden than is the expectation of returning in kind the support and care that was meted out in childhood and remained an obligation in adulthood. Children have become instruments of adult aggrandizement.

Political fights over schoolbook issues are not primarily concerned with the welfare of children as much as they are ways of venting a sense of political impotence and indignity. Perhaps nothing illustrates so well the confusion and contradictions in our attitudes toward children as our treatment of the children flown out of Saigon this year during the spring crisis of March–April. For years our servicemen had fathered and deserted children in Viet Nam, and our bombers poured death upon Vietnamese children. Then, at a moment when the United States was being criticized from all sides, what did we do? We tried again to take the children out, away from their own country, their own language, their own faith. Behind the evacuation lay, of course, great waves of indiscriminate humanitar-

ianism mixed with the desire for more adoptable children, now
so scarce in the United States. It is not surprising that so many
children suffered immediate physical harm during the poorly
conceived airlift—a prelude to the complexities of their ambiguous future as identifiable strangers in a society still glaringly
committed to the idea that character and intelligence are somehow related to physique.

In the face of our growing recognition that somehow the
methods we have used to protect children have failed—from
the first juvenile court to the last effort to compensate for the
segregated urban slum with Head Start alone, from our
elaborate and expensive ways of caring for a few children, to
our regimented schools for the many—we have thought of children with too little reference to the context in which they live.
This is vividly illustrated by the way we export our ideas of
public health to the developing countries while we focus all
our attention on infant welfare, neglecting the adults who are
needed to care for these children and who die young of preventable ills. Surely the care given to children is a measure of a
good society. But good care for children simply cannot be given
by a poverty-ridden, disease-ridden, crime-ridden, despairing
adult population. Nor can it be given by adults who find no
meaning to life beyond the purchase of equity in a suburban
house from which their children will move away, leaving their
lives, once narrowly devoted to their own children alone, empty
and meaningless.

We are moving into a period when there will be an attempt
to refocus our attention on the needs and rights of children.
Declarations of the rights of children, child-advocacy procedures, and child-abusing-parents-anonymous groups are pro-
liferating. There is one exceedingly good rationale for such a
change at a time when all the institutions of today's society are
being questioned, and when new ones, such as a family impact
statement or marriage insurance, are being sought. As trying to
save children *in vacuo* ends in failure, so greater involvement
of adults in the needs of children and greater attention to
changes in child-rearing practices are the surest ways of chang-

ing the attitudes of adults, and the direction of society. Called upon merely to pay taxes, make sentimental contributions to the welfare of children in other lands, or indignantly endorse some piece of legislation, adults are very little affected by our recurring campaigns, our Children's Days, our clean-ups of juvenile detention homes, or reforms of laws governing the quarters of inadequate day-care centers for the children of working mothers. If adult attention is actively, continuously directed toward children's needs for food, for love and trust, for conditions that will stretch their minds and stimulate their imaginations, adults also will have to think about food, love, and imagination.

Children seen at a distance are at best only wards or step-children—provided for out of guilt or sentimentality requiring no genuine personal effort. Only by involving adults, all adults —adults who have never had children and adults whose children have grown up—can we hope to combine reform in the care of specific groups of children—deaf children, crippled children, orphaned children, abandoned children—with a genuine attempt to rethink the way our towns and cities are built and the way our lives are lived. A family impact statement will be meaningless without an accompanying environmental impact statement. The most hygienic and well-provisioned orphanages are still places where babies die for lack of love and where adults who close their eyes and ears become reinforced in callousness and irresponsibility.

A crucial way of changing the condition of children in this country is by designing communities so that the childless see something of children and their needs, and so that those who have children of their own are provided with institutions that extend their concern beyond the well-being and advantage of their own biological or adopted children. There has been a spate of discussion about homes in which the mothers are so expansively loving that they can include other children—even those severely handicapped—inside their home also. But this is only another way by which society accepts a surrogate, like nuns in perpetual supplication for the sinners outside the gates.

These generous homes can serve as a way to excuse other people from parenthood. With zero population growth, if such mothers have borne five children and adopted three, then four of us are left to be non-parents.

Only as we redesign our life styles so that institutions for children are again play spaces within communities of adults of all ages and different economic and social status, will we have a more human, whole society in which the children who grow up will be safer and loved.

Therapist and counselor Ted Clark admits that his experience has driven him to the view that "the problems of young people are primarily the fault of adults." But he does not cringe from this conclusion, acknowledging that "yes, after careful consideration, I believe that the burden of proof is with adults." Here he explains what he means by the oppression of youth and why it is so pervasive.

The Oppression of Youth
TED CLARK

Everyone agrees that young people are often unhappy and discontented. Adolescence itself, the age from puberty to young adulthood, is assumed to be a natural series of identity crises involving emotional turmoil and conflicts with parents and other authority figures. The signs of discontent are clear; everywhere, one sees alienated youth. Symptoms of discontent and emotional conflicts include drug use, running away from home, unwanted pregnancies, the spread of venereal disease, withdrawal from all sexual relationships, delinquency, shoplifting and vandalism, and school dropouts. The most serious signs of difficulty may be chronic boredom coupled with despair; passivity, the capitulation to pressures to say and do nothing that makes large numbers of young people appear to be content simply because they do not dissent; and the egocentric attitude of many young people, their turning inward in an effort to gratify their needs at the expense of co-operative community-of-interest relationships with each other. Indeed, widespread *anomie* is seen in increasing rates of alcoholism, suicide, and other signs of endemic social problems for youth. The controversy is not about whether young people are troubled, but about *why* and about what can be done about it.

When we describe adolescence as having the main purpose of developing a sense of personal identity, what are we doing? First of all, a judgment is being made about a particular period of people's lives. The purpose of this phase, we are told, is to develop a "personal identity," as if this were intrinsic to this age group. In fact it is neither intrinsic nor is it actually the kind of identity being talked about. Young people in their families have a strong sense of personal identity, which is constantly confirmed by their parents and siblings. But this situation is changed for the young person after puberty. Societal authorities expect him to assume more responsibilities, to cope with sexuality and aggression along socially acceptable lines, and to fulfill the demands of society to achieve a *social role* instead of a familial one. Essentially, the youth is expected to move from a sense of self based on family authority to one based on societal authority. However, the social role is ambiguously defined. Furthermore, and unfortunately, society spends a great deal of energy defining the prohibitive limits of social roles while doing little to help the individual determine the *content* of a positive and socially sanctioned role.

The conflicts between the family's demands and the social pressures on youth are incredibly complicated and almost always in profound contradiction. Fantastic as it may seem, not only must youth begin, without much preparation or support, to change from child to adult roles in order to comply with the social imperative "grow up!" but they must *also* learn to distinguish between the rhetoric of the society and its real expectations and demands. Let us create some categories. The *family demands* will stand for whatever pressures parents and siblings are putting on the young person to comply with their needs, expectations, limits, and demands. The *societal demands* will stand for the real demands, standards, limits, and so forth demanded of the youth by social authorities, including school officials, community leaders, influences through the media, and the peer group. The *societal ideals* will stand for whatever ideology is propounded concerning the maturation process and on which the demands are supposedly based.

Let us take the example of Ann, a young girl about fourteen years old. She had an "identity crisis" concerning her desire to go out with a boy of fifteen. It was an identity crisis because the previous instructions about dating given to her were all family demands. What should she do? She was not expected to date at all: "you're too young," "wait until you are older," "we'll tell you when we think you are old enough to date." She knew all this very well, and as long as her sense of self was based on her family role, she was fine. But she also knew that "people" expected her to "grow up." These people represented societal demands. They included, "what's the matter with you, are you a baby or something?" and "you've got to start going out with boys sometime."

If Ann went out with John, few societal authorities would be upset. If Ann understood "make your own decisions" literally, she might let John "go all the way." She would quickly find both her peer group—through the bad-reputation tactic—and societal authorities—through allegations of immaturity, loss of control, and impulsiveness—didn't mean that she should make her own decisions at all. What they meant was: make the decisions *in terms of* societal rules and standards, not in terms of familial rules and standards. This conflict between societal ideals and societal demands is incredibly complex. Does society mean Ann should date? If so, is Johnny acceptable? What can she/they do, and what can't they do? Is Ann "old enough" to decide for herself? The point is that societal demands are vague and the limits are arbitrary.

If Ann is to "rebel" against her parents and try to get their permission to date John, is this being "grown up" or is it being a "baby" since she still is letting them decide? If she decides by herself to see John, what will her parents do in reaction? Punish her? Threaten her? Capitulate? Depending on how strenuously Ann's parents attempt to keep her in a child role, that is, dependent on their permission and punished for disobedience, Ann will have conflicts with her parents as she attempts to "grow up."

The peer group is both a source of support—everyone is going through the same things—and a source of pressure and punishment. By establishing limits, young people protect themselves against the possibility that someone will go further than they dare and hence demonstrate their own fear, feelings of helplessness, and insecurity. Ann knows that some kids her age date and others don't. It isn't clear whether she will suffer criticism for going out with John—some girls who date early are considered "sluts"—or gain prestige: "Boy, are you lucky to be able to go out."

Ann is also aware of the conflicting attitudes of society in general. Some adults permit and encourage children to date early, others don't. Such limits are often contradicting, vague, subject to inexplicable changes. Ann is still under pressure, partly from John, partly from her own desire to go out with him, partly because she knows that she has to begin making these decisions herself, partly because she knows that if she breaks any of hundreds of covert limits that she cannot imagine, she may suffer negative consequences. Ann is also frightened about what she has heard about sex and doesn't feel any sound and protective support being offered her—in fact, many people seem to assume the decision is an easy one. How will Ann decide?

Identity crises occur when the young person realizes that growing up means coming to grips with paradoxical injunctions offered by parental and societal authorities. On the one hand, parents expect obedience, while, on the other hand, society, through teachers, peer-group pressure, and its general pattern, expects the youth to become independent. Yet when the youth makes a move that contradicts parental authority, the state is usually willing to support the parents, not the youth. Invariably, neither the societal authorities nor the parents approve of many of the desires or inclinations of the individual. The results are self-oppression, conflicts with authority figures, and concealment of illicit attitudes, feelings, or behavior. Every youth experiences identity crises, often to the point where real emotional disturbances result.

Many of the "neuroses" of adolescents are the attempts young people have made to resolve the complex situation they are in regarding maturation. They love their parents, or at least are dependent on them; this situation makes them vulnerable to demands couched in terms of rewards (for example, the use of the car and spending money). They periodically hate their parents, feeling smothered by their own dependency needs and the parents' implied willingness to respond. Youths want to become independent but are fearful of responsibility. They make "impulsive" or unconsidered actions but deny that the actions are self-directed to avoid blame. Youths want acceptance of the peer group and act according to group demands, while selecting peer groups who represent their own desires and needs.

Identity crises are further complicated by other factors. First, oppression from the child role is intense, and adolescence lends societal support, however tenuous, to breaking out of its confines. Logically, the more oppressive the role the greater the effort must be to break out, which in turn means a greater punitive and repressive reaction from family and authorities. Second, the lack of clear-cut rules gives the young person some degree of choice, while the negative, extreme limits confine the choices to certain boundaries. This situation creates a desire for freedom by giving the individual a taste of it, while it is actually nothing but a more flexible version of the child role. The choice still cannot be made by the individual based on his or her feelings or on the realistic, probable outcome of the situation but is confined to the limits determined by societal authorities.

However, the taste for freedom is not quenched, and young people tend to continue even prohibited behavior if they think they can get away with it. They usually can; subversion of societal authority is widespread. When it is so widespread that some young people become blatant, society "cracks down" and institutes even more-repressive measures. Some young people are picked off as examples to the others. Third, identity crises are magnified by the stress authority figures use in promoting their injunctions. Fortunately, although early adolescence is a struggle, parents (at least many of them) accept the maturation process in late adolescence and let go. For those who do not, major family crises are generated. Fourth, the situation is usually a "no-win" for the youth. This can best be seen by looking at the choices open to Ann.

The most common choices a girl such as Ann makes are: (1) She can defy parental authority, giving preference to feelings, peer-group standards, and societal demands. Ann is left with guilt, shame, and probably conflicts with her parents if they discover, or she contrives to let them "discover," that she is doing what they disapprove of intensely. (2) She can avoid parental conflict by leaving home, often in a way that punishes the parents, for example by becoming pregnant, running away from home, marrying someone to legitimize leaving, or simply avoiding home except to sleep and eat. (3) She can avoid the conflict by accepting the reason for the parents' claim to be legitimate authorities—that is, she is too immature to make decisions for herself. Her feeling of immaturity may result in the loss of self-esteem, of opportunities for participation in peer activities, and the sacrifice of her own feelings and desires. (4) She can confront her parents directly and attempt to reason with them. She is unlikely to succeed with this method, since the ground of her parents' action is fear and anxiety, and the confrontation often leads to a fight, with all those involved being hurt. (5) Ann can join a deviant peer group that has a common bond, the rejection of parental authority—a counterdependent move, this may throw out the strengths of the relationship she has with her parents as well as the areas of conflict; she may conceal membership in a deviant group to avoid parental condemnation. (6) Ann can wait, passing the time until she is on her own, and at that point begin experimenting, exploring, and changing—a waste of time, a suppression of emotions and needs, and a poor preparation for the sudden "orgy" of freedom anticipated. (7) Ann can dissociate herself from her feelings, her parents, her society. In an extreme sense she can become schizoid. More often, girls and boys function adequately enough to avoid madness but live lives characterized by fragmentation, ritual-compulsive patterns, uncomfortable bodies (headaches, backaches, upset stomachs), preoccupations, rigidity, unsatisfaction, meaninglessness, and so on. If the crises are not resolved in childhood and youth, they often persist well into adult years, often for life.

The paradoxes thrust upon young people after they reach puberty are rarely constructive and helpful. Most youth are able to adjust to the demands well enough so that they are "let alone," and within this tiny niche, they attempt to find a reason for life. They retreat into couples, struggling to gain a mastery over life through the possession and control of another, or into small groups, where their loneliness and impoverished lives are camouflaged. Few young people survive youth without emotional and psychic damage, without areas of experience within which they are terror-stricken and helpless.

The best Ann can hope for is to be able to weigh all the alternatives open to her (surely the list is not all-inclusive) and make a choice that corresponds most closely to what she would like to do. Understanding the difference between the intrinsic risks involved in whatever she would like to do and the extrinsic risks created by the context adolescents are placed in by society would help decrease the anxiety. Supportive, non-controlling parents appreciative of the complex process of sorting out one's values amid the ideological confusion and illegitimate authority characteristic of society would also help. Unfortunately, many young people simply avoid identity struggles and the necessary risk and pain involved in attempting selfhood. They allow their identities to be co-opted by authority, doing whatever is expected of them in whatever situation they are in and failing to recognize contradictions of their own compliant personalities' deficiencies. Because so many young people choose this last alternative, adults—lacking personal relationships with young people in which issues of development are explored openly—are too often able to persuade their children that everything is basically okay.

We are also assisted in ignoring the destructive context within which youth exist by the assumption that the degree of difficulty they experience in simply being themselves is an expression of the biological characteristics of puberty. Puberty does function as an overt sign cuing adults when to change their demands and expectations for youth, but in itself it is not necessarily a conflict-ridden phase of development. The demands of parents, societal authorities, and the tantalizing "world of adults" offer youth double-bind situations, in which the majority of decisions are likely to be emotionally damaging. We can now explore these decisions and the contexts more completely.

Schooling was long thought of as a liberating force in young people's lives. But in recent years sensitive observers, acute researchers, and radical critics have joined to reveal that the conditioning that goes on as the student advances through his or her schooling enforce patterns of subservience.

"The most important social function of the schools," asserts sociologist and youth advocate Edgar Z. Friedenberg, "is in defining youth as a social role. . . . What compulsory school attendance does is to define young people as a subject category, and put on both their movements and their perceptions certain kinds of restrictions which no one else is subject to at all."

How Schools Subjugate Youth
EDGAR Z. FRIEDENBERG

1

The most important social function of the schools, it seems to me, is in defining *youth as a social role*. I would like you to consider what that may really mean. We generally think that youth is a natural category. There aren't any natural categories, however. There really are not *any*. I mean, if you are reasonably comprehensive in your survey of anthropology, you will find that even the living and the dead do not constitute for all societies, all cultures under all circumstances, two distinct categories or groups. In fact, with a different view of the supernatural there may well be little attention paid to the distinction. Obviously, a corpse presents certain practical problems, but they are not insuperable. The transition may be looked on as something having very little significance in the relationship of what we would call the survivors and the persona of what we would call the departed. The difference between men and women seems to be relatively more stable, but by no means always certain. The difference between races, however, is notoriously artificial. There are no Negroes in any part of Africa except Liberia and the Union of South Africa; for the rest of it there are black people who become Negroes if they fly to New York.

Youth is very much the same thing, and one reason that youth is youth is because (as with black people) it is subjected to certain specific, invidious, legally institutionalized distinctions, of which the school is the major source.

For example, since the War Between the States it has not been unlawful simply to be anywhere because you are black. But this is obviously not true of young people either in Canada or the United States. It is an offense to be anywhere but in school during school hours. Since it is an offense, you can be and will be apprehended, and you can be sent away to what we call a juvenile hall or detention home—the names vary. At any rate, there isn't any way you can hang loose. This isn't true of any other element of the population. It has even been elaborated in some jurisdictions in the states in ways that still astonish me. What compulsory school attendance does is to define young people as a subject category and puts on both their movements and their perceptions certain kinds of restrictions that no one else is subject to at all. It does so, moreover, in a way that is remarkably total, since even a veritable Samson has not the strength to grow out his hair within two hours between three and five in the afternoon, when he may want to pursue some activity among his own peers for which long hair is a desideratum.

The schools manage by virtue of manipulation of the authority invested in them by the education code. In other words they usurp or intrude upon their students' life space—not just his time in school—and this action they justify. In some ways America is getting a bit more liberal and the explanation of character building doesn't go down well in a society as heterogeneous as ours. It would have thirty or forty years ago, but there have been a few court decisions on the question, and American schools are not supposed to go around building your character without your consent. They have to say that long hair is so distracting that it interferes with the educational function of the school. The wife of one of the students who came with me to Buffalo from California and who is now teaching in the schools of a lower-middle-class suburb of Buffalo, had the odd experience of having the principal come into her room a few days ago and ask her to search a young girl. The principal said he was being distracted beyond his capacity to perform his duties by the fact that somewhere on her person this girl had a bell. She knew she wasn't supposed to wear a bell at school, so she put it under a sweater or something; but he could still hear it tinkle. It was found and confiscated.

It is reasonably clear that the hegemony of the school situation is really a good deal grayer than it would be if it were only a place to which you go of your own choice because you want to learn something you are curious about or that is useful to you for purposes of your own. Once you put it in the context of your being the client (society supporting you in this definition of your own role), then it seems obvious that education takes on a totally different function from defining a social role for youth.

2

The second major function of the schools, one that is obviously related to the first, is the legitimization of a form of economic discrimination.

The main thing the school is supposed to do for children is to guide them in investing in their own future. Once you get people to agree to this, then you can avoid the question of having to pay students for what is, after all, a form of involuntary servitude. By assuming that what goes on in school prepares young people to earn more money and have higher social status in the future, you can get out of any implication that they ought to be paid for the labor of doing it: the school, the argument goes, is already contributing to what the students are laying aside, if you regard their higher income as a return on capital investment; and what else could a good North American regard a higher income as? This makes everything perfectly just and okay.

However, pieces begin falling off the above little model as soon as you begin turning it around so you can look at it closely.

Now, all the books on the subject of income, status, and schooling, even the relatively sophisticated ones, will say that one thing about schooling is that it does indeed assist you in getting a higher standard of living; it contributes to social mobility; it is necessary if you are going to get ahead in the world. The best of the books may be rather wry about that and say, "Isn't it a shame that our traditional cultural faith in education seems to come to so little in comparison to the nitty-gritty issues of everyday life, and we wish people really were interested in ideas, but maybe we can't expect that. . . ." Yet once you've

shown a tight correlation between the number of years of
schooling completed and the average income for the rest of your
life and particularly, of course, for the highest level of income
achieved, what have you really proved?

What you've proved, it seems to me, if you've proved anything, is the existence of a conspiracy. Because you are faced
on the one hand with a very widespread agreement that you
are not going to hire people who don't have the credentials,
and on the other hand, if you don't hire people who don't have
the credentials you'll never find out if they could have done
the job or not, with no alternative ways of earning the credentials on the job. Increasingly we have no way outside the school
system of legitimizing participation in the process of growing
up, much less getting a license for a trade everyone agrees you
need a license for.

What we need to justify educational participation is not the
correlation of higher income to higher levels of schooling but,
rather, some direct indication of where or what the skills really
are that enable a person to make it through life, and to what
extent the school does in fact contribute to learning these skills.
Further, if there are such skills, and there is no other place than
school to get them, that still does not really prove that schools
are the best method of passing on these skills. In fact, the argument that schools are the only channels for opportunity in
American culture is a little bit like the argument that David
would have made a suitable and pious husband to Bathsheba.
There is still the question of his complicity in Uriah's fate and
whether there would not have been something even better available except for what he did. In this case it isn't the schools
themselves that provide the economic and social rewards, but,
then, in the biblical story David isn't the murderer either. He's
simply the influential administrative official.

If this were not enough to weaken the argument for schools
as places for getting ahead, there is the fact that the statistics
are interpreted in a kind of phony way. In the first place, most
of the arguments linking higher incomes and schooling are directed toward high school, concentrating on those who have or

have not completed high school. The data for completing high school include everybody who completed high school, which means people who go on and get university degrees. When you look at those who completed high school and didn't go on to college and those who didn't complete high school the difference in earning potential isn't very great. It averages out to something like an extra twenty dollars per month for those who completed high school—not enough probably to make up for the aggravation.

Of course you can say, "Yes, but we think everyone should go to college, and you can't do that unless you go to high school." But then you are faced with a couple of other things that a reasonably bright lawyer would raise in countering such an argument in a court of equity. You see, the financial value of a high school degree was great only at a time when the high school degree was relatively scarce and was a symbol of an elite position. So again we do not know that it was the high school education that caused the higher income. All we can say is that the people in the top 10 per cent of the society, with the resources to not earn money and go to school, are likely to earn more money over the long run than those who didn't have the resources and didn't go to school. Further, when education becomes universal, everyone going to college, then it's possible that its fiscal utility will diminish; this seems, in fact, to be what does happen. You can't, I think, use any part of this argument to conclude anything with certainty except that the schools are a sentinel. They provide the check points along which you progress.

From the point of view of the corporations, however, the schools do perform a useful function: they instill or induce you to develop certain characteristics that are marketable, the kind of characteristics that allow you to work comfortably within the corporation. Of course, if you have a mind to, you can then argue that this means that the schools constitute a subsidy for so-called private enterprise provided by the taxpayers' dollars. So maybe students ought to get paid much earlier, and by the people who use them.

3

I think probably in order to understand the relationship between our corporate society, our schools, and our students in a general way—as to how schools do what they do—there is no better source than the sage of Toronto and two of his most familiar aphorisms.

In the schools, more than in most of the other mass media, it is indeed true that the medium is the message, which is one reason I haven't said a word about curriculum. What is taught isn't as important as learning how you have to act in society, how other people will treat you, how they will respond to you, what the limits of respect that will be accorded to you really are. What the schools teach is the experience of being a school child, and once you get used to that it's unlikely you will run amuck among the inhabitants of your community.

The other McLuhan point that seems to me to provide an even deeper source of insight is the observation that we don't know who discovered water but we're pretty sure it wasn't the fish. What I mean by this is that the schools, by providing a continual social substrate—a kind that is, in effect, a caricature of the society—makes the society seem so natural that you don't notice the awful things that it does. In fact, even your ways of fighting the school are determined by what it teaches you to regard as propriety—or obscenity—whichever you happen to want to employ. In any case, it's essentially true that what the schools do is teach you how "it's spozed to be," particularly in a liberal democracy, where the schools embody the society's central contradictions.

In America, for example, we have a written Constitution to which the first ten amendments constitute the Bill of Rights. Most states have laws—laws made before the Supreme Court went over to the "Communists"—that compels you to teach the Constitution. However, if you learn the Constitution in the American public school system, you certainly are not going to go around thinking that the Bill of Rights applies to you. There has been a little research study, as a matter of fact, on what children really think the pledge of allegiance to the flag means, and there was a very wide divergence of opinion. A master's degree student who was more imaginative than most simply went around and asked children to tell him what the pledge said, to repeat it for him. The nicest result, I think, was "One nation indivincible, with liberty and death for all." We have been trying to fulfill that promise all right, but when it comes to promises, say of freedom of speech in situations in which it creates real social disruptions, we've been less than careful in keeping our word. I don't want to put down the quite remarkable and creditable degree of freedom of speech in the United States in the sense that you are unlikely to be subjected to official sanctions for anything that you say. The point is that the function of the school is to teach you about the unofficial sanctions, to prepare you for the blacklist, to make sure you understand the implications of being labeled a "troublemaker," which is the worst thing a school can call you.

The schools perform this kind of function, it seems to me, in a society that is lying about its traditions. A nicer way of putting it is to say the society still honors or likes to draw from components of its tradition that are nobler than it can in fact hope to institutionalize in everyday practice. But it still comes out lying.

One of the reasons this has happened is that we have included into the social process, with some degree of influence, people who would in an earlier, more conservative organization of society, have been *déclassés* and non-voting. Here, I think, we are at the heart of the matter. The schools have succeeded in becoming mass organizations, serving a much larger proportion of the population, and are as bad as they are because of their response to this process. The problem is not that they are serving people now who have less ability than before, but that they are serving people who in earlier days were treated by decision makers as victims. When a society becomes more democratic and no longer feels comfortable about treating people as victims, yet still retains essentially the same exploitative social arrangements, then it has to create institutions that will induce people to choose to be victims, choosing out of anxiety or out of a lack of sense of what their own resources might be or out of a realistic sense that they might not be smart enough to be rulers if they don't choose to be victims.

In the most general terms, then, the schools, like the society, hold in tension the contradictions of the liberal tradition as it grew out of British and, later, American society. They emphasize both the individual and the sanctity of getting rich, and so they obscure moral issues and at the same time tend to favor continual enlargement of the in-group.

There is real conflict, it seems to me, between provision through the school of increased economic opportunity and the support of cultural values that might treat all people more generously. The schools have been set up to avoid this conflict, although lately they don't seem to be having so much success. A serious polarization seems to be happening in America, for which I am glad, but, then, I'm not a liberal. The schools have tried to evade this polarization by defining the difference between the rich and the poor not in terms of their relationships to the means of production and the consequent real conflicts of interest but, rather, in terms of cultural deprivation. They take the sting out of this deprivation by making the authority of the things that really are associated with what is left of high culture so tenuous and so ridiculous that there wasn't much left but the implication that, of course, you must learn this culture just as you have to learn to put on a coat and a tie and comb your hair and have it short, because otherwise you won't get a job. Thus not having this culture doesn't have to mean you're inferior to anyone else. Now, it seems to me that a more valid human message would have been that you have the right to dress in a way you think becomes you, but no matter how you dress, it may indeed be true that you are inferior to other people. And this inferiority may be a consequence of experiences that happened so early and that were so intense that they will never be reversed. No school can be magical. There will be some things that you don't understand, that you will never understand, that certain kinds of schools could help cer-

tain other people understand if you would shut up. You have
been permanently deprived of something that is of inestimable
value.

*Our society is teeming with professionals who purport to be
devoting their lives to helping children. But could it be that
these adults, too, are actually oppressing and exploiting them?
That's the tough question that sociologist David Gottlieb poses.
He shows how even "well-meaning" adults often become en-
tangled in their own needs and desires, and lose sight of the
kids. To prove his point, he interprets what happened when
the nation's leading child-helpers gathered for the last White
House Conference on Children, for which he served as director
of research. While the conference "raised some strikingly advanced human service issues," according to the editors of* Social
Policy *magazine, Gottlieb feels it revealed how children become
victims—"victims of those who seek political power, victims of
those who seek control, victims of those who seek release from
their own frustrations, victims of those who seek to perpetuate
their own professional and personal ideologies."*

Children as Victims
DAVID GOTTLIEB

As we begin this significant national reassessment, let us re-
mind ourselves of our purpose.

This should be a conference about love . . . about our need
to love those to whom we have given birth . . . and those who
are most helpless and in need . . . and those who give us a
reason for being . . . and those who are most precious for themselves—for what they are and what they can become. Our
children.

Let us ask what we want for our children. Then let us ask
not less for all children.

We want for our children a home of love and understanding and encouragement.

We want for our children a full opportunity for learning in an environment in which they can reach and grow and take pride in themselves.

We want for our children the right to be healthy, to be free of sickness. But if sickness comes, to have the best care humanly possible.

We want for our children the right to have the respect of others.

We want them to have respect and dignity as a *right* because they are, not because of who their parents are.

We want for our children to live under laws that are fair and just and that are administered fairly and justly.

We want for our children to love their country because their country has earned their love, because their country strives to create peace and to create the conditions of a humane and healthy society for all of its citizens and is dedicating the resources necessary to redeem its commitment to these ends.

This we want for our children. Therefore this we must want for *all* children. There can be no exceptions.

To those who have food, it is intolerable that there is a child somewhere in our land who is ill-nourished. To those who live beneath a sound roof, it is intolerable that there should be a child who is ill-housed and without adequate clothes.

That we are well, so, then, is it intolerable that a child is needlessly sick or lives in an environment that poisons his body or mind.

That we have the knowledge, so, then, is it intolerable that there is some child who does not have a full opportunity to learn.

That we are a nation founded on equality, so must we not tolerate intolerance in ourselves or our fellows.

We must recognize that there is some child in special need. And he especially must be our child.

At a time when it is all too easy to accuse, to blame, to fault, let us gather in trust and faith to put before the nation that which is necessary and best. All this we say with the greatest sense of urgency and conviction.

Our children and our families are in deep trouble. A society that neglects its children and fears its youth cannot care about its future. Surely this is the way to national disaster.

Our society has the capacity to care and the resources to act. Act we must.

There is a need to change our patterns of living so that once again we will bring adults back into the lives of children and children back into the lives of adults.

The changes must come at all levels of society—in business, industry, mass media, schools, government, communities, neighborhoods, and, above all, in ourselves. The changes must come *now*.

We as delegates to the 1970 White House Conference on Children do now affirm our *total commitment* to help bring our nation into a new age of caring. Now we begin.[1]

This moving statement was the preamble presented to the assembled delegates of the 1970 White House Conference on Children. Unfortunately, as is so often the case, there soon emerged a marked discrepancy between the words expressed in defense of children and the behavior exhibited by those adults who had unanimously endorsed a "*total commitment* to help bring our nation into a new age of caring."

The self-serving desires and goals of different adult professional, ethnic, racial, and political groups contributed to an atmosphere of confrontation, dissent, and dysfunctionality. Having agreed to the need for a renewed crusade for children, the assembled adults then struggled to determine just who should lead the children's crusade. The end result consisted of hundreds of recommendations, numerous minority reports, and something in writing for each and every adult group and organi-

[1] *Report to the President: White House Conference on Children* (Washington, D.C.: U. S. Government Printing Office, 1970), p. 5.

zation attending the conference. No professional, social, ethnic, racial, or political group was denied. Advocates of education, of social welfare, of local, state, and federal government, and of day care did their thing. Each group made certain that the final report of the conference included a recommendation that would help perpetuate its particular ideology, profession, or approach. Recommendations were made for the establishment of numerous "national institutes"—an institute for everyone: an institute for the study of the family, the study of health, the study of education, the study of welfare, the study of environment, and the study of judicial processes.

Although the majority of delegates had agreed that past approaches and existing institutions were inadequate, there was little motivation to eliminate or restructure these arrangements as part of a comprehensive effort. And although most delegates expressed the opinion that we had overfragmentized child-centered services and were now competing for meager resources, few of them were willing to abandon their approach, their profession, their organization, and their demands for more funds in order to facilitate a more unified, holistic approach to the needs of children.

It is not surprising, then, that by the time the conference was concluded most participants felt it had been a hollow exercise. Few thought that the deliberations or recommendations would lead to societal changes in the treatment of children. It is significant to note that few delegates held themselves or their particular constituency responsible for the conference's failure to achieve its expressed goals; the failure of the conference almost invariably was attributed to some other group or to some other individual. The admission of failure is not a characteristic of professionals. Blame was placed upon others through such comments as "it was the minority-group people," "it's the establishment," "it's the system," "it's the old-timers," "it's the young radicals," or "it was poor organization."

Two years later, the prophecy of doubt and failure has been fulfilled. Nothing really has changed. The adult delegates have returned home and continue to function in the same manner and in the same institutional settings as in the past. The children continue to be dealt with as in the past. The children remain the victims.

The events and outcomes of the 1970 White House Conference on Children do not represent a freak or unique occurrence. On the contrary, there is abundant evidence to support the proposition that adults speak with hypocrisy. Again and again adult rhetoric rings with concern for our children even as adult behavior reflects indifference toward and exploitation of our children.

Various examples of the dichotomy between adult words of concern for the child and adult behavior patterns of indifference toward children are presented in the following pages. We begin with Martin Mayer's analysis of the teacher-community confrontation in the now famous Ocean Hill, New York, struggle over school decentralization. Following an in-depth review of the history of the confrontation, Mayer concludes with the following observations:

> But there were no real issues in the strikes—just slogans. What is ultimately disgusting about the teacher strikes and the public officials who failed to prevent them is that words like "community control" mean no more in dealing with the complex of relationships between school administrators and parents than words like "quality education" mean in dealing with the inadequate teacher training and severe multiple deprivations which combine to produce so much wretched work in our slum schools. On words like these, people who knew better created a confrontation.
>
> During the course of the crisis, a member of the Mayor's Urban Task Force told a meeting of architects that he thought the strikes would do good by showing people how important education is. One can, perhaps, be a little more precise about the impact of the teachers' strikes. They accelerated the flight from the city's schools—and indeed from the city itself—of those who can afford to leave. They made companies which had thought of establishing them-

selves in New York decide to shun the city. They poisoned
the wells of human decency which did exist in this cosmo-
politan and sophisticated metropolis, which the mayor only
three years ago called "Fun City." And they will very probably reduce to the condition of Boston and Alabama, or
some mixture of the two, a school system which was
wretchedly ill-organized and weakly led but relatively alert
intellectually and by no means so completely ineffective as
it has become fashionable to say—and which was almost
the only hope the city could offer for the future of hundreds of thousands of Negro and Puerto Rican children.[2]

In reviewing the public rhetoric surrounding the Ocean Hill
conflict, one can only be impressed with the continuous concern
expressed on behalf of the children. Each group emphati-
cally denied that it was an issue of its own power or self-
determination and sought to make clear that its behavior was
guided by the single goal of providing children with the education and training that would enable them to become productive, healthy, and dignified citizens. Each of the parties—
teachers, administrators, and parents—waved the child-loving
banner. Each questioned the sincerity and integrity of the others, no matter how similar the declared goals. Ultimately, as
Mayer points out, the issue was no longer what was best for
the children. Instead the issue became one of fulfilling the needs
of adults, even if these needs were not of direct benefit to the
children.

The events of Ocean Hill do not represent an isolated or
single case. Again and again we are able to note how children
are used as pawns in the political and social arena.

Some twenty years after the Supreme Court decision about
school desegregation, the President of the United States declared a moratorium on school busing. Once again the stated
intent was to protect the children from tedious travel and to

[2] Martin Mayer, "The Full and Sometimes Very Surprising Story
of Ocean Hill, the Teachers' Union and the Teachers' Strike of
1968," New York *Times Magazine*, February 2, 1969, p. 71.

enhance their educational growth. The welfare of "all the children" was the President's rallying cry. But even the most naïve of citizens recognized that the primary motivation for the busing moratorium was political.

In each case, whether the issue be education, employment, welfare, health, or busing, it is apparent that children are without power. It is equally apparent that children have little control over or influence with the social institutions that shape their lives. Yet somehow they must manage to live with the consequences of the actions of those who do have that power and control in our social institutions. If adults in our highly complex and impersonal society feel a sense of powerlessness and a lack of control over their destinies, it does not take much in the way of imagination to appreciate how removed and how insignificant children must feel.

Of course many would reject the argument that our children are exploited or treated with indifference. The counterargument is that our children are better off today than at any time in our history. After all, they have more toys, more recreation, more education, more "fun" than we ever did as children. If the quality of life for individuals is to be measured solely by material accumulation, then many of our children do have it made. If, on the other hand, the quality of one's life is to be measured by such factors as freedom of choice; control over one's educational future and environment; equal rights without regard to age, sex, race, and economic status; and access to alternative life styles—then our children are probably far worse off than in years past. For in reality our children are being increasingly segregated by age, race, sex, and socioeconomic status; blocked from pursuing alternative educational and socializing settings; isolated from the decision makers, whether in the home, school, community, or nation; insulated from the world of work and career exploration; and denied the opportunity to be listened to and taken seriously.

Whereas in the past our children were at least respected for their potential as economic contributors to the family, this is less and less the case today. Instead our children have become increasingly dependent upon us—economically, psychologically, and socially. The combination of extended economic investment in our children and the prolonging of their "adult preparation" contributes to the belief that it is our duty and right to control every aspect of the child's life.

Since children are seen as extensions of their parents, and since they are increasingly dependent upon their parents, they carry a double burden. As Bettelheim points out:

All this is only part of the attitude that expects American children to do better than their parents, and often, seen objectively, the task is even quite feasible; but to children and adolescents the demand seems emotionally impossible, because it comes at a time when their opinion of their parents' achievement is unrealistically high. Contrary to all psychoanalytic writings that teach clearly how the child and adolescent is overawed by his parents' power and wisdom, both society and his parents continue to expect the emotionally impossible of youth.[3]

Children are placed in a position in which they are victims of a social system over which they have little control or influence. In most cases society has arbitrarily assigned goals that children are expected to achieve. The means by which these goals are to be achieved are equally arbitrarily defined. Norms of appropriate behavior, dress, and language have also been established. The child is expected to act, think, feel, and believe in a prescribed manner. The established ground rules for expected behavior do not always represent what the child needs or desires. Nor do the ground rules frequently take into consideration the fact that many children, because of societal conditions, cannot possibly achieve expected goals, although they may be the very goals that they seek to pursue. The combination of arbitrary societal ground rules, social institutions that

[3] Bruno Bettelheim, "The Problem of Generations," in *The Challenge of Youth*, ed. Erik H. Erikson (New York: Anchor Books, 1965), p. 84.

pay only lip service to the needs and conditions of the young, and a lack of the child's involvement in decisions affecting his life can only lead to increased child failure, alienation, and emotional crippling. However, when the child does fail we do not examine the role played by the social system and its institutions. Rather, when the child fails to conform (that is, fails to behave in a manner deemed appropriate) he is considered deviant— he is the problem. Having classified the child as deviant, underachieving, or delinquent, we turn to strategies of individual rehabilitation and behavior modification.

Rarely do we implement strategies of institutional rehabilitation and modification. Rarely will we go beyond the making of statements about cold and indifferent bureaucracies and unfeeling and indifferent teachers, parents, social workers, and policemen. Despite the evidence that the failure of our children often flows from the inadequacies and injustices of our social institutions, we blame the child. Despite our awareness of the shortcomings of our child-rearing practices and policies, we continue to focus upon changing the child rather than the very institutions and laws that have created our "problem children."

The technique is one of blaming the victim. William Ryan, in his excellent book *Blaming the Victim*, illustrates how this technique operates when explanations are offered to account for the inability of poor children to compete with more affluent children:

> This is the folklore of cultural deprivation as it is used in an ideological fashion to preserve the care of the status quo in urban education—to forestall any questioning about the fundamental problems of recruiting and training teachers, achieving racial integration, and, in particular, governing the school system. Waving this banner, educationists can advocate Head Start, smaller classes, more effective schools, "scatteration" to the suburbs by one-way busing, teaching machines, or Swahili—almost anything that involves changing or manipulating the child. They fight to the death any proposal that implies there might be anything at all wrong

with the teacher or the teaching, and resist any exploration of, or intrusion into, the monopolistic control of public education by the teaching profession, particularly if it implies participation in decision making by laymen from the community.[4]

The child as powerless victim of adult needs and exploitation may also be noted in an examination of the mass media provided for the young. Clearly children do not control or directly influence the form and content of the media to which they are exposed. They are not the writers, producers, directors, or publishers. Whether it be periodicals, books, television, radio, movies, or recordings, they are the consumers. Given the quality of the various types of mass media directed at them, they are in reality victims both of innocuous and irrelevant content and in many instances of exploitative and false advertisement.

According to the report of the 1970 White House Conference on Children:

> Mass media have an overwhelming influence on the lives of our children and, consequently, the future of our society. Television, particularly, plays a dominant role; through grade school, children spend more time in front of their television sets than in front of schoolteachers.[5]

An awareness of the impact of television upon children has not generated much in the way of worthwhile programing for children. With the exception of token programs that are considered to be of some merit, the profit motive continues to be the salient factor.

The reluctance and indifference of those who control the media to change the content and focus of both programs and commercials directed at children are well documented. According to a report published in 1954 by the National Commission on the Causes and Prevention of Violence, television-industry

---

[4] William Ryan, *Blaming the Victim* (New York: Pantheon Books, 1971), pp. 34–35.
[5] *White House Conference on Children*, p. 325.

spokesmen took the position that the research evidence concerning the effect upon children of violent portrayals was inconclusive. Still, they did acknowledge that there was a possible risk of adverse effects and for that reason the industry had adopted standards and regulations to govern the portrayal of violence. The television authorities made two promises: first, to conduct systematic research in order to determine the relationship between viewing violence and exhibiting violent behavior; second, to reduce the amount of violence on television.

The report of the National Commission on the Causes and Prevention of Violence continues with this review of the efforts actually undertaken by the television industry:

> It is sufficient to note that although such promises (i.e., research) were made first in 1954 and continued through 1964, by October 1967 the amount of research sponsored by the industry on this issue was so small as to be insignificant, and that which was supported by the industry was, from the outset, clearly undertaken as a defensive move.[6]

With regard to the curtailment of programs depicting violence, the report goes on to note:

> Some studies in the files of the subcommittee indicate that the quantity of violent programs increased as much as 300 per cent between 1954 and 1961.
>
> After the tragic assassinations in the spring of 1968, there was much publicity in the trade and regular press about how the networks were reducing violence on television. Content analysis conducted by the Media Task Force indicates that there was no such reduction by October 1968.[7]

Criticism of children's television programs is not restricted to the issue of violence. Recent research by the new national organization Action for Children's Television showed that two

[6] *Violence and the Media: a Staff Report to the National Commission on the Causes and Prevention of Violence* (Washington, D.C.: U. S. Government Printing Office, 1969), p. vii.

[7] *Violence and the Media*, p. viii.

thirds of current television programs for children consist of chase/adventure cartoons. It is not being suggested here that chase/adventure cartoons are necessarily harmful to children; what is being pointed out is that such programs contribute little to the growth and development of the young. Such programs are rarely humorous or clever, and are frequently insulting to the viewer. To present these cartoons as children's programing is at best fraudulent. In reality they are relatively inexpensive fillers whose major purpose is to bombard children with countless "go after your parents" commercials. The commercials themselves are frequently misleading, with guarantees of power and prestige if only the child will purchase some brand of chewing gum, cereal, tooth paste, or soft drink.

The victimization and exploitation of our children is not always as apparent as it is in the case of the mass media. The current debate over the issue of I.Q. tests represents a more subtle, yet probably more insidious example of the way children suffer through the actions and behavior of even well-meaning, concerned adults.

Our purpose here is not to argue the merits or validity of I.Q. tests. There are already a sufficient number of scholars involved in that debate. It is clear also that while they continue their debate they have remained indifferent to the impact that their intellectual exchanges have had upon children. For while this debate rages, children continue to be labeled, categorized, and reminded that their failure to learn is not the fault of our schools or the methods by which we manipulate children but is due rather to their biological makeup, the incompetency or indifference of their parents, or their "social class."

The only ones to benefit from the I.Q. debate are the participating scholars (since it contributes to their prestige as productive scholars) and the educators who refuse to believe that the learning shortcomings of children might be explained by how and what they are taught. Any evidence that learning problems can be attributed to genetic factors, parental indifference, or ethnic and social class values will be readily endorsed by those who encounter difficulty with children. If the child fails, we do not look to the school. If the child is restless, we do not examine the content of the curriculum. If the child is angry, we do not study the impact of oppressive and frustrating rules and regulations. If the child fails, we do not send the teacher to summer school or deny salary payment. No, the child is the problem. Even for those adults who are reluctant to hold the child totally responsible for his behavior, there is always an abundance of blame alternatives. The child may then be perceived as the unfortunate recipient of an inferior culture or of inferior genes.

Still, no matter who is held responsible and whether or not there is consensus over the meaning of I.Q. tests, the children are the victims, and the burden of proof continues to be placed upon them. Finally, we might ask what differences does it make, anyway? Does it make a difference whether or not the nebulous quality we call intelligence is explained best by biological or by environmental factors? Will accounting in a methodologically approved fashion for the variations in human beings lessen the learning difficulties of children? Will agreeing that the cause is biological rather than environmental alter the fact that increasing numbers of children—I.Q. high-tested and I.Q. low-tested—are fed up with school at earlier and earlier ages? Will agreement among professors Jensen, Bruner, Kagan, Clark, and Herrnstein make any difference at all to the children? I think not.

Helen Baker has been a stanch friend of the young for years, fighting for their rights as a board member of the Ohio Civil Liberties Union. Her efforts on behalf of free speech and other basic constitutional rights in the schools have made a difference at the grass roots in Ohio. Undergirding her official efforts is the moral fervor that shines through this appeal to let the children be heard. When it comes to their own rights and needs, she points out, "As long as we decide, using our perceptions alone, what is best for children, we shall for the most part fail."

Growing Up Unheard

HELEN BAKER

I don't know how the First Amendment is doing these days for our adult population. I do know that it is a washout as far as young people are concerned.

Young people do not have a right to free speech, to a free press, or to petition for redress of grievances. No matter what the U. S. Supreme Court said in *Tinker* and no matter what most of the federal courts have said in the student press cases, in fact there is no First Amendment in the schools. And a great deal of the unwillingness to allow the First Amendment in schools, for instance, is based on the almost universal notion that what young people have to say is either unimportant, nasty, or the product of an immature and therefore irresponsible mind. If that is true, why encourage them in their expression? If that is true, no one has to listen.

Children are controlled and contained in our society because we don't really know what else to do with them. They are ignored or lightly dismissed, because it serves society's purposes to infantalize them into their twenties. It is much easier to justify control over persons called "young," "immature," and "irresponsible." This "strangling of the free mind at its source" —despite Supreme Court warnings—helps prepare a citizenry that is laregly passive and apathetic, willing to accept authority unquestioningly, willing to think of themselves as incompetent and incapable of making changes. On top of this gutting of the rights of citizenship, the racism and classism of our society permeate the system's treatment of children.

That is almost self-evident. What is not clear is why some critics of the system continue this same infantalization of young people. Why aren't we listening to—really listening to, dammit, not just "rapping with"—the young people?

Some time ago, a group of high school students ranging in age from fourteen to seventeen approached their school administration with a proposal for a school without walls as part of the school system. The students wanted to devise the curriculum, pick the teachers, and evaluate their own progress and the project's successes and failures themselves. They were told, with all the well-learned gestures of patronization (smiles, conciliatory hand movements, loving voice tones) that the school could hardly allow that. "That isn't sensible," the superintendent said; "we're the experts. After all, when you are sick, you go to a doctor, an expert, don't you?" "Oh, yes," the youngest of the students said, "and the first thing he does is ask me where it hurts."

Why doesn't anybody ask the children where it hurts? Why do we have endless collections of books *about* children, and endless seminars, endless workshops, endless research projects, all *without* the children?

I am here not to propose tactics or solutions; I am here to make a philosophical argument to underline the First Amendment rights of young people.

Adults who seek to describe the human condition of children hold reality in a sieve. No matter how sensitive the teacher, how innovative the administrator, how eclectic the psychologist, they are all describing the reality of *another* overlaid with the disadvantages of their disciplines. Adults tend to know things and concepts, to remember experiences, through a series of learned measurements. We tend to be labelers, cataloguers, measurers; graph makers, group makers, and omnivorous consumers of statistics and workshops.

We see the children through the filter of the measuring devices of our disciplines.

What we desperately need are the voices of the children. Not just their voices in the classroom, or the student council, or even in the pseudo-unstructured weekend retreat. Children say what adults want to hear—or, depending on the level of the child's hostility, what the adult does not want to hear. They seldom speak *their* reality to adults. *The risks are too great.*

Even their favorite teacher is often protected *by the students,*
who, out of kindness to the teacher, conceal their real frustrations and their real despair.

The *Harvard Educational Review* recently put out two heavy
issues on the rights of children, but none of the voices were
under eighteen, and all of the voices were of the educated professionals. Youth Liberation of Ann Arbor wasn't there; the
Children's Rights Organization of California wasn't there; the
editors of the high school underground newspapers were not
there. Just a whole lot of professionals picking over the same
old bones.

Someone is always measuring and cataloguing young people;
there is even an organization that prides itself on its "polls"
of young people. But adults ask children the questions that are
useful *to the adults;* they rarely ask the questions the children
want to answer.

Where children put out tentative feelers of trust, where they
are promised understanding, they are frequently betrayed.
Young people confide personal problems to school counselors
who frequently tell the principal, tell the child's teachers, or
put the information in the child's records. The juvenile courts,
built on a rationale of not punishing children but of helping
them, have so bad a track record that grown men recoil and the
ladies of the League of Women Voters in court-watching projects cannot believe their eyes.

If adults around the country are meeting in anguished workshops (and they are) about 1) the juvenile court, 2) definitions
of delinquency, 3) status offenses, 4) is rehabilitation possible
in an institution? looking for an answer to "juvenile delinquency," they will not find it in their workshops. They probably won't find it in their heads. The juvenile court has failed
to do what it set out to do, and even with the *Gault* decision,
little has changed for the child charged with an act that would
be a crime if committed by an adult. The child may have the
right to a lawyer, but frequently is told it in a left-handed
fashion. ("Now, you don't need a lawyer here, all that expense,
and we can handle this among ourselves"—the benevolent

judge guarding his immense discretion from the invasion of those upstart young lawyers.) The right becomes only a paper right. The case against the juvenile court has been well made in other places. My point is only that the same people who made the juvenile court are now into "diversion" and other neat-sounding names to solve the problems the court has only made worse. Why should we assume *their* perceptions will create effective programs now?

At a conference on runaway children in Columbus, Ohio, in 1974, Jerome Miller, who wiped out the juvenile jails in Massachusetts, spoke about the children, the ones for whom the juvenile-justice show is presumably about. And he said a most interesting thing: that we set up enormous, costly, bureaucratic structures, that we people them with all kinds of professionals including the most dedicated social workers, and the end result of their actions is *disaster* for the child. He warned that the professionals are going to have to stop just doing their piece of the action and take a look at what the result is. When Miller moved to the Illinois Family and Children Services, he was appalled to discover that hundreds of Illinois children were being sent to *substandard* institutions in Texas (because the Illinois ones were full) at a cost of over twenty thousand dollars per child per year.

If anyone had asked the children, they could have enlightened the professionals years ago. But our society is full of people who are convinced they know what's best for other people. Some of them go to work for the state in the capacity of official interveners in the child's life. Some are presently engaged in some charming research (funded by the amiable federal government) including testing of kindergarten children to spot "future delinquents." These records will go—and I hope this shocks you, because if it doesn't, I'm in the wrong place—to the FBI. A kind of preventative surveillance, beginning at age five. Children are presently, in the guise of being "helped," forced to undergo psychosurgery for hyperkinesis (whatever that is), for minimal brain dysfunction (whatever that is), and for the greater glory of university-based research. (It isn't only beagles that "scientists" experiment on.) That may be the grossest kind of thing that *trained professionals* are doing, but there are lots of others. In some school districts teachers are asked to make character studies of young students, with the teachers filling out a questionnaire. These are submitted to the Diagnostic Education Grouping people, who then class children as "oedipally conflicted," "developmentally arrested," or "ego-disturbed." *All* children need help, according to this method, but therapy focuses on the last two groups. Using this test, some 40 per cent of the children tested nationally, two years ago, needed therapy. The whole theory is to identify children who will be "high risks" in their ability to adapt to society's rules and institutions. Is the therapeutic state any different from the old-fashioned police state?

We have gone berserk with our measurements, with our passion for grouping people, with our labels. The natural outgrowth of all the categorization is behavior modification. What behavior mod is really saying is that our society cannot afford all this damned individuality and we can't control it; instead we will devise programs to produce conforming behavior. We will do it with tokens, candy bars, privileges, Ritalin, and so on. The society is giving up on its polyglot population, in school and out. Of course, behavior mod will fail. There is no system devised by human beings that will control all human beings; there will always be people who escape, no matter if it is Ph.D.'s who build the jail and no matter what the prison is called.

Of course, the children could also tell you that. They are escape artists. They escape their parents even while their parents are speaking to them; they escape their teachers; they escape their probation officers. Teachers rage at the child who is looking right at them and not hearing a thing. Children are much smarter out of school than they are in school, and that fact alone should have alerted professionals long ago on how wrong they are in the way they deal with children.

Professionals get exasperated, however, because the children don't react the way they should. Counselors get mad at students who don't like any curriculum that is set up for them; it is the echo of the parent's cry: "How could he . . . after all I've done for him." Nevertheless, the professionals seldom doubt their own perceptions. They poke and probe, they cajole and punish, they watch and they restrict, and most of all they categorize. Those who measure, group, and label children do so to prove some hypothesis, or with some hoped-for result (such as better control). Research on children is grossly value-oriented. Children are especially labeled by the institution that touches all our lives: the school. The school measures children for the school's sake, to make it easier for teachers and textbook manufacturers. School labeling, like juvenile-court labeling, is destructive per se to children whose reality is not anesthetized by the kind of hypocritical semantic gymnastics so normal in adult life.

Rousseau once said, "We have physicists, geometricians, chemists, astronomers, poets, musicians, and painters in plenty, but we have no longer a citizen among us." In much the same way, we have all kinds of child professionals, but do we have enough human beings around willing to treat children as human beings and not just as persons-in-need-of-supervision? Adults deal with children from the point of view that children are so different from adults. Children would suffer less if adults looked to their similarities. Adults need encouragement, love, identity, friends, kindness, societal rules they can depend on, equal treatment, and so on. Children need no less.

There is in our society an inability, perhaps just an unwillingness, to validate the perceptions of children. We give them token recognition: we make a fuss over their fourth-grade poetry, we praise their artistic endeavors. But we give them no voice on stage; they are merely allowed to paint scenery.

If children see study hall as a restraint, that is what it is. It is, for most students, not a *study* hall; it is something to be either endured or escaped. If children view incarceration in state youth commission facilities as imprisonment, that is what it is. It is not a home away from home or in place of home; it is not a girls' school; it is not a vocational school; it is not rehabilitative. It is jail. Creating a layer of "in" definitions does not change reality. The "hole"—and there are such places in juvenile institutions—is still a cruel and destructive and dehumanizing technique, even when it is called "milieu therapy."

No amount of adult newspeak can change the children's raw perception, although in time many children will, in order to survive, adopt adult "truths" about themselves and about the world. But until they do they ask, like Alice, "What if I never commit the crime?" and from that perception they view all the regulations that box them in. (After all, study hall *is* a form of preventive detention: "If we let them out, they'll do all kinds of wicked things.")

Children in school are viewed as "in need of supervision" in much the same way the juvenile court views its charges. The school does not trust the students; why is it such a surprise to school people that the students don't trust them? The slogan "Don't trust anyone over thirty" was the mirror image of a society that does not trust its children.

Nowhere are the students' perceptions more outlawed than in the high school press. Censorship of regular school newspapers and banning of underground newspapers, to prevent young people from expressing themselves on issues that concern them, reflect the schools' unwillingness to allow any perception except the adult perception to seep into the schools. It not only demonstrates a total disregard for constitutional principles, and for case law, but is insulting to the students' intelligence.

Some young people, frustrated by their inability to make adults treat them as sentient beings, become passive, resigned. There is nothing like coming to class stoned in order to warp time and redefine the surroundings. The student's body remains properly present, pen in hand, while his head is untouched by the clock or the class. Oddly enough, what most students know about high school—that it is intolerable—is reflected in a bizarre way by educators who claim that students are intolerable, especially in the early grades, where educators (and I use the word loosely) would like to have 20 per cent of the children on Ritalin or some other drug that removes the ability to resist the mind-subverting business of the school.

Part of a child's reality is his/her size. Would children be treated differently if at age six they were as tall as adults? Adults' ability to think of children as small tends to also allow the assumptions of fragility, incompetence, immaturity, helplessness. These assumptions are very necessary to adults; it certainly helps justify their control of young people. But high school students, who are frequently taller than their teachers, are still considered incompetent, immature, irresponsible, because it is easier to justify controlling high school people if you make these assumptions.

Every generation of children speaks a language for which there are all kinds of self-styled interpreters, most of whom are over thirty and remember their own childhood only occasionally and not necessarily accurately. No one's memories are a substitute for the child's own perceptions of his time and place. We use our rulers, when their world has no inches; our clocks, when their world's time runs in a different dimension; our disciplines, which try to dissect, when we need not measurers and cataloguers and endless seekers of Ph.D.-thesis statistics but poets and clowns and other human beings who try each day to deal with reality in its uncategorized state. To children who tend to see their own issues as matters of life and death, the adult preference for an infinite mañana is intolerable.

How the children suffer because our ears cannot hear except in ritualized discipline-vocabularies! The horrors visited upon the young become the commonplaces of our everyday adult life. We create our own hells (and call them good!) and insist our children suffer them because our analyses, our definitions, *our perceptions*, our decisions, are so mature, so educated, and so correct. Adults are afraid to allow children to speak in the language of youth, uncluttered with whatever today's "in" language is, the special words and phrases, the language of probability, of psychology and sociology, all dripping in a superior fashion over the unschooled and unsophisticated pain of the

young. Each hunter—rationalizing the pin he sticks the speci-
men with—glorifies the usefulness of his group while he de-
stroys the child with his labels, programs, solutions, institutions.

Children—or most of them—learn to walk and to talk without the help of professionals. For their own reasons, from the
motivations of their own perceptions of reality, children crawl,
then stand, then walk. Perhaps they just want to be able to
reach more things; it does not matter. What matters is that
without study groups, teachers' colleges, workbooks, learning
methodology, curriculum directors, classrooms, grades, and
lesson plans, children learn to walk and talk. Can you imagine
the horror that would be visited upon children learning to walk
or learning to talk if these two useful techniques were *taught*
by the same people who bring us the school systems of America? Can you imagine what would happen to the children in
Cleveland, Ohio, for instance, if the school system taught them
walking and talking? Cleveland's children are on the average
above the national norm in ability but alarmingly below in
performance. By the tenth grade, although their ability is at
the fifty-ninth percentile, their performance is at the twenty-
ninth. By the third grade, Cleveland children are falling behind
national reading norms. By the sixth grade, one half of the children are reading below a fourth-grade level. The "professionals," of course, have decided that it is the poverty-and-mobility
factor that prevents the children from learning to read. But a
1974 survey by the Cleveland Task Force on Literacy proved
that children in schools with widely different poverty rates
came out essentially the same on reading-comprehension tests.
Can you imagine what would happen to poor and minority
children if the adult perceptions of the Cleveland education
community were visited upon the children in their early years!
Children do not originally perceive themselves in classist and
racist terms; in time, adults will convince many of them of their
"unworthiness." Can you imagine what speech difficulties
would develop in children if the education community taught
"talking"? Can you imagine the children who would never stand
if the educational community taught "walking"?

196   HELEN BAKER

Nowhere is the cruelty and disabling effect of adult perceptions more evident than in the schools. Nowhere is it more important that each child define himself or herself, and his/her needs, than in the *compulsory* environment only a few of them escape. To the snappy retort usually fired at me: "You mean, you want the children to run things, to tell the teachers what to do!" I can only say that the speaker has deliberately missed the issue. It is simply that the teacher should not decide who the child is and what he/she can do; I want the child to determine his/her own identity. A word a child sees or needs is more important than a word the teacher thinks the child needs. A teacher can add to a child; no one has the right to subtract from a child.

It is the adult world that separates children into groups, so labeled as to provide some children with permanent inferiority feelings and some children with arrogance. It is the adult perception of the child, measured against arbitrary and not necessarily reasonable goals, that makes some children outcasts not only in their own eyes but in the eyes of other children. Nothing we do to children is so cruel as the tracks we put them in, or the labels we paste on to "help" them. And no matter how adults view special classes, the value of those classes to the children is determined by *their* perception of where they are. Special classes, despite all the positive language of funding proposals and progress reports, are of use to the school. They are rarely of use to the child.

Is there a way to protect the child from the adult world? The U. S. Supreme Court has tried. There is no doubt that students are persons under the Constitution. There is no doubt the Court says they have First Amendment rights in or out of school. There is no doubt the Court says young people in juvenile court who can be committed for their alleged offenses must have certain due-process rights.

But young people find out that in real life these are paper rights. The principal stands jaw-deep in discretion, and the student who tries to exercise his rights may well have to go back to court to win what is rightfully his/hers. It is a very discouraging state of affairs. A recent U. S. Supreme Court decision gave students the right to a hearing before suspension, but what the Court defined as a "hearing" is so insufficient that it is almost meaningless. Even so, at least one superintendent in an Ohio city has told his principals to "ignore" *Goss* v. *Lopez* unless they are challenged.

In February 1975 the U. S. Supreme Court held that students could sue individual school-board members if the school board knowingly violated a student's rights—and they defined knowingly as "knowing" or "if the person reasonably should have known." This *is* a significant victory. But none of these victories speak to the real issue, because none of them deal with *power* or with *definition*. As long as children are *compelled* to go to school, no matter how many court decisions there are protecting student rights, we will find 1) that the school administrators ignore the decisions, 2) that most students never hear about the court decisions, 3) that most systems do as they damned please, knowing that few students know their rights and very few parents will defend their children if it means going to court. What makes a good citizen, according to school administrators' perception, is a student who knows he/she has *no* rights.

There are some things the courts have not done; and there are some things that courts and/or legislatures can do. One of the ways to curtail the infantalizing of our young people, for instance, is to destroy status offenses. An act that would not be a crime if committed by an adult should not be an "offense" if committed by a child. We should remove the incorrigible, the unruly, and the runaway child from the juvenile-justice system. Young people should be allowed to leave home if they so choose, and to live where they choose. Until such time as they commit a crime, society should keep its hands off. Young people should be able to get food stamps and welfare; they should be able to have their own lawyers. Children should always have their own counsel in any court proceeding in which their bodies are involved: divorce/custody proceedings, adoption proceedings. The juvenile court should never be allowed to institution-alize *any* child unless that child was represented by counsel. No child should be committed to a mental institution who was not represented by counsel. Many times, the interest of the parent and the interest of the child are quite different; without his/her own counsel, the child is unrepresented.

Giving juveniles in all states a right to a jury trial would be helpful. Although the U. S. Supreme Court has said this is not a constitutional right, that decision does not prevent individual states from legislating a right to jury trial for juveniles, and several have done so. Young people should have a right to bail; the right of appeal has to be better developed so that it isn't a totally meaningless right.

Children should be able to get medical advice and care without parental permission. Young people should not be penalized by the law for having sexual relations.

What this takes, of course, is a rather overwhelming change in the perceptions not only of the American people but of the child professionals. There is no other way to validate children's perceptions of reality than to allow them to act upon, and to present, those perceptions. There are some 60 million young people in school; there are an awful lot of people earning a living off children. That may not be a nice way of putting it, but, for instance, just what are the manufacturers of Ritalin doing? They are living off the discomfort some children have in school. Look at all the courses, materials, special teachers, and Ph.D. research projects on minimal brain dysfunction, a "disease" recognized *nowhere else in the world*. It is, of course, not the children who are dysfunctional; it is the schools. But the per-ception of the schools controls, and the schools are not about to admit that they really aren't very good. So if they are having trouble with the children, they can dope them, push them out, and develop behavior-modification projects to pacify the rest of the school population.

Millions of people feed off the pain this society inflicts on its children. We create for children the lives they must lead: we make the shoe, with highly trained professionals every inch of the way. We make it from a variety of fabrics, we lace it, buckle it, or snap it—but it does not fit. If it pains the child, if it cripples the foot, perhaps it is time to ask whether we need the shoe at all, not whether we need a new fabric (the alternative school), a new design (the open classroom), or a new set of specifications (from the measurers).

It may be time for the children to raise their voices and shout, "This is where it hurts." It certainly is time for us to listen.

For the past ten years, I have been a listener. I am not a professional: I am not now and never have been a teacher or a psychologist or administrator or sociologist. Although I listen, I do not presume to speak for the young. They are quite capable of speaking for themselves. The question remains whether adults are capable of allowing the child's perceptions to determine what we as adults try to do for children. As long as we decide, using our perceptions *alone*, what is best for children, we shall for the most part fail. When one generation measures the air that another generation is allowed to breathe, there is impermissible destruction.

Most educated people simply resist this notion; they are quick to say that a child cannot possibly "know better."

Ah, but it is not that the young know *better*. It is that they *know*.

3.
Birth of a Movement

In response to the destruction and oppression documented in the preceding sections, a movement for children's liberation has begun to take form. Because the conditions that damage or constrain the young are so diverse, so are the initiatives on their behalf.

This section explores the scope of the movement at present, and the ideas that propel it. The range is wide: from national overviews to personal manifestos. Some authors try to define the basic rights and needs of children, while others envisage new options that will provide alternative routes to adulthood. Some speak primarily to policy makers, others to parents, still others to young people themselves. Some offer facts; others, informed convictions forged through study or struggle, or, in the best cases, both.

Together, these documents attest to a ferment of thinking, feeling, and action. Undeniably, a movement is commencing to recognize, articulate, enhance, and enforce the rights of the young.

A balanced overview of the movement for children's rights is provided by Peter Edelman, who has been in the midst of it from the beginning. While serving as the vice-president for policy of the University of Massachusetts, he was instrumental in the pioneering child-advocacy work of the Massachusetts Task Force on Children Out of School. He is currently director of the New York State Division for Youth, which supervises research and programs to combat juvenile crime and delinquency. He is married to Marian Wright Edelman, director of the Children's Defense Fund.

The Children's Rights Movement
PETER EDELMAN

Black people, women, and children share a similar status in American law historically—all were regarded as chattels. If that status has at last begun to change in some tangible ways for blacks and women, it is only just beginning to change for children. Building upon the movements of the sixties, a "children's rights" movement is gradually emerging. It consists of a loose coalition of concerned parents, older students, citizen and professional advocates, and public officials, both executive and legislative.

The aim is not to create a total parity of rights for children—or to lower the voting age to zero. Rather, the goal is to extend some adult rights and improve government programs so that children will be assured protection and dignity and the chance to develop their maximum potential.

Limited Accomplishments

Education is one of the most active areas of endeavor for the advocates of children's rights, although so far, as elsewhere, the accomplishments are limited. For the most part, the children protected up to now are the unusual ones—exceptional children, minorities, or nonconformists.

Following are the main areas with which the movement has been concerned:

¶Freedom of religion. The nonconformists came first, long before anything called children's rights or students' rights existed. As long ago as 1943 the Supreme Court held that a Jehovah's Witness child did not have to salute the flag in school if it interfered with his religious beliefs.

¶School desegregation. Black children came next, still precursors to children's rights generally.

¶Freedom of expression. The Vietnam War brought an explicit students' rights case when the Supreme Court held in 1969 that high school students could not be punished for wearing black armbands in an antiwar protest.

¶Procedural due process. Over the past twenty years, the Supreme Court has woven an intricate tapestry of due-process protections never visible before, benefiting accused criminals, prisoners, mental patients, and a host of others. In the past five years a number of courts have applied this concept to classification of children in special classes for the retarded and handicapped, requiring that a hearing must be held in which the school must prove the need for the assignment before it can take place.

¶School discipline. Twenty years ago no court in America would have intervened in an expulsion or suspension from school. Yet in the past fifteen years, beginning with cases that arose at the college level, a significant number of courts have held that expulsions and suspensions must be preceded by a hearing to determine the truth of the allegations against the student.

¶Right to education. This is the slowest area to develop, and ultimately perhaps the most important. A number of courts have held that retarded and handicapped children have a right to educational services. Elsewhere, some courts have ruled that placement tests for educable mentally retarded classes cannot be linguistically or culturally biased so that they affect Spanish-speakers or blacks disproportionately.

Landmark Legislation

Massachusetts has declared in landmark legislation that every child has a presumptive right to be in a regular classroom, every child must receive an assessment of his or her need for special programs, the school must prove that a special classification is warranted, and the programs must be provided.

¶Right to privacy. The Buckley amendment dealing with who should have access to school records raises still another issue of children's rights in school.

Here the courts have not been involved although they may be someday. Tradition has had it that education professionals in their discretion could put anything in the student's file that they wanted, keep it from the student and his or her family, and show it to anyone else they wanted to.

Congress set out to change that with the Buckley amendment, which would give parents and adult students the right to examine school records and restrict which outsiders can see them.

Whether the institution involved has been the juvenile court, the jail, the welfare office, or the school, there has been opposition—not uniform by any means—from the professionals involved. All say the same thing, and with understandable, if misguided, conviction: "I know how to do my job, and I don't need outside interference."

Where the children's rights movement—if it is indeed a movement—goes from here is a question. It is still unclear just what rights one applies from the adult sphere and what modifications are necessary. The full dimensions of protection that the child needs from his own parents are also unclear, as is the proper balance between parents, professionals, and children in a variety of institutions.

What is clear is that in a wide range of areas—education, justice, mental health and retardation, health, products, child abuse, television, and many more—children are in need of far greater attention and protection than they have received up to now. There is more than enough for a movement to do.

It will probably never be a "movement" in the mass-action sense that the civil rights, the women's, and the peace movements have been. Even so, the growing effort is showing enough potential strength and effectiveness that it may soon be worthy of the term.

Suddenly, so much is happening so fast in this field that even those who want least to hear have been compelled to take notice. This account from a conservative news magazine (U.S. News & World Report) provides a swift journalistic survey of the new thrusts to give young people the right to have their own counsel, sue their parents for neglect, choose their own guardians, leave school, handle their own finances, exercise free speech, not be beaten in school, and have their privacy protected.

Nationwide Drive for Children's Rights
U.S. NEWS & WORLD REPORT

On the rise across the United States is a "children's liberation" movement that is forcing the nation's elders to sit up and take notice—often in disbelief.

At least four national organizations of attorneys and countless public-welfare groups have joined the fray in behalf of the 68 million Americans under eighteen years old—whom some libertarians call the country's "most oppressed minority."

Young pickets. In Washington, D.C., there were echoes of the 1960s protest marches recently when children aged eight to thirteen—some of whom have been veterans of antiwar parades since the age of four or five—picketed a dime store that barred all minors, unless accompanied by an adult, because of growing shoplifting and rowdiness.

Mostly, however, the new campaign is being waged through legal channels with help from professional activists, liberal parents, and other interested adults.

As children get lawyers, lobbyists, and political sympathizers, the growing trend is to view them as at least semi-independent persons with their own rights—not automatically subservient to parental or official authority.

Keystone of this new "kid power," say leaders, is the U. S. Supreme Court's so-called *Gault* decision.

In that case, the justices ruled that a young suspect tried in juvenile court is entitled to have a lawyer, to cross-examine witnesses, and to enjoy other safeguards guaranteed to adult defendants by the Constitution. Rena K. Uviller, head of the Juvenile Rights Project of the American Civil Liberties Union, summed up the impact this way:

"That was really the first time the Court recognized that children were human beings and that the Constitution is not for adults only. Since then, everything has been aimed at expanding that concept and seeing how far it can be taken."

Full court rights. Today it has been taken far enough that at least one advocate believes any child can tackle an adult in court if he has a sound case and a good lawyer. Gabe Kaimowitz, a public-service attorney who has successfully handled cases in behalf of children in Detroit, said:

"Theoretically, I can win anything for a child in court where an adult has a comparable right—but whether or not the law is enforced is another question."

A series of court decisions has eroded the traditional doctrine that minors can't sue their parents, raising the possibility of damage claims by children who feel they have been abused—or simply neglected.

F. Raymond Marks, a lawyer with the Childhood and Government Project at the University of California, Berkeley, said:

"A trend away from immunity [for parents] altogether—even in negligence cases—can be discerned. By eliminating the immunity rule, courts recognized a degree of intrafamilial autonomy for the child."

As the precedents pile up, parents find they are no longer guaranteed complete sway over their offspring just because they provide financial support.

New laws and court decisions in some states, for example, give minors—even those living at home—the right to get medical help without their parents' knowledge or consent in certain cases. At least forty-eight states grant such freedom when a teenager has venereal disease. Other states extend it to pregnancy, abortion, contraception, drug addiction, mental disorders, or severely contagious diseases.

The Maryland Court of Appeals has upheld the right of a sixteen-year-old girl to refuse to have an abortion ordered by her parent. Mississippi allows any child to make all medical decisions as long as he or she is "of sufficient intelligence to understand and appreciate the consequences."

In Michigan, a sixteen-year-old youth who was expelled from school for long hair won his lawsuit over the opposition of both the school and his parents.

After years of compromise, educators are making further concessions on students' dress, extracurricular activities, smoking, and disciplinary procedures. Much of the pressure for these changes developed after a U. S. Supreme Court decision in 1969 upholding an antiwar protest at a Des Moines, Iowa, school. The High Court ruled that students do not "shed their constitutional rights to freedom of speech or expression at the schoolhouse gate."

No censorship. In Illinois and elsewhere, school officials have published new freedoms in booklets of "rights and responsibilities" that often end hair and dress rules except for safety reasons, and prohibit disciplinary action over the contents of student publications. As a result, young journalists in public schools from Columbia, Maryland, to Berkeley have been putting out special issues on sex and drugs, with features ranging from a review of the X-rated movie *Deep Throat* to an illustrated article on how to use birth-control devices.

Because of court rulings, some of the educators hesitate to search students or their lockers for drugs, weapons, or stolen money. One faculty member at a New York City school for problem children said:

"A search happens very seldom today, because we are so conscious of the youngsters' rights. We have been made aware of them."

Paddlings banned. Spankings by teachers and principals are also a thing of the past in many school districts—especially without parental permission.

This autumn, Illinois will become the third state, after New Jersey and Maryland, to impose an antispanking rule on all schools.

Houston, Texas, on the other hand, has reinstated corporal punishment by teachers—after much debate over disciplinary problems.

California reported more than forty-six thousand paddlings last year. But 7 per cent of the state's districts forbid them, and most of the others urge restraint.

Suspensions are being curbed, too. Litigation has made formal hearings the rule before students are suspended for long periods as a disciplinary move.

Even so, some libertarians want to end suspensions and expulsions altogether. In North Carolina a suit has already been filed claiming government has no authority to remove unruly children from school without providing an alternative means of education.

Similar attacks are being made on educators who try to keep retarded youngsters out of school or to group children into "slow" and "fast" classes.

System abolished. In the District of Columbia, judges abolished the traditional "track" system and ordered reinstatement of all students excluded because of mental or physical handicaps. A Pennsylvania court ordered "due process" hearings before a child is judged "uneducably retarded."

Most attempts to establish an absolute right to an education have failed. But in Illinois the new state constitution gives children the right to be "educated to the extent of their capacity."

And a San Francisco high school graduate has filed an "education malpractice suit"—demanding $1 million from the school district for failing to teach him to read properly.

Use of amphetamines to quiet hyperactive children in schools and other institutions is also under review.

The U. S. Department of Health, Education, and Welfare is still embroiled in a storm of controversy that greeted its suggested regulations on the subject last autumn. Among other things, the draft rules would require personal permission from all children aged seven years and older before they could be used in federally funded drug-testing programs.

William C. Smith, a lawyer with a new advocacy group called the Children's Defense Fund, said:

"I don't think even a parent should have the right to deliver a child up to a non-therapeutic drug experiment."

Fund Director Marian Wright Edelman, in an interview with *The Harvard Educational Review,* added:

"It is a sad fact that there is a better government policy to protect animals than children from experimentation."

Disclosure move. Latest targets in the drive for pupils' rights are school files containing potentially damaging medical or psychological information on students. A Congressional conference committee has approved legislation to make these confidential records available for inspection at the demand of parents, who could challenge the contents at a hearing and prohibit their distribution to police, prospective employers, banks, or credit bureaus.

The advent of computerized data banks compounds the threat to children's privacy, said the Defense Fund's Mr. Smith. He cited a Maryland program in which teachers, psychologists, and other "instant experts" put defamatory labels on students, choosing from a list of computer codes for characterizations such as "sexual deviation" or "paranoid." The information is stored in a data bank to help government agencies looking for ways to aid children. Mr. Smith continued:

"Only certain officials are supposed to see the reports. But the codes can be cracked, and the information is practically useless compared to the danger of its falling into the wrong hands. A kid could be branded for life because a teacher thought he acted sort of weird back when he was seven years old."

For the same reason, legal fights are being mounted against programs that give public school pupils psychological tests and ask personal questions about their family lives in an attempt to identify those who might turn into drug abusers or delinquents.

"Worst of both worlds." The informal manner in which juvenile trials have been handled stirred controversy even before the celebrated case of Gerald F. Gault, a fifteen-year-old boy sentenced in Gila County, Arizona, to a six-year term in reform school for allegedly making an obscene telephone call.

In an earlier decision, then-U. S. Supreme Court Justice Abe Fortas wrote:

"There may be grounds for concern that the child gets the worst of both worlds; that he gets neither the protection accorded to adults nor the solicitous care and regenerative treatment postulated for children."

Today the American Civil Liberties Union is challenging a Georgia law that allows juvenile-court judges to send chronic offenders to adult prisons without the safeguard of grand-jury indictment or jury trial.

In Washington, D.C., a judge has ruled it unconstitutional

to incarcerate juveniles who have committed no crime but who have been declared too unruly for their parents to control.

Similar laws allowing the detention of "unmanageable" children have come under fire in various states—especially where runaways or rebellious youngsters are jailed with young robbers and drug addicts because there isn't enough space in more humane institutions.

Custody rights. Children's rights are also being asserted in custody cases.

Activists are pushing a model state law to require courts to consider the child's best interests and personal wishes in divorce cases—even when they are uncontested. In the past, the activists say, courts usually rubber-stamped agreements between the mother and father, allowing children to be parceled out the same as the couple's furniture.

Neither do all parents who turn their children over to foster homes any longer have inalienable rights to reclaim them.

A court ruling in Georgia gives judges what Juvenile Court Judge Tom Dillon calls "an almost frightening amount of discretion" in terminating the parental rights of adults for the psychological well-being of the child. Before, say officials, such children were denied permanent adoption unless their natural parents had physically abused them.

More authorities are agreeing with the Georgia adoption worker who said: "We feel children have the right to be members of a stable family."

Mr. Marks, of the Berkeley children's project, points out that teen-agers actually had much of the social and legal independence they are now seeking until juvenile courts, compulsory school attendance, and child-labor laws were instituted, around the turn of the past century, to protect them from the new threats of the industrial revolution.

The result, he says, is an artificial strain on parents and society—as well as adolescents—because youngsters are kept in legal childhood long after physical maturity.

Mr. Marks suggests granting formal independence at an earlier age for the good of both children and adults—provided child-labor laws and customs are also changed so adolescents can get along in the outside world.

The National Commission on the Reform of Secondary Education, reasoning along the same lines, recently recommended lowering the top compulsory school age to fourteen.

On the whole, controversy over children's rights has been peaceful compared with the violent wars across the "generation gap" of the 1960s.

Government still generally upholds the right of parents to dictate to children on questions ranging from what they receive in the mail to whether they get a driver's license. The Court of Appeals of New York allowed a father to stop supporting his college-age daughter unless she agreed to live in a dormitory instead of an apartment.

The new interstate compact on runaway juveniles is so strict on requiring their summary return to parents that one activist compares it to the fugitive-slave laws of the 1800s.

Ms. Edelman, head of the Children's Defense Fund, conceded that a balance must be struck between treating children as human beings and giving them the protection needed because of their immaturity. She said:

"The narrow legal approach of merely extending adult rights to children is not the answer. Children do have, in my view, special needs and require special protections in certain regards. Defining the working medium between the extremes must be done carefully."

"The social and political structures of almost every nation still tend to treat children as possessions of their parents." The denial of basic human rights to young people is a world-wide phenomenon. Combating it unremittingly is the organization that has been rightly called "child advocate for the world's children." Here Joan Bel Geddes, of UNICEF, argues that "human rights begin in childhood."

The Rights of Children in World Perspective

JOAN BEL GEDDES

When the United Nations General Assembly issued its *Universal Declaration on Human Rights*, in 1948, the nations of the world were implicitly expressing concern for the rights of children. However, children have special rights and needs of their own, in addition to those they share with the rest of humanity, and human progress is incomplete unless it provides explicitly for these.

The Human Rights Commission of the United Nations Economic and Social Council therefore drew up an additional document, a few years later, to focus the world's attention on children's rights. The *Declaration of the Rights of the Child* was adopted unanimously by the General Assembly in 1959—and in an accompanying resolution the United Nations Children's Fund (UNICEF) was assigned the special responsibility of working to implement those rights, to try to make them meaningful realities in the life of every child on earth.

The Declaration of the Rights of the Child states that "the child, by reason of his physical and mental immaturity, needs special safeguards and care, including appropriate legal protection, before as well as after birth." One of the central purposes of that *Declaration* was to apply, in a specific way, the principles of the *Universal Declaration on Human Rights* to children.

The *Declaration of the Rights of the Child* also asserts that "all children, without any exception whatsoever"—regardless of race, sex, national origin, or the political or religious convictions of their parents—are entitled to such rights as special protection, adequate medical care, nutrition, housing, free education and recreation, and equal "opportunities to develop physically, mentally, morally, spiritually, and socially in a healthy and normal manner and in conditions of freedom and dignity."

For the most part, however, the principles of the United Nations *Declaration of the Rights of the Child* have not yet been translated into the constitutions and legal codes of individual nations, with the result that clear affirmation and protection of the child's rights is still lacking in the world today. Policies that affect children are often formulated primarily to respect the interests of adults, of society, or of specific institutions within the society (such as the educational or welfare institutions).

Although there has been considerable progress in recognizing the human rights of all persons, especially those of minority groups, the welfare of children is still very much ignored or overlooked. There has been a gradual expansion of educational and social-welfare programs to benefit children, but large numbers of children still suffer from malnutrition, disease, neglect, and the lack of educational and social opportunities.

The growing number of young children, especially in the developing nations, tends to distract from the recognition of each child as a uniquely valuable, individual person. Moreover, the social and political structures of almost every nation still tend to treat children as possessions of their parents.

There are parts of the world in which children are not accorded the full respect to which they are intrinsically entitled as human beings. In most countries, while the rights of the child are fully honored in theory, in practice many children are innocent and helpless victims of destructive social or economic forces. All efforts, both governmental and non-governmental, to aid the children whose rights are thus threatened or denied deserve the co-operation and support of all people of good will.

Establishing and protecting children's rights is often, very literally, a matter of life and death. For example, the *Declaration of the Rights of the Child* says *all* children are entitled to adequate medical care—yet, in the developing nations, four out of five children receive no trained medical attention either at birth or later, and in some areas the death rate for children between the ages of one and five is actually forty times higher than it is in other areas.

As one of many ways by which it attempts to impress the needs and rights of the world's children on the world's conscience, UNICEF sponsors every year "Universal Children's Day." The basic purpose of the day each year is to emphasize the universality of children, to foster international friendship among children, and to make both governments and the general public more aware of the needs of children, by organizing seminars, conferences, radio and television programs, and other special events around the basic theme of the universality of children and a special educational theme that varies from year to year. The vital importance of caring for infants and children and their mothers is stressed and explained in countless editorials, articles, speeches, and discussions as the occasion is commemorated in more than 110 countries.

Children are small and powerless in comparison to adults. They cannot protect themselves. They rely on the grownups, who brought them into the world and who are thus responsible for their very existence, to provide for their needs and to protect their rights. As the *Declaration of the Rights of the Child* asserts, mankind *owes* to the child the best of what it has to give.

UNICEF is firmly resolved—not only on one day of the year but during all the days of all the years to come—to do what children instinctively and trustingly expect adults to do: protect children and prepare them for the future, fostering their wellbeing and growth in every way we can. It is futile to speak of implementing human rights unless at the same time we make every possible effort to establish and protect the rights of every child, because the child is humanity's future. Human rights begin in childhood.

Mary Kohler, who as director of the National Commission on Resources for Youth has been a long-time driving force in giving young people broader scope for their talents, here suggests a broad platform for the movement. She argues that the "rights

of children" must go beyond the increasing expansion of legal
rights.

Existing institutions must be held accountable, and existing
rights enforced. Here she envisages "various forms—ombudsman, child advocate, enlarged access to counsel, etc.; perhaps
some combination of these and other means may be best. In
addition, ways must be developed to involve the children themselves in protecting their own rights" (emphasis added).

She warns against "a tyranny of services" and urges that we
must protect "every child and his family from social institutions
that are abusive even when well-meaning."

To What Are Children Entitled?
HON. MARY KOHLER

Children constitute one of the largest and most vulnerable
minority groups. They have no voice in the political process.
They participate directly in no lobbies on their own behalf. At
a time when they are particularly weak and easily intimidated
and manipulated, their rights are particularly vulnerable to in-
fringement, perhaps at least as often as not by those who de-
claim that they act in the children's regard.

The spate of recent court decisions (In Re Gault and others)
has brought into question the view of the state as parens patriae
—the benevolent protection of the vulnerable child. And whatever the procedural safeguards won, there are entitlements of
children that go much further—the right to protection against
neglect, abuse, poverty, discrimination, or degradation. Especially when rights are infringed upon in the name of rehabilitation or treatment, the latter must in fact be benevolent and
therapeutic, not merely avoidance or shunting aside of the problem, to say nothing of incarceration or imprisonment.

So far these entitlements are only unachieved aspirations. We
have still to develop the means and mechanisms to assure them.
The experience of the past makes it clear that neither fine laws
nor benevolent administrators are sufficient. Children's rights

at law are only a prologue to a delineation of those specific rights that control the well-being of our children. So far the purely legal focus has left unexplored the whole area of "pre-court" rights, in which the child is often a victim of those whom society has designated as his protectors—parents, guardians, teachers, physicians, and lawyers. Thus I am concerned here with precourt rights and those rights beyond the ken of the court; I am concerned with the problem of who protects the child from his protectors, who guards against the guardians.

Much of the law now governing the relationship between parent and child relegates the child to little more than the status of a chattel. Parents are described as having "property" rights in children. Children's economic interests are made subservient to those of the parent in almost every instance. Legal concepts of parental control and legal requirements of parental consent leave the child little opportunity for self-determination. The time has come for re-examination of such fundamental issues as the extent to which a child is entitled to seek medical and psychiatric assistance, birth-control information, and even abortion without parental consent or over parental opposition. The desirability of subjecting children to the stigma of juvenile-court proceedings merely because their conduct does not seem to accord with parental standards of governability should be the subject of careful study.

A Serious Commitment to Children

Divorce, child-custody, and adoption laws and regulations, while paying obsequious obeisance to the "welfare of the child," are often—advertently or not—the means for playing out adult interests, the venting of adult anger, the serving of adult convenience, the fulfillment of adult desires. A serious commitment to children calls for a re-examination of the laws, statutes, ordinances, rules, and regulations governing marriage, divorce, custody, support, paternity, adoption, dependency, guardianship, and property rights in order to bring some clarity and coherence to a confused and often contradictory whole and to ground these policies and procedures in the primary of the child's interests.

Even though the state compels a child to attend school, his ability to attend, to be cared for, and to be given access to school are depressingly subject to considerations of color, sex, race, class, physical condition, or behavior. No child should be excluded, expelled, or suspended from such services for more than a few days unless alternative provisions for his education are available and arranged.

The rights children have in school—and out—are not those which have to be earned, but are ones whose exercise is their privilege even if they have poor judgment, are ill-informed or ill-mannered, or have contributed little or nothing to their class, school, or society.

If the choice is ultimately between what is least detrimental to the child and what is least detrimental to the adult, I profess a bias in the child's interest. I see the exercise of this preference as a means of interrupting the transmission of conflict and pathology from one generation to the next. The well-nurtured child is most likely to be the nurturing parent. We must also ask to what extent the right to be wanted, in an affectionate sense, is undercut and interfered with by our tendency toward violent resolution of conflict, both internationally and domestically.

One cannot simply assume that persons who father and mother a child are adequately prepared to be parents, to have wanted children. The opportunity for children to serve (as volunteers or workers) in a day-care program or other child- and youth-serving activity can be an important means of observing behavior and learning patterns at various ages; it provides the ideal preparation for parenthood.

It is, in a sense, to state no more than a truism that this (and any) nation's most precious natural resource is its children. To state this truism is not, however, to affirm that we have always acted in keeping with it. Nor is it to assume that the current tension in our society permits us the capability and the will so to act. From the legal point of view, we seem still to be in need of such drastic action as a new constitutional amendment, for example, to establish that all other constitutional amendments apply to young people as well as to their elders. From the extra- and supra-legal point of view, we must first acknowledge the right of all children and their families to respect and dignity. And before that can happen we must be ready to protect every child and his family from social institutions that are abusive, even when well meaning. We must free ourselves of threat of domestic and foreign turmoil if the inequities of hierarchies based on race, sex, and class are to be effectively engaged. The rights of children can, in the final analysis, be attained only in a society whose institutions, public and private, are open and humane.

At this point it is possible only to offer guidelines for evaluating current practices and developing strategies for their improvement. New approaches are needed, not simply the modification and expansion of current practices and services. We have to develop and support sound options based upon the following principles:

The birth, growth, and developmental needs of children and their families must be met as these needs are manifested among children at different ages, in differing sequences and patterns, in differing circumstances.

The needs of all children must be met regardless of socioeconomic status, race, sex, or residence.

Both the family and the society share the responsibility for meeting these needs. The responsibility of the child—self-discipline, respect for others, full development—that is necessary for the child's development results from the family's and society's responsible behavior toward him.

Services must be equal—in access, control, and quality —without regard to the financial circumstances of the family. They must be tailored to the needs of the individual and delivered by persons and institutions fully and directly accountable to the individual recipient and the community of which he is a part.

Against Tyranny of Services

In the active pursuit of the conditions to facilitate the development of the child into an adult able both to influence and to adapt to society, emphasis must be placed upon the design and establishment of opportunities, not the creation of a tyranny of services. In so doing it must be assured that the availability of the service not become a requirement for its utilization.

A system of multiple sources of support and protection would seem more likely to assure the expression of children's rights. Those persons and institutions—parents, school, social-welfare agency, public official, governmental unit—charged with the duty of promoting, protecting, and implementing the rights of children must be held legally accountable for their failures and deficiencies in so doing. A variation on this point is to make it a positive obligation of all school personnel and others who have authority over students to take specific steps to protect the students' exercise of their legal rights. Citizen complaint suits could be brought in cases of dereliction.

Persons and agencies need to be established and charged with the obligation of seeking the enforcement of the rights of children. Various forms are possible—ombudsman, child advocate, enlarged access to counsel, etc.; perhaps some combination of these and other means may be best. In addition, ways must be developed to involve the children themselves in protecting their own rights.

Basic Rights

The categorization of rights that follows is neither unique nor original, as one can see by comparing the basic rights listed both in the Children's Charter of the White House Conference of 1930 and the Joint Commission on Mental Health report *Crisis in Child Mental Health: Challenge for the 1970s.*

THE RIGHT TO GROW IN A SOCIETY
THAT RESPECTS THE DIGNITY OF LIFE, FREE OF POVERTY,
DISCRIMINATION, AND OTHER FORMS OF DEGRADATION

Children must have the opportunity to live and grow in a society free of war and ever-present threats of war, a society that demonstrates its commitment to its children by wiping out hunger, poverty, racism, and sexism—in other words, a child must have the opportunity to live in an ordered world, a world in which there is an opportunity to anticipate the consequences of action, the effect of effort.

THE RIGHT TO BE BORN A WANTED CHILD

We define a wanted child as a child who is wanted, in an affectionate and nourishing sense, on a continuing basis by at least one adult—a child who can feel that he is, and will continue to be, valued by those who take care of him.

It is well known that there are unwanted pregnancies that result in wanted children; that there are wanted pregnancies that result in unwanted children; and that there are unwanted pregnancies that result in unwanted children. The child who is wanted begins life under conditions that favor his development. Nevertheless, his parents will need various kinds of assistance and services in order to sustain his healthy growth and development over time and through the vicissitudes of life. Particular emphasis must be placed on developing psychological supports and tangible services on a neighborhood and community basis.

For those who wish to prevent a pregnancy, there should be easy accessibility to information on contraception and family planning. Abortions should be available; they should be neither prohibited nor compelled. The parent who brings a child into the world and discovers he does not want him should not be forced or shamed into keeping him. There should be available nurturing adults who become the real parents of the child whose biological family is unable to take care of him. Ritualistic adherence to the biological or blood tie has frequently led the law to preclude the child's having an opportunity to be wanted.

The financial incapacity of the new parent should not, as it too frequently does, preclude the assurance of continuity of adequate, nourishing care of the child. Laws should assure financial and other tangible supports so that adults can fulfill the parental role. The arbitrary categorizing of the nonbiological parent as a "foster" parent, which carries with it vulnerability to interruption and discontinuity of the relationship, could be largely alleviated through changes in existing laws and policies. When children's institutions or other group-care settings need to be available, they must be so staffed as to ensure closeness with, and continuity of care by, significant adults.

All pregnant women, regardless of their class, location, or marital status, must have adequate nutrition, excellent prenatal care, and skilled delivery, in order to ensure healthy children. Our technical skills and economic capability make such care possible.

All newly delivered mothers should be under the care of specially trained nursing personnel; and paraprofessionals trained to the needs of mothers, fathers, and children should be made available to help parents with home and child on an ongoing basis. The services of these paraprofessionals can be supported, as needed, by those of nurses, social workers, and physicians.

Taking the concept of a wanted child seriously also requires us to find ways, without intruding upon the rights of adults, to identify unwanted (i.e., very poorly nurtured) children as early as possible in order that their opportunities to grow and develop in a healthy way may be ensured. Although the interests of the parents as well as those of the child must be safeguarded, we leave many children too long in a desperate situation in their own families. Our capacity to identify maternal depression and early mother-child alienation, for example, means that we cannot in good conscience, and must not, permit psychotic children and depressed parents to develop when we know and can provide the cure via intervention by paraprofessionals with professional consultation.

Other children, we take out of their families too soon. By "too soon" I mean that we take children away from their families without having mobilized the kinds of help that might enable the family to maintain or reconstitute itself, and the parents, through such help, to function adequately as parents. In temporary placements and in foster care we are often confronted with a similar problem. Frequently we must ask at what point the biological parent has, in a psychological sense, lost his status as a real parent. The law must come to recognize that "foster" parents can become "real" parents.

To take the concept of being a wanted child seriously requires re-examination of many of our current policies with regard to compulsory education, the concept of truancy, schools for boys and girls under juvenile proceedings, etc. If these were examined in terms of what it means to be a wanted child, there is reason to believe we would modify or reorder many of our ideas about such "solutions."

THE RIGHT TO GROW UP NURTURED
BY AFFECTIONATE PARENTS

Here we see an instance of the interconnection between the first rights we have set forth: if a parent is degraded by society or if the absence of birth-control or abortion facilities results in an unwanted child, the likelihood of the child's growing up nurtured by affectionate parents is sharply diminished.

The special possibilities for natural parents to play a nurturing role should not blind us to the possibility, if the child's best interests call for it, that this role may be played by one or more other adults. This possibility should not be hampered by the stigmatizing of "foster parents" or the tenuousness and lack of permanence that today too frequently are made inherent in foster-home or other, similar placements.

Child-centered divorce laws should be required to ensure that the welfare of the children of the marriage is primary. This would mean that the capacity for nurturing and loving of the child that is required for child development would determine the parent most capable of exercising custody. It would also mean that when parents were using the child against each other, the court would provide a nurturing and loving foster home and an adoptive family, under continuous professional supervision. Here anticipatory guidance of new parents would be provided to ensure an optimal environment for the child.

One of the most effective ways to help young people experience closeness and affection in preparation for marriage is through group projects. Group projects, beginning in the fourth and fifth grades, that involve children in the practice of participatory democracy in the classroom, where they assess their own learning and teaching and gather data and make recommendations on issues of major concern to their community (e.g., better housing, pollution control, safety measures in the streets, multiple use of school plants for community functions) teach children how to obtain facts, evaluate them, and come to rational, workable conclusions. Such preparation for responsible citizenship is essential. Older children can act as resource persons and guides to resource materials and thus enhance the relationships between age groups. Such close involvement around actual problem-solving experience in the schools and community brings about mutual respect, a sense of warmth, closeness, and regard for the contributions of others. A sense of intimacy and working together permits people to express their feelings, both verbally and non-verbally, and sensitizes the participants to a range of feelings and their varied expression within themselves and others.

Disruption of the family and weakening of the family structure and bonds of affection should rarely be permitted. Child-centered criminal and civil law would not, as happens now, remove parents from their families for minor crimes and misdemeanors, i.e., failure to pay parking fines, rents, etc. The court would be enjoined to consider the primacy of the family and be obligated to strengthen it in any consideration of punishment for minor crimes or misdemeanors. Opportunities to make restitution by meaningful weekend work designed to clean up and beautify the environment should be considered by courts as more beneficial than imprisonment to the defendants' learning citizen responsibility and parental responsibility. In some instances conjoint work projects with teen-agers in the family may enhance family unity and decrease criminal tendencies, especially if other opportunities to maintain one's job and do it more effectively are part of the court's injunction, as is current in some county courts.

When parents have been imprisoned, maintenance of some degree of stability in family ties requires the utilization of liberal visiting privileges or provision of live-in situations in order for the mother to care for small infants, as is currently the practice in some modern institutions. Similarly, the effect upon children should be a factor in the implementation of the Selective Service laws.

THE RIGHT TO BE A CHILD DURING CHILDHOOD AND TO HAVE MEANINGFUL CHOICES IN THE PROCESS OF MATURATION AND DEVELOPMENT AND A MEANINGFUL VOICE IN THE COMMUNITY

Too-early forcing of choices, too-quick labeling and categorizing of children, and all-encompassing and permanent record-keeping and stigmatizing rob the child of the opportunity to be a child, the right to play, investigate, explore, relate, test, try out, experiment, rebel. The balance between gathering and recording information about the child, his activities, feelings, and attitudes as a means of aiding and abetting his growth and the very same activities as a means of stigmatizing, categorizing, labeling, and shunting the child into one or another "track" is too tenuous to allow mere expression of good intent or goodwill to justify such activities. Continuing attention needs to be given to how and by whom such information is collected, by whom and for what purposes it is used, and for how long and in what way it is maintained. Prevention of abuse is promoted by openness concerning the existence of such records, access to them by the party concerned, opportunity to comment upon and challenge particular items, and positive legal sanctions to assure their non-harmful use.

A child has the right to learn through trial and error, to try a variety of educational experiences, and, if necessary, to fail without acquiring stigmas or labels that carry the force of a continuing burden. Laws and police practices, school regulations, and social welfare agency procedures must not stigmatize children as criminals, deviates, or disruptors.

In a rapidly changing, pluralistic society we have a vital need to help children learn flexibility, openness, tolerance of others, capability for leadership, and capacity for living with the dissonance and differences made inevitable by technological change. The right of children to such an upbringing faces us squarely with the need for basic respect for differences through respect and understanding of minority groups. We must not only allow and enable minorities to preserve their heritage as a basis for stability of children but we must, more importantly, be committed to their self-determination and economic security so all children can face a rapidly changing future with the security of having parents who know their origins and can communicate them and thus provide the heritage and history that offer the flexible stability so necessary for meaningful change and ready adaptation to solving new problems. This requires a new and flexible educational system, ready to help children learn flexibility and problem-solving, unlike today's rigid schools.

Children raised in their own culture and capable of valuing it, seeing their parents as dignified and significant adults, are secure enough to make free choices about their own future. They need assurance of a decent standard of living themselves in every setting to choose the best values of each world and to love and provide security for their own children.

Future shock, with resulting apathy and immobilization, occurs primarily in children and adults whose heritage and relations with their parents have been insecure, who have shrunk from involvement and feared commitment, since they had no parental and adult models to follow. Their health and mental-health problems are myriad as they seek escape from change and responsibility through meaningless work, uninvolvement as citizens, and addiction to drugs and TV. We must provide:

(*a*) self-determination through community control of the institutions that serve the citizens and development of indigenous community participation and leadership in these institutions;

(b) a culturally relevant education in the family, related to the values of the family, to reinforce self-esteem and a positive self-image;

(c) models of effective parents through economic security and a meaningful voice in decisions that affect the parents' lives. Such parents are the living embodiment of the history and culture of their people and are able to give their children a sense of continuity, security, and free choice about how they will live their lives and rear their own children.

THE RIGHT TO BE EDUCATED TO THE LIMITS
OF INDIVIDUAL CAPACITY AND THROUGH
PROCESSES DESIGNED TO ELICIT THEM

Children learn best by active involvement, by doing, experiencing, engaging. Children have a right to learn through participation in making the decisions that affect their lives and in significant tasks of sharing and being of service. They develop social responsibility as participating citizens. They have a right to guidance from models whose love and concern are expressed in ways that lead to self-reliance, self-discipline, and self-realization.

Too often, education stifles the spirit of inquiry, curiosity, experimentation, creativity. These are qualities that must be nurtured and encouraged.

A child has a right to learn through trial and error, to try a variety of experiences. Educators and others with responsibility for the child's education are obliged to use their observations on behalf of the child, to help him use his talents in ways most satisfying to him and most useful to society.

Differences in children—in their sex, age, and degree of maturity—require differing approaches to their education. For example, the earlier stability of the autonomic nervous system in girls and the instability in boys result in early learning readiness in girls and an unreadiness on the part of many large-muscled, hyperactive boys to sit still long enough to be able to begin to learn to read and write. The school, with its uniform curriculum, may contribute to such youngsters' increased hyperactivity and learning difficulties.

Society has an obligation to provide educational experiences in which every child can, and does, succeed. And those who deliver these services, school personnel and others, must be responsible to the children and their parents. As part of this sense of accountability, the participation of the child in the planning, design, and implementation of educational activities is of great merit.

THE RIGHT TO SOCIETAL MECHANISMS TO MAKE THE FOREGOING RIGHTS EFFECTIVE

Schools, welfare agencies, police and courts, and mental-health and health institutions are all enmeshed in undermining individual and social differences and abusing their clients' rights through a system of non-service or, at best, brutalized service, as black, Indian, Spanish-speaking, and Oriental adults and children can all testify. To prevent further alienation, social institutions must be controlled and directed by those whom they are to serve. Inherent here is our commitment to meaningful employment and a decent standard of living for all American citizens. Only under such conditions can social institutions actually reflect the citizen's concerns and needs in a changing scene.

Most observers would agree that our present system falls far short of this standard and that

> service delivery arrangements are geared more to professional and field needs than to those of children;
>
> we deal with crises more than prevention;
>
> we reach only a fraction of the population in need and, all too often, with too little, too late;
>
> we know that problems often begin in infancy, yet we develop programs that intervene after this critical period.

To establish systems that carry out our stated commitment to children, we need to revise the basis upon which services are offered, provide instruments and agents who act on behalf of children, bring those to be served into the governance of programs, and train and utilize new personnel.

Individuals, agencies, and public bodies providing services to fulfill children's rights must be legally accountable for their performance. Such a recommendation has consequences for malpractice liability, sovereign immunity, the defenses of legislative domain, and professional standards and practices. It is not enough, for example, to assert and enforce the right of a child to education; the right sought, the one to be asserted and enforced, should be the right to *quality* education. And as with the other rights described, the assertion of the right must include a standard of performance and a positive obligation of the service-giving party to deliver it.

Child-advocate services should be established to assert children's rights. Such services must be accessible and available to every child, able to operate effectively within the context of each of the institutions that impinge upon the life of the child— schools, courts, police, child-care agencies, etc. Such advocates should seek redress through both individual "casework" approaches and more general social action. Such an advocacy service should include both local and national components: what is called for is both a national "Office of Child Advocacy," operating at the highest governmental level as an advocate and inside "lobby" on behalf of children, and local child-advocate services responsive to a local constituency.[1]

[1] The recent White House Conference on Children, making child advocacy a key recommendation, proposed a Presidential Advocacy Commission to monitor and analyze existing program activities, to study proposed legislation as to its effect upon children. According to this proposal, the key activity would take place at the local community level, where neighborhood councils on child advocacy would be established. They would be similar to the antipoverty program's community-action-agency governing boards, combining broad local participation with a tie-in to the national structure, which, in addition to its role regarding national policy, would also provide training and technical assistance. The council's

We have often limited those who may serve children by arbitrary and irrelevant standards regarding formal training, credentials, etc. The experience over the past several years in the utilization of paraprofessional workers in schools, health and welfare agencies, courts and counseling programs, etc., argues for a broadening of the definition of those who can and should serve.

Training must also provide for understanding the contingencies of any professional's or paraprofessional's actions on the child's next stage of development and their effect on the integrity of the family. Thus teachers, judges, and medical personnel must be aware of their importance and impact on the child and family and of how their behavior serves as a model of adult behavior for the child and influences his anticipation of future dealings with adults; his reaction to adults is determined by each contact with meaningful adults in his life.

Training of adolescents to serve children in various paraprofessional roles not only is excellent paraprofessional experience but also enables the child to learn from a person near his age and to model himself after a peer.

Mutual respect of adults for one another—co-operation on behalf of a child—should be part of training experiences. These foster the child's respect for adults and the development of self-respect and self-discipline.

Sufficient paraprofessionals and trained volunteers, including parents and older children, can provide individual attention. Nurse practitioners and trained paraprofessionals can provide individualized well-child care and refer sick children to physi-

---

authority would include determining policy, contracting for services, and hiring the child advocate and other staff. The primary focus would be upon the individual child—his or her rights and needs in the context of the family, the school, the courts, the police, etc. Working with any of these, the family, for example, the child advocate would initially seek to be a resource or backup to the family, with a primary concern to maintain it; where that was not in the child's best interest, the advocate would intervene on behalf of the child.

cians. Our failure to take extensive action in this direction
means we do not care to do what is possible for the health,
mental health, and well-being of all children.

*The work of the Carnegie Council on Children was a major
contribution to rethinking our national policies with respect to
the young. Kenneth Keniston, chairman and director of the
council and Mellon Professor of Human Development at
M.I.T., distills his own conclusions from the council's work.*

Change the Victims—or the Society?
KENNETH KENISTON

I wish to pose a question that has preoccupied me for the
past couple of years: Do we Americans *really* like children?

After considerable reflection, I suggest that the answer is:
Yes, *if* our sentiments are to be taken as evidence. Yes, we do
like children, and even love them—if the test is in the values we
profess and in the myths we cherish, celebrate, and pass on
from generation to generation. However, I am prepared to assert that in spite of our tender sentiments, we do *not* really
like children. We do not as a nation really love them in practice,
and I am sure that all of you will agree that what we do must
finally provide the evidence that answers the question.

Why *is* it that we, as a nation, allow so much inexcusable
wretchedness among our children in practice, while at one and
the same time we, as individuals, nurture and profess such
tender and loving and solicitous sentiments for our children?

Broadly, I think that the answer is this: Our sentiments for
children have been rendered ineffective by the stronger influences and forces of the economic system that have grown up
willy-nilly among us.

I have been preoccupied with the subject of American children since I joined the Carnegie Council on Children three years ago. The council has been attempting to understand the unmet needs and problems of American children and families. Such is the assignment that sent me looking for an answer to the question, Do Americans *really* like children? Now let me give you a bit more detail about the practices that impel me to the negative answer I just offered.

Let me start by mentioning our scandalously high infant mortality rate. Our rate is the fifteenth among forty-two nations having comparable data, which is almost twice the rate of Sweden. Infant mortality rates for American non-whites are much higher than the national average, and mortality rates for non-white infants born in America's twenty largest cities approach the rates in urban areas of underdeveloped countries. We are among the very few modern nations that do not guarantee adequate health care to mothers and children.

Next let me mention malnutrition. A United States Department of Agriculture survey shows that between 1955 and 1965, a decade of rising affluence and agricultural productivity, the percentage of diets deficient in one or more essential nutrients actually increased. Millions of American children today remain hungry and malnourished.

So it goes, our sentiments of caring to the contrary notwithstanding.

We say that children have a right to the material necessities of life, and yet of all age groups in America, children are the most likely to live in abject poverty. In fact, one sixth of them live below the officially defined poverty line. One third live below that level defined by the government as "minimum but adequate." And we are the *only* industrialized democracy that lacks a system of income supports for families with children. In this area, we are an underdeveloped nation.

Our school system, of course, is supposed to equalize opportunity for all children, poor and rich. Yet, on a variety of standard achievement tests the absolute gap between rich and poor, and between black and white students as well, is greatest at the twelfth-grade level. Far from equalizing opportunity, our school system augments the inequalities with which children enter schools.

Why are such things so? I have suggested that the answer lies in our economic system. Let me examine this suggestion in the context of three problems, which I will call the depopulation of the family, the intellectualization of the child, and the perpetuation of exclusion.

The depopulation of the family is a label for what others call the disintegration of the family, the death of the family, or the rapidly changing family. I personally believe that American families are alive and kicking, though struggling against enormous disintegrating pressures.

It is a simple fact that last year, for the first time in our history, more than half of all mothers of school-age children in two-parent families worked outside the home, mostly full time.

Another trend is the disappearance of non-parental relatives from families. In 1949, about 50 per cent of single-parent families with children under six were headed by a relative other than the mother or father. By 1973, this proportion had dropped to 20 per cent.

Let me cite a final statistic: In 1960, about one out of every twenty women giving birth was not married; by 1972, this ratio had increased to one out of every eight.

Taken together, these statistics mean that more and more children are spending more and more time in homes empty of people to look out for them.

What has replaced the people in the family? For one, television has become a kind of flickering blue parent for many children. Indeed, this technological baby sitter occupies more of the waking hours of American children than any other single influence—including both parents *and* schools.

A second replacement is, of course, the peer group. Other, unrelated children play a larger and larger role in socializing the young.

The third replacement for the child's family members includes schools, preschools, and the various child-care arrangements that must be made by working parents.

And, finally, growing numbers of children simply receive no care at all. These we call latchkey children. They stay alone in empty houses, often locked in, while their parents work. For those who run loose, the street is their playground.

Although many factors have helped transform the American family from the largely self-sufficient unit it once was, the forces of our economic system are the most fundamental of all. Indeed, our very perception of the family—and the dramatic change in that perception—can be traced to shifting economic imperatives.

In colonial times, the family functioned simply as a single production unit. But this changed with the emergence of, first, a national agricultural market and, second, the industrial epoch.

Soon the family was redefined as a nurturing oasis set apart from the workaday world, a retreat to which the man of the house repaired at day's end. And a funny thing happened to Mother along the way to industrialization: She now became the guardian of the hearth and the primary socializer of the children.

Meanwhile, and also back in the nineteenth century, we developed the first universal public school system to replace many of the family's traditional functions. From the start, this school system was explicitly justified in economic terms by early advocates, such as Horace Mann. School was a way to provide trained workers and to socialize all children further into American values.

And what happened to Mother after her exaltation? Was she free to remain at home and fulfill that heroic role? No way. In great numbers, she pioneered the entry of women into the paid labor force.

Mothers went to work back then for the same reason that most mothers do so today—they needed the money. The highest rates of female participation in the labor force occur in families of average and below-average income.

The entry of mothers and other women into the occupational

system seems to me irreversible. In many cases, it is desirable. To my knowledge, no one on our council believes women should not have the same opportunities for productive work that men have.

Our effort is not to condemn but to try to understand. Certainly, we have come to understand that the economic forces at play on us are sharply at odds with our sentiment that children should receive consistent care and nurturance in and from the family.

If families in America become little more than dormitories, quick-service restaurants, and consumption units, we must look not to the negligence of American parents but to the pressures of the economy for the main explanation. And if this is allowed to happen—and it is happening at a hastening rate—what does it say about our *real* attitude toward children?

Now I move to another subject and ask this: While we have been depriving our children of what they might obtain from a complete and vital family, what have we been doing to them at school? Lately we have been accomplishing what I call the intellectualization of the child.

I believe we are witnessing a growing emphasis upon the child as a brain; upon the cultivation of narrowly defined cognitive skills and abilities; and, above all, upon the creation, through our preschools and schools, of a race of children whose value and progress are judged primarily by their capacity to do well on tests of intelligence, reading readiness, or school achievement.

Although children are whole people—full of fantasies, imagination, artistic capacities, physical grace, social inclinations, cooperation, initiative, industry, love, and joy—the overt and, above all, the covert structure of our system of preschooling and schooling largely ignores these other human potentials in order to concentrate on cultivating a narrow form of intellect.

Our inordinate preoccupation with intellectual development and our presumption that it can be handily measured have not only shortchanged the general population of children in our schools but have also tended to hamper such efforts as we have made to give special help to those children needing it most.

I am thinking of those programs, such as Head Start, that were launched in the 1960s, after our rediscovery of poverty and racism. And I am thinking of our subsequent evaluation of those programs or—to keep it specific—of Head Start.

Most of us know that evaluators examined the results of Head Start and deemed it gravely wanting simply because it failed to raise—permanently—the I.Q. scores of the children in the program.

Well, the fact is—according to the testimony of its architect, Julius Richmond—that Head Start as originally conceived had many purposes, among which the raising of I.Q. scores and the developing of reading capacity were only secondary. This program was intended, more fundamentally, to give power to parents, to broaden the experience of children in non-cognitive ways, and to provide them with many services such as health and dental care. It would seem that the critics were impelled to overlook these other factors by the veritable obsession of our society with cognitive development and with standard tests as a measurement of the educational well-being of the young.

The fashionable theory underlying much of the valuation of Head Start attributes the plight of those children to something called "cultural deprivation." I'll concede that this is one way of looking at the situation, but it seems to me that we need to get at what is *causing* the cultural deprivation. It is certainly easy to see that the term *culturally deprived* has come to be just another euphemism for poor and/or black. And it seems clear to me, at least, that the reason some families cannot provide their children with intellectual stimulation at breakfast and cultural riches at dinner is that they are blighted by and bogged down in poverty.

Now I, for one, see poverty as a manifestation not of our cultural system but of our economic system. So I suggest that it is extremely odd to speak of cultural deprivation as the primary problem facing destitute families whether in inner-city ghettos or in impoverished Appalachian hollows.

The cost of not properly identifying the roots of our problem is manifold. In the case of Head Start, we often stigmatized those whom the program was intended to help.

I have emphasized Head Start, however, to underscore the tendency in our society arising from our obsession with cognitive development, with test scores. It is our tendency to rank and rate children, to reward and stigmatize them, according to their ability to do well in the narrow tasks that schools (or we psychologists) believe can be measured quantitatively.

This tendency to rank and rate is to be found at every level of education. The ability to do well on tests is a primary determinant of the child's progress and position in the world of school and, to a large degree, later on in the world of adults. We talk a great deal about the other human qualities of children, but when push comes to shove, the child who has learned to master test-taking gets the goodies—promotions, special tracks, educational credentials. Indeed, our schools are so structured that without the ability to get good "objective-test scores" or high "grade-point averages," a child is condemned to almost certain failure.

Ironically, this fact lives next door to our professed devotion to the qualities we say we value: physical vitality, caring, imagination, resourcefulness, co-operation, moral commitment.

Why is this? Once again, I would not blame teachers or parents but would point to the pressures of a modern technological economy, to our assumptions about measurement, and to the tracking and selection procedures for our occupational system.

Ours is a highly developed technological society in which we have adopted, usually without knowing it, the implicit ideology of what has been called "technism." This ideology places central value on what can be measured with numbers, assigns numbers to what cannot be measured, and redefines everything else as self-expression or entertainment. The development of so-called objective measures (which are, in fact, not at all objective) of I.Q. and performance is an expression of this broader propensity.

Thus, we measure the effectiveness of education by whether or not it produces income increments, not by whether it improves the quality of life of those who are educated. And we measure the success of schools not by the human beings they promote but by increases in reading scores. We have allowed quantitative standards, so central to our economic system and our way of thinking about it, to become the principal yardstick for our definition of our children's worth.

A related characteristic of our highly developed technological economy is its need for some mechanism to sort individuals into various occupational slots. By the time a poor, black, handicapped, or uncared-for child reaches fourth or fifth grade, a consistent position in the bottom track of the grade has become an almost inescapable adult destiny. The intellectualization of the child reflects the school's role in classifying and sorting the labor force.

Now let me turn specifically to the problem of the children born in the cellar of our society. Our sentiments in their behalf are always touching; our treatment of them is heartbreaking.

The tragic truth is that this one quarter of all American children today are being brought up to fail. This figure is an estimate, but we believe it to be on the conservative side. I am talking about children who are being deprived of the opportunity to realize a significant portion of their human potential.

One out of every seven children in America is non-white, and these children must somehow cope with the persistent institutional and psychological racism of our society. One out of every three children lives below the minimum adequate budget established by the Department of Labor and must face the multiple burdens of poverty.

One out of every twelve children is born with a major or minor handicap, and all of these children face the stigmas and social disabilities that accompany any handicap. One out of every ten children has a learning disability.

Approximately one quarter of all American children do not receive anything approaching adequate health care, nor did

240KENNETH KENISTON

their mothers before they were born—whence our disgraceful infant-mortality rates. Millions of children live in substandard housing. Millions attend deplorable schools.

The process by which children are disabled in our society is no mystery. Physical vitality, emotional caring, resourcefulness, and moral commitment in the child are undercut.

The process is cumulative. Inadequate prenatal care of mothers increases the chances that children will be born dead, defective, or sickly. Early malnutrition decreases the chances for robust physical vigor. Inadequate health care increases the chances of illness or transforms minor illness into permanent handicaps. The child born poor, non-white, handicapped, or of emotionally drained parents faces steeper odds against survival to adulthood.

Children of poverty are denied those needs that most Americans consider fundamental. They live in a world more dangerous by far than that of the prosperous. It may be a ghetto world of broken stair railings, busy streets, lead paint, and prowling rats, or a rural world where families cannot maintain the minimal levels of public health considered necessary a century ago.

Such a world turns off initiative and strips children of the eagerness that more fortunate youngsters can bring to learning. And it teaches many children that the best defense against a hostile world is constant offense—belligerent aggressiveness, sullen anger, deep mistrust, and a readiness for violence.

Such children are systematically trained for failure. They learn that the best strategy for coping is never to venture out, to take no risks, or to be constantly on the attack. This pathetic sense of self and this view of the world is in fact an accurate perception of the messages our society gives these children.

Success stories—the poor boys who made it, the Blacks who became a tribute to their race, the handicapped who made contributions to our society—reassure us now and then that the poor *can* get ahead. But such stories are exceptional.

The fact of exclusion would cause us no grief if we were a society dedicated to gross inequality, if we were eager to waste human potential. But once again I am only reminding you of realities that sharply contradict our sentiments and values.

The themes that dominate our social and political history sing with our commitment to equality and fair play. Nothing in our constellation of basic values even hints that our society should impose special burdens upon special children. How, then, can we understand the perpetuation of exclusion?

One answer, put forward for almost two centuries in America, is that those at the bottom belong there because they lack virtue, merit, industriousness, or talent. But no thoughtful person can accept such an unjust explanation. And here I suggest, once again, that the excluded are not the result of individual inadequacy or immorality but, rather, of the way our society works, the way it has worked for more than a century.

Let me point to one cold and significant fact: The distribution of wealth and income in this nation has not changed materially in 150 years. It has not been changed by our promises of equal opportunity, by our efforts at schooling, by general increases in our national prosperity, or by all of our efforts to reform and change and uplift those at the bottom of our society.

And thus it seems to me that the key explanation of exclusion lies in the nature of our economic system and of our unthinking acceptance of the ideology that buttresses it. Our system, as it has worked, has needed a large pool of drudges—and we have provided them. By the customs and laws and policies that perpetuate exclusion, we have created individuals and families driven by economic need to accept menial, dead-end, low-paying, insecure, hazardous, and boring work.

There are menial and boring jobs to be done in every society. The question, therefore, is not whether such jobs exist; the question is whether they are to be filled by paying decent wages to those who do them or by impelling them to be done by those desperate souls we keep in chronic need.

We must acknowledge how well our system has worked, given its goals. It has made us the most prosperous and technologically advanced nation in world history. Materially, we have profited, but we must realize that the profit has been reaped at costs that do not appear on corporate ledger sheets. These hidden costs consist of the misery and despair and neglect and hunger and want of that vast segment made up of those of us whom I have called the excluded.

In the long run, the price of exclusion is enormous—not only in dollars laid out for remedial services, prisons, and mental hospitals but also in the anguish and pain exacted by social tension and unrest and discontent. And, finally, this nation pays a moral and human price simply by tolerating a system that wastes the potential of many of the next generation.

In each of the three problems discussed—the depopulation of the family, the intellectualization of the child, the perpetuation of exclusion—I have suggested that the search for causes leads us not to blame the individual but the workings of that economic system, which for better and worse, pervades our national existence. And now let me conclude simply by stating and underscoring my belief that if these problems mentioned here are to be effectively solved, we must start to change the workings and assumptions of our economic system.

I believe that the beginning step is to recognize the way in which families and children have become the victims of our system. But even this first step is not going to be easy, for we Americans have been profoundly influenced by a tradition of individualism that makes it hard for us to perceive the larger causes of social ills.

Since our very founding we have emphasized the freedom of the individual, the opportunities of the individual, and the responsibilities of the individual. And, historically, we have also invariably tended to credit primarily the individual for his or her place on the social ladder. And this, of course, has given rise to our long custom of blaming individually those of us who have wound up suffering financial or social or moral perplexities. Out of that perception has come the long—and largely unsuccessful—history of our efforts to cure our social ailments by reforming and uplifting those individuals whom we have viewed as short on character or morality.

I believe it is time to see that there are certain social and economic forces that none of us individually can resist. And I think it is now indispensable for us to see that millions of American children and their parents who suffer unmet needs should not be blamed for crippling situations that are in fact caused by us all within this system.

No doubt individualism can and should continue to be a cherished value of this society. But it seems to me that it is time for us to behave like a family of related people rather than like a collection of competing individuals. It is time for old-style individualism to give way to some old-style sense of community.

All that this would entail, in fact, would be for us to translate those abundant and tender statements of ours into *practice*. Then it might be said that we *really* like children.

A spate of reports over the past few years have struck a common chord. They have come from diverse groups, public and private: the foundation-sponsored National Commission on the Reform of Secondary Education, the professional National Association of Secondary School Principals, and the Department of Health, Education, and Welfare. All of them have agreed that high-school-age youngsters have outgrown the schools as a way to grow up, that young people should not be isolated for so long from the larger society, that other avenues for growth need to be recognized and supported and new ones created.

The most notable of these reports was Youth: Transition to Adulthood, *a report by the Panel on Youth of the President's Science Advisory Committee, headed by James S. Coleman. It provides the most extensive documentation and the broadest proposals.*

Needed: New Routes to Adulthood
THE COLEMAN REPORT

Every society must somehow solve the problem of transforming children into adults, for its very survival depends on that solution. In every society there is established some kind of institutional setting within which the process of transition is to occur, in directions predicated by societal goals and values. In our view, the institutional framework for maturation in the United States is now in need of serious examination.

The purposes of this report are to examine the contexts that now exist for youth, within which they come to adulthood, and assess the fitness of those contexts for the accomplishment of the developments necessary to full maturity, and then to propose alternative settings that seem to be preferable ways of accomplishing that assignment.

Although we recognize that the process of maturation begins in infancy, and in some senses never ends, we have chosen to confine our attention to the age span fourteen to twenty-four. The justification for that arbitrary choice is that essentially none can be classified as adults prior to their fourteenth birthday, and essentially none can be classified as children subsequent to their twenty-fifth birthday, whatever the operational definition of the transition.

When ours was still an agrarian society, the needs of youth were necessarily subordinate to the economic struggle, and the rudimentary occupational requisites permitted them to be brought quickly into adult productivity. The dominant institutional settings within which they grew up were the home and the workplace. Choices in the occupational sphere were few: the future roles of the children were generally well exemplified by those of parents. In short, the task of socialization was resolved by early and continual interaction with the parents and nearby adults.

But as our society moved into the modern era, the occupational structure became progressively more a matter of movement into activities different from those of the parents. A long period of formal training, under specialized instructors, was initiated to provide the cognitive skills seen as necessary for satisfactory performance as an adult, and equality of opportunity itself required postponement of decision. To accomplish these tasks, institutions to provide the instruction were designed, and rules were formulated with respect to school and work. Specifically, schooling to an advanced age became compulsory, and automated promotion, age by age, became the norm. Laws were established against child labor, and minimum wages were specified. These latter not only served their prime function of protecting the economic security of the breadwinner but also delayed the entry of the young person into the labor force.

In consequence, the schools and colleges have come to provide the general social environment for youth. The world of the maturing child, formerly dominated by the home, is now monopolized on the formal level by the school and on the informal level by the age group. The typical young person has a long preparation for his occupational future, within a highly structured school system, interrupted only by some work at marginal tasks (either part-time after school, or during the summers) and terminated by entry into the labor force or motherhood.

Our basic premise is that the school system, as now constituted, offers an incomplete context for the accomplishment of many important facets of maturation. The school has been well designed to provide some kinds of training but, by virtue of that fact, is inherently ill-suited to fulfill other tasks essential to the creation of adults. Indeed, it would be unreasonable to expect any institution to suffice as the exclusive environment for youth. Signs of dissatisfaction abound, from parents and taxpayers who have an inarticulate sense that something is amiss, from school administrators and teachers who are experimenting with methods and objectives and forms that differ from those of the established system, and from youth themselves, many of whom are showing individual initiative in the search for extracurricular experiences.

The school now shares the socialization task with the family and the peer group. Because the family has become limited in its effectiveness with respect to the age group of our concern, it is a minor part of the social environment of many youth beyond early adolescence. And the peer group is not only an unsuitable source for development toward adult goals, it also attenuates the invaluable lines of communication and culture transmission across the generations. The way of life we have institutionalized for our young consists almost entirely of social interaction with others of the same age and formal relationships with authority figures.

To summarize, society has passed through two phases in its treatment of youth. In the first, which may be characterized as the work phase, young persons were brought as quickly as physical maturity would allow into economic productivity, to aid the economy of the family. In the second phase, which may be described as the schooling phase, young persons are being kept as long as possible in the school and out of the labor force, to increase their potential for productivity.

We think it is now time for a third phase in society's treatment of its young, including school but neither defined by nor limited to it. We think it is time to reappraise the contexts of youth, to question even the most accepted and ordinary aspects of their current institutional settings, and to consider the reformation of existing structures and if necessary the creation of new ones. We are proposing the establishment of alternative environments for the transition to adulthood, environments explicitly designed to develop not only cognitive learning but other aspects of maturation as well.

The discussion of environments for youth appropriately begins with a discussion of the kind of objectives toward which they should be directed. These objectives represent the criteria by which to assess the present system and the proposed alternatives.

The objectives to which environments for youth should be

addressed consist of two broad classes. One is essentially self-centered. It concerns the acquisition of skills that expand the personal resources and thus the opportunity of a young person. Schools have traditionally focused upon this class of objectives, and often narrowly so within this class. But a second class of objectives is important as well, in which youth is centered on others rather than self. This class concerns the opportunity for responsibilities affecting other persons. Only with the experience of such responsibilities can youth move toward the mutually responsible and mutually rewarding involvement with others that constitutes social maturity. Whatever the set of specific objectives within each of these classes (and those we shall list are certainly not exhaustive), we believe it important that environments for youth address directly both of these classes, not merely the former, as schools have traditionally done.

First among the self-centered class of objectives are those *cognitive and non-cognitive skills necessary for economic independence and for occupational opportunities.* Although survival in the modern world requires as a minimum a considerable capability in the use of words and numbers, the range of necessary skills beyond that minimum varies as widely as the distribution of occupations within the labor force.

Beyond the acquisition of marketable skills, a second objective consists of developing the *capability of effective management of one's own affairs.* The emergent adult faces an increasingly complex world, in which self-direction and self-management are prerequisites to success. The current environments imposed on youth by society, in the form of schools, provide little experience with self-management, in large part because, where there is little freedom of choice, there is little self-responsibility. The need for such experience is manifested in the frequency with which the freshmen entering college, and seniors leaving college, experience shock as a consequence of the enlargement of choice. Environments for youth should provide experiences that develop one's capability for managing one's affairs in an organizationally complex world.

A third objective within the self-centered class is to develop *capabilities as a consumer not only of goods but, more significantly, of the cultural riches of civilization.* The store of cultural achievements, whether art or literature or music or science, and whether experienced from the standpoint of creator or performer or simply appreciator, enrich the experience of one's life. Some people continue to assimilate these throughout their lives, in a continual expansion of their horizons, but only if they have acquired in youth a sufficient basis of taste and motivation. Environments should provide youth with the kind of experience with cultural achievements that will enable them, as adults, to pursue their tastes in those directions.

As a final objective in this class, environments for youth should also develop in youth the *capabilities for engaging in intense concentrated involvement in an activity.* The most personally satisfying experiences, as well as the greatest achievements of man, arise from such concentration not because of external pressure but from an inner motivation that propels the person and focuses his or her attention. Whether the activity be scholarship, or performance (as in dramatics or athletics), or the creation of physical objects, or still another activity, it is the concentrated involvement itself, rather than the specific content, that is important.

The objectives of the second class, with activities directed toward other persons, are equally important. Adulthood cannot be accomplished merely by the acquisition of self-serving capabilities. These must be augmented by capabilities for mutually rewarding involvement with others.

First, it is important for each person's horizons to be enlarged by *experience with persons differing in social class, subculture, and age.* For some young persons this has been accomplished by national service in the armed forces or in such activities as the Peace Corps. But, for most, the opportunities for a broad range of experiences with persons from backgrounds other than their own are simply unavailable.

A second facet of social maturation concerns *the experience of having others dependent on one's actions.* All persons throughout most of their youth are cast in the role of a dependent on others, while only a few, largely because of family circumstances, have others who are dependent on them. Although a few current school situations do provide appropriate experience of this kind by giving older children some responsibility for the teaching of younger children, this opportunity is atypical. It is important that environments for youth provide opportunities in caring for others who are younger, sick, old, or otherwise dependent, and to engage in activities that are responsible in the sense that they have significant consequences for others. This is a most important apprenticeship for prospective obligations as spouse, parent, and citizen.

Social maturity also develops in the context of involvement in *interdependent activities directed toward collective goals*, in which the outcome for all depends on the co-ordinated efforts of each. A cognate advantage of such joint enterprises is that it provides the individual with the opportunity of serving in the capacity of leader as well as follower. All young people are presently subject to the authority and the directives of others, but only a few gain the experience of guiding and leading. Yet those capabilities are necessary for the management of their future families, as well as in their work and their community activities.

These kinds of social maturation are now accomplished haphazardly if at all. A prime criterion for assessment of present and prospective environments for youth is their efficacy for filling this void.

It is important to develop in youth an additional set of attributes that arise from both classes of objectives: a sense of identity and self-esteem. These are attributes toward which environments for youth should be directed, for such identity and self-esteem form the foundation on which an adult life is built. Further, environments for youth can be assessed by these criteria just as well as by the objectives discussed earlier.

We hope to initiate discussion and debate concerning the capabilities that constitute adulthood, as sketched in the foregoing account, and also concerning the institutional forms that are best designed to achieve the various components of adulthood. The times may seem unpropitious for the announcement of far-reaching goals. In recent years our educational institutions have been in continual crisis, and our efforts at improvement have been frustrated by an inordinate increase in the numbers of youth. Yet times of trouble offer the opportunity for major restructuring that would be resisted were the times tranquil. Also, we are now on the brink of a demographic moratorium in which the number of youth will remain approximately constant, permitting us to seize the opportunity for reformation without the apprehension of being numerically engulfed.

The process of social change requires that discussion and debate begin, that nuclei for social inventions be tentatively formed, that experiments be designed with meticulous attention to comprehensive recording of their consequences for all those whose lives they touch, and that forthright decisions then be made when the evidence is in.

The audience for such discussion is obviously broader than the federal governmental structure. Indeed it may be that the joint responsibility, first of assuring that young people acquire a set of capabilities to serve them well in adulthood, and second of assuring that they retain the freedom and opportunity to move in diverse directions, is best shared between different levels of action, the first at the federal and state levels, and the second through local community and private channels. A central emphasis of this report is the importance of encouraging as wide a variety of environments for youth as are compatible with the enforcement of criteria to safeguard their development.

That is the conclusion of Cornell psychologist Urie Bronfenbrenner, based on his career-long monitoring of trends in the American family. Reviewing virtually every phase of our society that impinges on the welfare of children, he has discovered that the factors that make for contentment, health, growth, and a decent life are being weakened. On the other hand, the factors that make growing up hard, damaging, and dangerous are in-

creasing. *The disintegration of the family is at the center of this ominous process, according to Bronfenbrenner.*

To help revive the American family, Professor Bronfenbrenner proposes one practical remedy: that we revamp our workplaces so that parents and children can be together more. Through changes in the patterns of work and leisure, and through such innovations as child-care facilities at the workplace, he would attempt to alleviate the pressures that pull families apart in the process of earning a living. His argument makes it clear that there is hardly an office, factory, or service enterprise in this society that could not help, through changes in its work regulations, to strengthen the family life of its employees.

"Our System for Making Human Beings Human Is Breaking Down"
URIE BRONFENBRENNER

The Critical Effect of Business on Family Life

It is American business and industry, more than any other institution in our society, that has the opportunity of determining the fate of the American family and the American child. More than any other institution, they have the power to reverse the present trend and to place families and children at the center rather than the periphery of our national life. They can do so by:

recognizing the full measure of their responsibility for the way in which families are forced to live,

changing the organization and demands of work in such a way as to make it possible for children and parents to live and learn together,

actively providing opportunities, resources, and facilities that will increase the involvement of parents and all employees in the lives of children in the community, and

developing ways for children and youth to engage in meaningful activities in the world of adults.

Minimizing Out-of-town, Weekend, and Evening Obligations

A parent who cannot be at home when his children are,
no matter how excellent he may be in other respects, cannot
fulfill his role as a parent. And the organization that keeps him
away is undermining the welfare of his children. The introduction of a family-oriented personnel policy that minimizes such
obligations would not only counteract these effects but—if offered as a fringe benefit—would help attract and hold more able
personnel, for the most capable and responsible staff are also
likely to be those who care most about their families.

Reducing Geographic Moves

The policy followed by some large organizations of transferring personnel every few years from one city or region to another
is highly disruptive to family life. The impact is hardest on children, since healthy psychological development requires some degree of stability and continuity in the social environment from
childhood through adolescence. A pattern of life that repeatedly
tears the child away from familiar friends, schools, and neighborhoods increases the likelihood of the child's alienation both
inside and outside the family. Accordingly, moves should be
kept to a minimum.

Increasing Number and Status of Part-time Positions

We recommend that business and industrial organizations
and government agencies increase the number and status of
part-time positions so that employees who wish to give a larger
part of their time and energy to parenthood or other activities

with children can do so without sacrificing their career opportunities and rate of income.

Leave and Rest Privileges for Maternal and Child Care

Business and industrial organizations share with other institutions in society responsibility for the birth of a healthy child. In view of the cost to society of welfare and institutionalization of children born with prenatal damage, these organizations have the obligation to develop policies of leave and rest for mothers during pregnancy and early months of infant care without jeopardy to their employment or income status.

Day-care Facilities

To increase opportunities for parents and other employees to spend time with their children, day-care facilities should be established within or near the place of work, but with completely independent administrative arrangements that allow parents a determining voice in the planning and execution of the program. Parents and other employees should be encouraged to visit the day-care facility during the lunch hour or coffee breaks and to participate in activities with the children.

The evidence indicates that American society, whether viewed in comparison to other nations or to itself over time, is according progressively less attention to its children. The trend is already apparent when the child is born. America, the richest and most powerful country in the world, stands thirteenth among the nations in combating infant mortality. Even East Germany does better. Moreover, our ranking has dropped steadily in recent decades. The situation is similar with respect to maternal and child health, day care, children's allowances, and other basic services to children and families.

But the figures for the nation as a whole, dismaying as they are, mask even greater inequities. For example, infant mortality for non-whites in the United States is almost twice that for whites, and in several states the ratios are considerably higher. Ironically, of even greater cost to the society than the infants who die are the many more who sustain injury but survive with some disability. Many of these suffer impaired intellectual function and behavioral disturbance including hyperactivity, distractibility, and low attention span, all factors contributing to school retardation and problem behavior. Again, the destructive impact is greatest on the poorest segments of the population, especially non-whites. It is all the more tragic that this massive damage, and its subsequent cost in reduced productivity, lower income, unemployability, welfare payments, and institutionalization, are avoidable if adequate family and child services are provided, as they are in a number of countries less prosperous than ours.

But it is not only children from disadvantaged families who show signs of progressive neglect. For example, a survey by this writer of changes in child-rearing practices in the United States over a twenty-five-year period reveals a decrease, especially in recent years, in all spheres of interaction between parent and child. A similar conclusion is indicated by data from cross-cultural studies comparing American parents with those from Western and Eastern Europe. Moreover, as parents and other adults move out of the lives of children, the vacuum is filled by the age-segregated peer group. Recently, my colleagues and I completed a study showing that, at every age and grade level, children today show a greater dependence on their peers than they did a decade ago. Our evidence indicates that susceptibility to group influence is higher among children from homes in which one or both parents are frequently absent. In addition, "peer-oriented" youngsters describe their parents as less affectionate and less firm in discipline. Attachment to age mates appears to be influenced more by a lack of attention and concern at home than by any positive attraction of the peer group itself. In fact, these children have a rather negative view of their friends and of themselves as well. They are pessimistic about the future, rate lower on such traits as responsibility and leadership, and are more likely to engage in such antisocial behavior as lying, teasing other children, "playing hooky," or "doing something illegal." In short, we see here the roots of alienation and its milder consequences. The more serious manifestations are reflected in the rising rates of youthful drug abuse, delinquency, and violence documented in charts and tables specially prepared for the White House Conference. According to these data, the proportion of youngsters between ages ten and eighteen arrested for drug abuse doubled between 1964 and 1968; since 1963, juvenile delinquency has been increasing at a faster rate than the juvenile population; over half the crimes involve vandalism, theft, or breaking and entry; and, if present trends continue, one out of every nine youngsters will appear in juvenile court before age eighteen. These figures index only detected and prosecuted offenses. How high must they run before we acknowledge that they reflect deep and pervasive problems in the treatment of children and youth in our society?

The institutions that take care of children who lack permanent homes depend for their income upon reimbursements for each day each child is in care. So they have a vested interest in keeping children under their jurisdiction for as long as possible. Rena Uviller, the dynamic director of the Juvenile Rights Project of the American Civil Liberties Union, argues that "the child-care industry stands as a virtually impenetrable barrier between children and their right to a permanent home."

There is a role for non-lawyers in breaking the back of this deeply damaging incarceration: finding local instances of abuse and mobilizing community pressure to demand reform.

Doing Well by "Doing Good"
RENA UVILLER

There is a large unregulated and unpublicized industry in this country which I shall call the child-caring industry. Like any industry, it provides jobs for many people—social workers, psychologists, and non-professional staff. And like any industry it has a vested interest in its own survival and growth. In some states child care is publicly operated through departments of social welfare. In other states the child-caring business purports to be privately run by charitable and/or religious institutions that bristle at the very suggestion that they have anything but the welfare of their young charges at heart. In other states, a complex network of public and private agencies assumes care for dependent and neglected children. Under their auspices, it has been conservatively estimated, one hundred thousand homeless children in this country are in foster care or in institutions.

These children are an unseen and unheard-from population —unheard-from, that is, until they intrude upon our consciousness as juvenile delinquents or "incorrigible" adolescents. They have been deprived, during their formative years, of the permanent home that would give them half a chance at normalcy. They have no permanent home, the child-caring people tell us, because their natural families are non-existent or hopelessly inadequate and the children themselves are unadoptable because of their racial, mental, emotional, or physical handicaps, and because they have become too old to be candidates for adoption.

What the industry does not tell us is this:

Child care is a lucrative business and depends for its financing upon reimbursements through welfare dollars for each day each child is in care;

In many instances so-called private child-care agencies, which purport to be financed by private contributions, depend upon these same tax dollars for most of their operations;

Each child who returns from child care to his own family or is adopted represents a loss of income to the child-caring agency;

Many of the children in care need never have been removed from their homes if the money that supports the child-care business were used instead (at less cost to the taxpayer) for services (e.g., homemakers, public-health nursing, day care) to the child in his or her own home. Many children presently in care could be returned to their families with proper supportive services;

For those who cannot be with their families, there are thousands of people in this nation who stand ready, willing, and able to adopt handicapped children, older children, and minority-group children. Their adoption efforts are stymied because of agency control of the criteria for adoptive parents and the fundamental differences of opinion as to what criteria should govern (e.g., interracial adoptions, single-parent adoptions, older adoptive parents, homosexual adoptions, subsidized adoptions, relevance of past criminal records, etc.).

The statutes governing children in care are a confusing maze and vary from state to state. Indeed, in many states, no statute governs the removal of many children from home, since their placement in child care is supposedly "voluntary" by the parents. Even if it is genuinely voluntary in the first instance, the parent finds it impossible to retrieve the child. (Compare the nature of "voluntary" commitment to mental hospitals. It may be voluntary in but not voluntary out.) Where statutes do govern the removal of the child from home, they are typically so vague and open-ended as to provide virtually no check on state officials in their discretion to divide families. And once the children are in care, however they have gotten there, they disappear from public scrutiny and responsibility altogether. Rarely do statutes mandate automatic periodic judicial review of child-care cases. Or if review statutes do exist, they contain no articulable standards. The consequence is that a vast population of children exist in this country who are wholly at the mercy of a bureaucratic network of child-caring agencies.

The child-care industry thus stands as a virtually impenetrable barrier between children and their right to a permanent home—either through return to their own parents or through adoption. Lest any of you think that penetrating the barrier is easy, that vindicating something so American and apple pie as a child's right to a family is non-controversial, you must speak to CLU lawyers in Iowa, New York, and South Carolina who have taken on the child-care business, to understand the nature of the resistance.

I have devoted so much space to problems of children in care, because they bring into focus the tensions between wanting to "do good" for children and the nature of the obstacles. By doing so, I hope I have also suggested the obvious role of non-lawyers in reform of the system. Each state, each community, has a different maze of statutes, administrative practices, and customs. No meaningful challenge can occur without data. Some of the information-gathering occurs when litigation is initiated. But, more often than not, it is through legislative reform and community pressure that this unseen and unheard population of children are brought out from shadows.

Mark Gerzon was a radical student during the fiery sixties and wrote the best-selling The Whole World Is Watching *while a sophomore at Harvard College. Since graduating, he has become sharply aware of the challenge facing his generation as many of them become parents: how can their idealism and commitment be translated into their roles as nurturers of the next generation?*

Having thought this through to his own conclusions as elaborated in the neglected but pioneering A Childhood for Every Child: the Politics of Parenthood, *Gerzon issues this challenge to his fellow activists. "Unless the insights we gained during youth are practiced during parenthood," he points out, "these insights will be lost with the birth of our children."*

"Good Parents Must Think More Like Radicals"

MARK GERZON

By its very nature, youth is a time of life preoccupied with its own unfolding. The search for identity, the questioning of values, the rebellion against authority, the raising of consciousness—these are all admirable, but self-centered, quests. Unless the insights we gained during youth are practiced during parenthood, these insights will be lost with the birth of our children. If our generation as parents does not free its children to redesign the fatal technological trajectory on which "spaceship earth" has been launched, children throughout the world will face bleak prospects of surviving as human beings. Only if the values of radical youth are sustained and expressed in parenthood will the human strengths that gave birth to our generation's creativity survive. Our reactions *against* technology must grow into actions *for* our children. Otherwise our revolt will die as soon as our adulthood begins.

The oppression of children by adults has continued after every previous revolution that adults have engineered. Our youthful revolution will fail in the same way unless the values of youth culture come to embrace the virtues of parenthood.

The members of our generation have often been simplistically divided into a vocal, radical minority who seek revolution, and a patriotic, conservative majority who simply want to work and raise their children. Perhaps as young people we were so divided, but as parents we can no longer afford to be. Neither part of our generation will succeed in their aims unless they embrace the concerns of the other.

Good radicals must think more like parents, and good parents must think more like radicals.

Barbara Bode, president of The Children's Foundation, in Washington, explains how each of us can become advocates on behalf of children.

Citizen Action for Children
BARBARA BODE

Day-care centers, runaway houses, lead-paint-poisoning programs, and new government agencies, a nearly endless list of projects and programs all have been achieved through the concerted efforts of citizen groups in communities across the country. Parents, professionals, and in some cases the children themselves have seen a problem and have organized to meet a whole range of children's unmet needs.

In the twentieth century, citizen action for children has become an American tradition. Few middle-class parents, mothers particularly, have not participated in a PTA meeting or a March of Dimes campaign. But in the 1960s a new style of children's advocacy developed. With the support of grants from the Office of Economic Opportunity, funds from the Department of Health, Education, and Welfare, and seed money from foundations and churches, groups of low-income community people and ethnic minorities were able to garner the kind of financial assistance necessary to begin their own projects for children. Other, similar groups, without any kind of outside funding, took hold as well, as the spirit of the civil rights movement began to extend to include children's rights.

This mood was recognized by the government. For example, Title I of the Elementary and Secondary Education Act, the special education assistance for schools serving disadvantaged children, required that low-income parent advisory committees be established to oversee programs and curricula. It was reflected through the use of parent and community aides in Head Start programs designed to even the chances of low-income children in public school systems. It was felt by such groups as a few poor parents in Mississippi who began a tutorial program

for their children which has grown over the years into a major
health and child development center. And for some it culminated in the Children's March for Survival, sponsored by the
National Welfare Rights Organization in the spring of 1972.
In short, a new sense of awareness developed with an emphasis on children's rights as well as services.

Today there are local groups and organizations for children
throughout the country monitoring programs, evaluating problems, assessing needs, initiating new programs and facilities, and
engaging in legislative lobbying. National organizations have
been established to provide supportive services: organizing
help, information, technical assistance and even legal aid. At
times the groups work in tandem, the state or national group
fulfilling an advocacy role and the local group concentrating on
services. In other cases state or national organizations act as
clearinghouses and simply replicate the work of local groups on
a broader scale. Some are focused on a single issue while others
work to serve the range of needs of a single group of children,
such as the handicapped. All began, however, with one or two
people who saw a need and were concerned enough to try to
meet it. Such local action is the key to effective advocacy and
services for children. Several representative organizations and
advocacy efforts are cases in point.

Model: Concerned Mothers Club, Augusta, Georgia

Mothers in Augusta, Georgia, concerned about the low grades
of the children in their housing project, joined together in 1971
to start a tutorial program in their community center. The
tutoring, they found, was constantly disrupted by children clam-
oring for something to eat. After questioning the children and
conducting an informal survey they found that most were going
without breakfast. Calling themselves the "Concerned Mothers
Club," they met with the school superintendent to request a
school breakfast program. The superintendent was immovable
and adamantly opposed to the program. The children continued
to go unfed.

Obviously, the little money the mothers could contribute among themselves was not enough. Working as volunteers, they began to solicit food donations. Churches, local merchants, and others contributed and soon they were feeding breakfast on a regular basis to more than five hundred children. The tutors soon found they were working with much more attentive children. Parents were pleased and even the school reported a dramatic decline in vandalism. Nevertheless, school officials continued to refuse to institute a federally supported breakfast program.

Realizing that donations can last for only a limited time, the Concerned Mothers Club sought the help of the Southern Regional Council and The Children's Foundation. They incorporated, gained tax-exempt status, and applied for federal food assistance funds. After struggling for more than a year with the Agriculture Department bureaucracy, they were finally approved for participation in the Special Food Service Program for Children. At present they are feeding and tutoring over a thousand children each morning in Augusta. Tutoring is a fine first step for those concerned about the educational needs of children, and tutorial programs provide concerned citizens with a revealing initiation into the broader issues of quality education and other community problems.

Model: Voice of Calvary, Mendenhall, Mississippi

The pastor of the Berean Baptist Church in Mendenhall, Mississippi, started a volunteer tutorial program, called the Voice of Calvary, in the early 1970s for local children dropping out of school or having difficulties with desegregation. It soon became clear that help with school work alone would not substantially improve classroom performance. Health and nutrition problems were affecting the children's ability to learn. Reaching out into the community, the Voice of Calvary brought in support to develop a learning and health center for the children of Simpson County. Now with the help of foundations and some government funds they offer a total health-care program for children and their families along with nourishing meals, an expanded tutorial program, library, and field trips.

Model: United Bronx Parents, New York, New York

Similar concerns led a few Puerto Rican parents in the South Bronx of New York City to join together to improve the learning opportunities for their children. They found a rigid school administration, inadequacies in the curricula, and the school's lack of responsiveness to the needs of Puerto Rican students. As volunteers in 1965 they began a group called United Bronx Parents, which has gradually expanded its influence throughout the city and widened its focus to include health needs, housing, summer recreation programs, and the juvenile justice system. Essentially they monitor programs, particularly those in school, and train parents to evaluate curricula, teaching performance, and administrative efficiency. Parents are organized to intervene on behalf of both individual students and groups of students. They also sponsor such services as youth drop-in centers, summer recreation programs, and day-care programs.

Model: Day Care Crisis Council, Chicago, Illinois

One of the most critical areas of children's needs in every town and city is day care. There are simply not enough centers to accommodate all the preschool children whose mothers work or are away from home. Moreover, many of the centers that do exist are unlicensed, understaffed, and dangerous. Such national organizations as the Child Welfare League of America, the Black Child Development Institute and the Day Care and Child Development Council of America are among those working to improve the quality of child care nationally while offering technical assistance to local centers and to those wishing to open centers.

In Chicago, the Day Care Crisis Council fills this same role on a local level. Started in 1969, in response to such horror stories as a mother who was forced to drug her three preschool children daily with sleeping pills so that she could go to work, the Crisis Council brings together individuals and organizations in a city-wide forum with a community-action orientation. Members of the council, parents, and representatives of church and civic organizations work as volunteers to upgrade and expand day-care services for all children in the Chicago area who need them. They have led the fight for expansion through increased federal and state appropriations and continued advocacy for fairer eligibility requirements in order to open up more programs to low-income working parents.

Low-income parents themselves have started a number of day-care centers in churches and community buildings throughout the country. In five southern states, Alabama, Mississippi, Georgia, North Carolina, and South Carolina, these community-controlled centers have banded together in federations to help each other, to encourage similar centers to open, and to get more clout in dealing with recalcitrant state bureaucracies.

Model: Citizens Councils for Children, Massachusetts

The problems of unresponsive bureaucracies and recalcitrant officials on all levels, local, state, and national, eventually becomes an issue for almost any citizen endeavor for children. Most groups find they must decide initially between providing services for children and becoming involved in government decision-making on behalf of children. In Massachusetts, however, forty Citizens Councils for Children have the best of both worlds. In response to the efforts of the Massachusetts Children's Lobby and the need for co-ordination of state services for children, legislation was passed in 1972 establishing an Office for Children. The office opened in January 1973 and began by sending organizers across the state to organize councils for children. Anyone in the state who is interested can join a council and vote to elect the board. Board membership is open to anyone, with the one requirement that a majority of the members be consumers (parents or children). The members must also represent a cross section of children's interests. The councils themselves do not provide direct services, but they support those who do. Each year, the over-all budget ($5 million this year) is divided among the councils to be used in supporting innovative projects to meet the *unmet* needs of children in the area.

The Massachusetts councils are continually in the process of examining their communities, evaluating local programs, and setting priorities. One of the most active ways they accomplish this is through community hotlines, called "Help for Children," staffed by paid child advocates. They offer a means of keeping a finger on the pulse of the community and finding out how well services for children are actually functioning. In the first year of operation, with only about half the lines installed, six thousand calls came into the hotline. In response, the councils get involved in projects ranging from support of children with special education needs, to day care, juvenile justice, and lead-paint poisoning. No other state begins to approach this close relationship between citizen initiative and government programing, although it makes much more sense than the confusing, conflicting, and overlapping programs that generally exist. The Massachusetts model combines almost all the basic varieties of citizen action for children: monitoring, intervention or advocacy, initiation of new services, and even lobbying.

Lobbying

Lobbying, in a general sense, is where everything begins and ends. If successful it gains the authorization of new programs and blocks regressive ones. It can be as simple as writing a congressperson or as multifaceted as drafting the legislation for a new program.

Lobbying is influencing legislation, convincing elected officials to pass a law to meet an unmet need or to defeat a law that would be harmful. It is also initiating legislation. The most important thing to remember is that anyone can do it by following some basic steps.

BECOME INFORMED

1. Get copies of all bills concerning children or a particular aspect of children's needs (from your legislator or the legislative committees that handle issues affecting children).

2. Analyze the bills and decide what position you or your group will take.

3. Draw up a position paper that you endorse and that can be endorsed by other individuals and organizations (ask them if they have a position you might consider adopting or endorsing).

4. Find out if there will be hearings where you can speak or submit written testimony.

PLAN YOUR STRATEGY

1. Make a list of all the legislators representing your area, including their home and office addresses and home and office phone numbers, and distribute copies to your group or friends.

Make and distribute a second, similar list of "key legislators" with major responsibility for bills affecting children.

2. Put one person in charge of co-ordinating lobbying efforts and compiling results of contacts and the responses of legislators.

3. Mark your lobbying calendar to focus on the dates when

the bill is in committee,

the bill is before the House,

the bill is before the Senate, and

the bill is ready for the governor's or President's signature.

4. Make lobbying assignments so that just before each stage your group will be in contact with your representatives and key legislators in one or more ways:

visit them in person with a copy of your position paper if you have one, or

write them explaining your position and the effect of the bill on children in their district, or

send a telegram stressing the critical importance of their support, or phone them or follow up your contacts with a phone call explaining your position and urging their support.

5. At every stage, the person in charge of lobbying should assess the responses to your contacts to decide whether or not your lobbying efforts should be stepped up (more personal visits, more telegrams, etc.).

FOLLOW UP

1. Keep a record of the positions of the legislators you contacted and how they voted.

2. Send thank-you notes to legislators who supported your position.

Probably the best-known citizen lobbying groups are the League of Women Voters and Common Cause, but children have their own, special lobbyists as well. The American Parents Committee is the oldest. Representing concerned citizens across the country for twenty-eight years, it is still an active force in Washington on behalf of children. A lesser-known but equally effective lobby is the Washington Research Project Action Council, focusing particularly on the needs of poor and black children. The churches, of course, are active lobbyists, as are the groups representing children with special needs, such as the handicapped, the autistic, and the retarded. In several states there are active children's lobbies. In Minnesota, the Children's Lobby has concentrated primarily on day-care problems. California's Children's Lobby, with about one thousand members, has had a similar focus. Both are now seeking to expand their areas of concern.

Monitoring

A natural next step from lobbying is monitoring services for children. Monitoring is keeping watch over programs to see that the programs are available and that they are implemented properly, successfully, and in accordance with the law. A monitoring effort can begin with one or two people knowing that some service is being provided but that many of the children are not being adequately helped. Generally, monitoring combines research and action with the goal of improving the delivery of services. Interested community groups can easily follow a basic pattern of approach.

DEFINE THE NEED

1. Get a thorough understanding of the laws and regulations authorizing the program.

2. Get copies of the agency policies regarding the program and compare them to the laws to see if there are any gratuitous restrictions or illegal rules.

3. Decide what methods you will use (surveys, visits, interviews, etc.).

4. Decide how many weeks or months you will spend on this first phase.

CONFRONT THE BUREAUCRATS

1. Decide what problems you will focus on (missing services, poor response to needs, unnecessary delays, abusive treatment, etc.).

2. Send a letter to the local bureaucrat responsible for handling the service, briefly describing some problems you have found, and ask for a meeting within two weeks.

3. If you don't hear from the bureaucrat within a week and a half, call to find out why and arrange an appointment.

4. If she/he refuses, send a second letter with copies of the first to the supervisors at the local, county, and state levels; the mayor; local and state elected officials.

5. Try to arrange a meeting with the supervisor.

6. If all this fails, use the records of your attempts as part of your report.

REPORT YOUR FINDINGS

1. Compile your findings in a written report to be mimeographed or printed for distribution, including:
a general statement of the need,

explanation of how the program should work,
horror stories (examples of abuses),
chronology of your meetings or attempts to meet with
bureaucrats, and
recommendation for change.

2. Go public with the report by presenting it to
the press, and
a civic or community meeting or
the school board or agency advisory committee, and
local, state, and national elected officials.

NEGOTIATE WITH THE BUREAUCRATS

1. Send your report to the supervisor of the bureaucrat responsible for administering the program and request a meeting with him and the person who turned you down—or refused to meet all your earlier requests for action—within two weeks.

2. Do not be intimidated by them or taken in by their flattery; you pay them through your taxes and you should demand good performance.

3. Insist that their responses be specific and that they agree to make changes within a certain specified, short time limit.

4. Get their agreements in writing.

FOLLOW UP

1. Continue to monitor their progress in correcting abuses and inadequacies.

2. If necessary, contact a legal-services office or the ACLU to bring a lawsuit.

Monitoring services for children can be the most effective way of ensuring children's rights and heightening public awareness of their needs. For almost any issue there is a national organization ready to offer suggestions. Help for ending the practice of suspending children from school for long periods of time with little or no cause comes from the Children's Defense Fund in Washington, D.C., or Cambridge, Massachusetts. Help in organizing efforts for equitable implementation of children's food programs in school and out of school is available from The Children's Foundation situated in Washington, D.C., and Atlanta, Georgia. Information to achieve non-sexist education for children can be obtained from Women Associates in Reno, Nevada, the Women's Action Alliance, or any chapter of NOW, the National Organization for Women. Assistance in combating corporal punishment of children in public schools is ready from EVAN-G, End Violence Against the Next Generation, a national organization situated in Berkeley, California, which provides speakers, radio and television spots, counseling, and consultation to school systems, as well as expert witnesses for hearings and court cases. The New York Citizen's Committee for Children offers a superb example of a local monitoring or watchdog committee.

Support in improving the quality of children's television programing and in bringing an end to seductive television advertising aimed at children comes from a group that exemplifies the extent to which local monitoring can grow. Action for Children's Television (ACT) was started in 1968 by a group of mothers in Newton, Massachusetts, concerned about violence in children's TV shows. Beginning as a small group of volunteers, it has grown to a large voluntary organization with representatives in most states. It has published materials and studies, proposed specific guidelines to the Federal Communications Commission, filed briefs with the Federal Trade Commission, and engaged in extensive public education through workshops, conferences, monthly newsletters, and constant proselytizing. While maintaining a single focus, representatives from ACT sit on the boards of any number of national projects working on behalf of children.

COALITION ADVOCACY

Single-issue monitoring and organizing, as ACT clearly demonstrates, can make an impact even though it is undertaken by just a few people. However, individuals and groups have also found that it is often most useful to work in coalition with representatives of other organizations. A new monitoring and advocacy project, the Philadelphia School Breakfast Campaign, is just beginning under the joint leadership of the Philadelphia Nutrition Council and the Philadelphia Jaycees. The Nutrition Council will mobilize coalitions in low-income areas to join with the business-community half of the coalition being organized by the Jaycees. A similar kind of short-range coalitional campaign was organized by the Children's Rights Project in San Francisco last year with great success. Instead of planning to expand into a national organization, it had a specific short-range goal. Both groups hope to provide local models that can be adapted by similarly concerned citizens working with groups in other communities.

A key element of this kind of monitoring is advocacy and intervention—intervening with government bureaucracy on behalf of a child or class of children. Often, however, there are no existing programs from which to demand services. In such cases the only avenue of action available for citizens is to initiate their own services.

PROVIDING DIRECT SERVICES

In Birmingham, Alabama, the AFL-CIO and the Red Cross have joined together with other concerned citizens to open a runaway house for teen-agers. Similar homes have been established in Las Vegas, Los Angeles, and virtually all across the country. Some are the result of work by adults, while others have been organized by young people themselves. This is also the case with drug treatment centers. RAP (Regional Addiction Prevention), in the Washington metropolitan area, is one of the best examples of young people and former drug users organizing to help themselves. Supported by foundation funds and community contributions, the several RAP centers are run as a collective, with all decision-making and daily operations being carried out by the group of young people being served.

Another kind of co-operative effort at providing children's services is seen in the day-care and baby-sitting co-operatives springing up all over. Parents in northern Virginia, for example, who were at a loss to find sitters with a concern for children, organized to trade sitting services in two different towns. Now

they have joined forces to promote developmental child care for
their children and have become involved with the quality of
education in their schools.

While there are no instant formulas for success in organizing
to provide direct services, there are certain factors that are
critical:

an obvious need,

a group of dedicated individuals, and

an overriding faith in the ability to succeed.

The winning combination is concern and common sense.

Whatever avenue of citizen action is taken, it is above all
important to act. The horror stories, abuses, and bureaucratic
bungling are compelling. After meeting with a few friends and
analyzing the problems confronting children, a group must
simply decide how it can be most effective in a way that is most
comfortable for its members. Advice and assistance are widely
available. Some groups join a national organization, others call
on state or national organizations for help, still others work
entirely on their own.

The key to all is to become involved.

Children are the most vulnerable and powerless group in our
society. Advocacy on their behalf is vital and rewarding.

The most popular and respected authority on bringing up children explains how he has learned some important things by living through the past few years in America.

Some Things I've Learned
BENJAMIN SPOCK

To feel confident about how to bring up your child, you've
got to know what you stand for, what you want for your family
and community and for your nation. If you know what you're

in the world for and what the world needs, how you raise your child will fall into place. If you haven't any idea of what you're in the world for or what people should be striving for in America at the present time, then it's terribly hard to put into perspective what you should do with your children.

Don't be ashamed of your spiritual side. Man is a spiritual being, and if he doesn't have a spiritual side of one kind or another or doesn't have beliefs of one kind or another, he's miserable. I think many of our contemporaries, especially the most highly educated and most sophisticated, are the ones who most sadly lack anything to believe in. This produces something like depression, or at least apathy, in these people. That would be all right if nothing needed to be done in the world, if all of human life were going along smoothly and people were enjoying the fruits of technological advance, but that isn't the case. We've got the means to make a heaven on earth, and yet there are more hungry children in the world now than ever before.

Parents are quite hesitant about telling their children what they believe, because they wonder whether it's old-fashioned and out of date to do so. They're also afraid that if they're too firm they'll make their children hate them, or their children won't love them as much as they would like them to. Parents have been assailed by these doubts in a society that to a considerable degree has lost its bearings except in purely materialistic terms.

One of the significant developments of this century has been all the advice coming from such professional people as psychologists, child psychiatrists, and educators. American parents have craved this kind of advice in large amounts, presumably because we don't have any grandmothers around to turn to in our society and we don't have so many traditions. So Americans have turned eagerly to the professionals, who have tried to be helpful with the best intentions in the world. But all their advice has had the unanticipated effect of robbing American parents of some of their own assurance. Some of the professionals are saying, "Now, wait a minute, let me tell you what's the right thing, let me tell you the dangers to avoid in bringing up your child." This gives Americans—especially those who've gone through a university and gotten what I consider a respect for academic knowledge—the feeling of *"I don't know whether that's the right answer; I have to turn to somebody else."* So all my career I've been telling parents, *"Don't pay too much attention to the experts. If you've got a particular problem, sure, go to an expert. But also learn to believe in yourself, because, ultimately, that's the way you have to raise the child anyway."*

The balance has swung so far toward understanding of children and being tolerant of children that some parents allow their adolescents to be quite rude and inconsiderate. It's time for these parents to say, "I agree that we have to discuss all these things. I agree that I'm not to be arbitrary as a parent. But I don't want you to be rude to me and I don't want you to be disagreeable to me."

I agree with those critics of the family who say it's too ingrown in America at the present time. I have to say Nature with a capital N never intended a mother to sit all day enclosed in a separate residence with two or three small children, not seeing other people of her own age until her husband comes home in the evening. But it's premature to jump to the opposite extreme and say that the family is over or that it should be over. I think many young people have an impatient attitude about the family, as if it were a purely artificial institution that was imposed on our poor human race in prehistoric times by some tribal priest or somebody who said you've got to get married if you're going to have a good time with sex. From my particular slant, I believe the family has tremendous appeal still, and always will, for the simple reason that practically every human being grew up in a family. One of the strongest drives in children is to learn how to grow up and to behave like one's parents and to be able to give to children of one's own the love and security that one experienced in childhood. There is a drive that one sees all through early childhood, the conflicts visible in later years of childhood, a drive to grow up to be a mother or father and have children. This is why children play with dolls.

This is why they insist that the youngest one among them should get into the baby carriage and act as a baby so they can be parents. Now, I do think there are going to be changes. I think there ought to be considerable changes. It's marvelous that more people who don't feel ready for a commitment to marriage, or who don't want children, are resisting social pressures to do so. This doesn't hurt anybody. But I'm old-fashioned in feeling that if you are going to have children, you ought to make a commitment, whether you call it marriage or something else, to try to stick together. I'm not against divorce, but I think it's so easy to differ and to spring apart. When getting into child-rearing, child-raising, one should say we're going to try to stick together in order to have a family and to give security and stability to the children.

The only hope for America is in our young people who dare take a four-footed stand. Many of them are saying, "Why not live by brotherly love instead of by ruthless competition? Why not try to live simply instead of living as ostentatiously as we can possibly afford?"

You can't hold parents totally responsible when they are harassed by economic insecurities or if they've had a very inadequate education and therefore are not able to give their children a conviction about the importance of going to school. The society owes good housing, good recreational facilities, a good job, and I would say pay for the parent who stays home to take care of the children. I don't think that it's right that a family has to penalize itself financially if somebody's going to stay home and take care of the children.

I used to take it for granted that we have to have a certain amount of poverty. When, in my sixties, I got a little wiser, I found that in Scandinavian countries they don't have poverty. These countries have decided that if a country can support those who can't fend for themselves, it isn't decent not to do so.

We've got to have a fundamental change in our economic system in which it is assumed that industry will produce for people's welfare rather than the sole ambition of making profits. I'm not pointing a finger at any one industrialist. This is how industrialists are judged by their peers and by the people who buy the stocks—are they making a profit. We've got to change that.

There's violence on the part of young people, at least a minority of young people. Juvenile-delinquency figures are still going up and up. There are more robbery and more murder and more rape. This is a very unhealthy aspect of our society. But I think you shouldn't blame youths for this. The fact is, we're a violent society. We always have been somewhat violent and we've grown more and more tolerant of violence. America is going to continue to have more and more violence until the whole society, or the considerable majority of it, turns around and says, "Let's have a decent society."

"We will grow our own," proclaims Berkeley radical Michael Rossman in this impassioned statement on the birth of his son. His manifesto expresses the extreme of an impulse many people have: to enable their offspring to grow up truly free.

Declaration on the Birth of the Child Lorca
MICHAEL ROSSMAN

We will not send our child to a public school, or even to a private one in the usual sense. Together we have managed to learn much the schools couldn't teach us, and unlearn some of what they did. The heart of our knowledge is ours now, and it tells us we must be responsible ourselves for the conditions of our child's growth. This is no romantic, hippie daydream. It is a full political act: grounded in theory, chosen as strategy, implemented with all the skills of our consciousness.

We chose to move on the future by freeing our child from the control of the present state. We declare independence from its essential instrument, the system of education. We will not give our young over to be conditioned in obedience with its programs by any of its representatives, however unofficial, informal, and liberal. *We will grow our own.* And we will grow them as free as we can manage, in situations in which we have only to contend with what is in ourselves of the lives we are trying to leave behind.

Several years ago we left the educational system, where we were cut off from our many selves. We sidestepped the institutions that continue it in society, and began to come together. Now we know that other lives of learning are possible. We can name them. Crippled as we are, we can create their initial conditions: we understand what is involved and have the skills and the power. For we have been learning to be what we imagine: to live in our bodies, make art with our lives, realize cooperation, and fight fascism by any means necessary, including the creation of alternate realities, guerrilla enclaves of life in the state of death.

Good life learning means understanding is integrated in action. We display our knowledge of the culture of specialized roles, with its destructive systems of education, competition, and authority, by how we manage to be each other's teachers, siblings and lovers, parents and children, by how we tend and heal and share each other's growth. We must focus at home through this if we are to focus anywhere else and into the future. *We will grow our own.* And we ourselves must be directly involved in what and how our children learn, for no one else can represent our interest in the future.

For this we must make our lives over: rearrange the ways we work, the styles of our play, the priorities of our time and our love; and move beyond the roles that still bind us from within. To replace what we reject, we must learn anew what we have to share, and grow to make it adequate. The price of making of our lives a school for our children is our own transformation. We believe it is possible, because it is already begun.

Our parents were forced to abandon their children to the part-time uses of the state because they were integrated into its economy and culture, because they saw no alternative, because they were isolated in marriage and privacy and could not organize their lives to be also a school. We know now that no couple can cope alone with even their own relation. We learn in a larger community. To free our young, many must come together, to share their powers in critical mass and intimacy. We believe it involves all entering equal as children into the school of a larger family.

It also means learning economic co-operation, to free space and resources. And it means committing ourselves to political identity and struggle. At present here, one elementary credential can front for up to fifty kids, leaving us with only our own limitations. But when many choose to use this freedom it will be curtailed, and that will be only the beginning. For fascism is rising softly in this land; you have seen its sign in the black headline of the sky.

The state registered our son with a number at his birth and designs to own him. Our growing up prepared us for integration into its army, its civil and industrial bureaucracies, its systems of consumption and exploitation, decision and power. It cannot afford to let us grow our son unprepared, let alone prepared for something else. It will not give him over to the gropings of our freedom without a deadly struggle. This will take many forms. To meet them, we must realize together who we are and the politics of our necessities and choices. And prepare to resist, to fight for the cradle of the future, and to flourish in and beyond our resistance.

1 June 1970

4.
Young People Act— for Themselves, for Others

Every once in a while, the remarkable things that young people are thinking and doing break into the newspapers or make the evening news on TV. Perhaps a Nader-related group exposes local malfeasances, or young people mobilize behind an ecology drive, or a young inventor or artist wins an award, or a high school group starts a "hotline."

These are valid achievements, and should indeed be heralded. But there is a vast and pervasive undercurrent of action by youth throughout the country that quietly goes on between the periodic headlines: modest projects that help hold communities together, bold interventions that save troubled individuals from desperation, engaging business enterprises, or just personal acts of fellow feeling. Such projects reveal what youth could do on an even broader scale if our institutions and attitudes welcomed and supported their energy and inventiveness.

In this section are reports of a small sampling of such projects. We have purposely eschewed two kinds that are familiar to most readers: in-school projects through which students play a role in improving their own educations, and social-action projects such as those mentioned above, which are well covered in the daily press and the literature. We have focused instead on somewhat unusual projects and activities.

Not all of these projects are still in existence, but in the case of projects by young people this is not unusual. Change is inherent in youth-initiated and youth-run programs: the individual young people are growing fast and may move on to take up new and different challenges. "New ideas emerge and new energy creates new projects," as Ralph Tyler says. But viable ideas and workable projects may be useful elsewhere at a later time. And their achievements certainly leave no doubt about what youth can do.

Under the imposing name of the National Commission on Resources for Youth, Mary Conway Kohler co-ordinates a far-flung network of activists and volunteers who together document and stimulate projects by young people. Started almost a decade ago as a kind of spontaneous action by a group of humane educators, social scientists, and businessmen, the commission has specialized in spreading the word about innovations that "nurture and utilize young people's talents in ways meaningful to themselves and their communities." NCRY functions like a switchboard: plugging into youth projects, validating their effectiveness, and transmitting them to practitioners across the country. Here Judge Kohler surveys the range of projects the commission has discovered.

Community Service Projects
NATIONAL COMMISSION ON RESOURCES FOR YOUTH

NCRY has collected reports on over eight hundred participatory learning projects. Excerpts from these reports have been made available to educators across the nation in a free quarterly newsletter. Exemplary projects have been preserved on film and videotapes which are circulated to interested groups. The commission provides workshops for the training of teachers and arranges conferences at which representatives from youth participation projects—both young people and adults—meet with people from other existing and prospective programs.

The programs collected by the commission fall into several categories, which are described in a recent NCRY publication, *New Roles for Youth in the School and the Community*. The examples that follow hint at the variety and originality that characterize them:

Youth as Curriculum Builders. A social-studies lab cart with multimedia presentations prepared by students was invented and has been operated by students in Enfield, Connecticut, for the past seven years. High school youth in Philadelphia, Pennsylvania, provide a traveling puppet show to educate younger children about the dangers of drugs, VD, and alcoholism. Another group of high school students in the same city have developed an environmental curriculum that they use with younger children.

Youth as Community Manpower. Irreplaceable Indian artifacts were rescued from the path of a housing development by diggings conducted by high school students in an archaeology class in Atlanta, Georgia. The state education department of Vermont established a program called DUO (Do Unto Others), in which students receive academic credit for a wide variety of service in community agencies. Students in Darien, Connecticut, operate an emergency ambulance service. In San Francisco students staff the Exploratory Science Museum.

Youth as Entrepreneurs. Home-economics students at Portland, Oregon, opened a restaurant in their school and prepare daily meals for teachers and students. Teen-agers in Cornwall-on-Hudson, New York, created and maintain a natural-science museum that provides education and recreation for themselves, younger children, and the rest of their community.

Youth as Community Problem Solvers. Students of a Denver, Colorado, high school developed a community car-pooling operation to meet the gas shortage. In New York City, young men in the Teen-age Tenants Council have learned to spot and report housing violations in their neighborhood. A youth-run ecology organization in San Francisco bought equipment and recycled twenty-five hundred pounds of aluminum in its first year of operation. In Hoffman, Minnesota, students visit regularly the town's nursing Home for the Aged and an activity center for the mentally retarded. Their school compositions reflect the experiences with their institutionalized companions.

Youth as Communicators. Navajo youth in Utah interview the old people in their tribe and preserve their traditional tales on film and in books. City Arts Workshop, in New York City, have helped young people in ghetto communities create huge outdoor murals expressing the pride and history of their people. In Guildford, Connecticut, junior high school students research the history of their town and produce it in a booklet entitled *Twelve Spoons and Two English Coats.*

Youth as Resources for Other Youth. Students in Philadelphia, Pennsylvania, run an Unwinding Room, where young people can drop in for informal counseling by their peers. Youth Advocates, a crisis service in Seattle, Washington, trains teenagers to staff a hotline and rap center for other young people. In Palo Alto, California, high school students counsel foreign and transfer students as well as new students and elementary students.

In a frankly capitalist society it is natural that many talented young people will be attracted to trying their hand at profit-making enterprises, particularly if they promise more than just profit. Journalist Jo Ann Levine describes three who have shown what energy and ability can achieve in the worlds of the theater, publishing, and manufacturing.

Three in Enterprise
JO ANN LEVINE,
Staff correspondent of The Christian Science Monitor

Scott Rudin will be a senior in high school next year, but already he has worked on such plays as *The Wiz, The Good Doctor, Thieves, Words and Music, The Hot L Baltimore,* and *Equus.*

Around Broadway, they call the job a "gofer"—someone who

"goes for" food, scripts, and just about anything, while a play
is in the preproduction stage.

However, Scott, who plans to be a producer, has turned the
job of "gofer" into someone who types script pages, cues actors,
obtains rehearsal props, and handles payroll. He is listed on the
playbill of *Equus* as "production assistant."

Scott explains that he serves as "assistant to everyone." And
then, "after the show opens, I become obsolete."

He obtained his first "gofer" job in the summer of 1973. He
was fifteen years old, and the play was *The Wiz.*

As Scott moved from play to play, he didn't advertise his
age, and in fact most people thought that this fellow who was
running over with both knowledge and questions about the
theater, this eager beaver who called producers by their first
names, was someone much older.

Scott's goal to be a "quality" producer received some encouragement this season—a season that he sees as a turning point
and an indication that perhaps Broadway will deal more seriously with modern scenes and lean away from nostalgia and
light entertainment. *Equus*, he points out, is an artistic as well
as commercial hit.

Scott, who has been paid bonuses as well as train fare from
his home in Baldwin, Long Island, admits as he heads toward
college, "I have an unusual advantage over people with similar
goals. Many people I see going into the theater have an ideal-
istic sense. But it is not all fun and games, it is a serious business that demands a lot of passion. A lot of kids go to school
and hope that what they do will help them. I have more knowledge than to hope."

Denise Yuspeh, sixteen, makes all the editorial decisions for
a magazine with a circulation of sixty thousand.

She says simply, "The magazine is written by kids. We just
stick what they write in the paper."

Kids Magazine, which is sold only by subscription, publishes
eight issues a year and receives five hundred letters a week.

"Working for *Kids*," said Denise, "you get to do everything—
layout, editing, proofreading, reporting."

During the school year, she does her magazine work between one and three in the afternoon and in the summer between nine and five.

"If I have a lot of mail one day, I may grab a bunch of kids in the school hallway to help," she said. Editors are paid five dollars a day and contributors six dollars per published contribution. There are three adults who work on the magazine, but publisher Sandra Brown insists that Denise has full editorial power and a better relationship than adults with readers who range from age five to fifteen.

Reporting jobs include one story that focused on an agricultural school in Queens. "New York has everything," said Denise, who attends the United Nations School and is planning to take the international baccalaureate her last two years in high school.

How did Denise, who is from Manhattan, get into the UN school?

Well, we went for an interview with the principal, said Denise, "and when he asked about our international connections, my mother grinned and said, 'Would it help if my husband were Jewish and I'm an Arab?' The principal put that in his report, and I got in."

Denise is not sure if she will go into journalism as a career, although English has always been one of her favorite subjects.

President Harris could not be interviewed on a Thursday. That is the day he goes to drivers' education.

David Harris is president of the city, state, and regional organizations of Junior Achievers. He is also treasurer of his manufacturing company, which makes lamps. It is one of 7,500 Junior Achievement companies in the United States, involving 175,000 high school students.

A JA company is formed at the beginning of the school year and liquidated in the spring.

"Our company liquidated Tuesday," reports David, who is also the treasurer. "We had $1,060 in sales," he said with satisfaction. "One thousand dollars is like a plateau—that's the biggie." After having sold stock for one dollar a share, his company is paying back its stockholders $1.16.

"No program, not even high school economics, can give you an idea of what business is like as well as Junior Achievement," said David. (That, of course, is what the founder of Junior Achievement decided back in 1919.)

"We go through all the pain and struggle of making products and selling door to door. We sit through board meetings and we know we have been through business." [sic] The company pays wages of twenty-five cents an hour, and employees work two hours a week, although as president of three organizations, David thinks he probably spends about forty-eight hours a week on Junior Achievement activities.

He explained that although some of the JA products are sold to manufacturers and wholesalers, most of them are sold door to door. He says that out of every eighty house calls, there are ten sales made. ("You figure out of eighty, forty are at home, and out of forty, only twenty will let you in, and out of twenty, only ten will buy.")

David, who lives in the Bronx but attends school in Manhattan, stresses that there are many personal benefits in JA, as well as educational ones. He has met executives of many major corporations (as well as Bob Hope), has traveled a great deal, and has been invited to an annual meeting of the J. C. Penney Company. He has also learned to budget his time, set up schedules, and speak in public.

"A lot of teen-agers come into this program and have a very negative attitude about business," said David. "They think that business is ripping everyone off. JA shows what big business is like; they see it is very hard to make a profit."

"What would happen . . . if children between the ages of five and ten could take over all the decision-making regarding the future of Covent Garden and Piccadilly?" That is the question that inspired Professor Simon Nicholson, who is on the faculty of England's TV-based Open University, to undertake this experiment.

Children as Planners
SIMON NICHOLSON

When we are very young, many of us believe that our world is fairly egalitarian, and that we are free to experiment, draw, paint, invent, play, plan, and create. Many institutions will allow children this kind of equality, for example, the institutions that we call preschool play groups, play buses, adventure playgrounds, and some primary schools. To the extent that these situations allow the child the freedom to create his or her ideas, we might call the situation a non-institution or "de-institution" and when a situation becomes more rigid, and less loose and creative, we may try to de-institutionalize the child's environment. An example of this is the process of de-schooling.

However, as we grow older, and as we approach the age of eleven, we are transferred from a world that may allow for abundant creativity to a world of infinitesimal creativity. It is not relevant whether this transition occurs with the aid of an 11+ examination, or not. What happens is that from the age of eleven years, the child is successfully imprisoned within strict environmental boundaries and times, by law. Within these prisons the child may study other people's ideas and their literature, poetry, science, art, theater, and so on, and when the child ventures outside of such a prison, it is with an "environmental permit" to go to a museum, gallery, etc. (such as Tutankhamen or Royal Academy Chinese exhibition) so as to passively look at the creative work of others. The idea that children can create their own culture, whether as a microcosm or macrocosm, is considered by most people to be an insane one.

The transition from a relatively active and creative early childhood to a relatively passive and inert secondary school takes place apparently naturally, and children rarely discover the true nature of this transition until later in their lives. Thus our culture successfully conditions us to believe that we are not capable of playing much part in the shaping of our lives, and that a small minority of "exceptionally gifted" people such as artists, scientists, city planners, teachers, psychologists, economic experts, etc., will do this for us. A few people are singled out as active and creative, while the rest are conditioned to be passive (even if well-*read*) observers of the world.

To put the point simply, people have behavioral choice between being either *inert* or *inventive*. The inert person reads other people's books, becomes able, within limits, to criticize and understand the work of others, and watches performances by others, such as, for example, watching one-way TV. Contrasting with this, the inventive person writes books, generates ideas, cooks meals, has theories, makes art, and shapes and builds the environment that is his or her own. In theory we all have the choice to be either inert or inventive, but in practice our physical, social, and political environment conditions most of us to be inert.

This condition of inertia is expressed three-dimensionally in our culture in the form of cities and streets and buildings, and even smaller constructions, such as sculptures, that are invented by the active few and which are "fixed." The property of fixedness is important, because it is by being fixed that the rest of the community remains in an inert state. Inert people may wander through the new shopping center, new town, or new exhibition, but under no condition try to evaluate it, modify it, pull it down, start again, or try to come out of their passive state by thinking enough about the environment to want to try to change it in some way. Thus we have a vicious circle, in which the "inventive few" create environments for the inert that will further their inertia. Moreover, the inert environment is usually high-cost, in order that it can be claimed to be irreversible.

The distinction between inertia and invention, although a simplified one, applies to a great many situations. Although it can be maintained that we can be inventively inert, or inertly inventive (for example, getting musical ideas from listening to the compositions of another person), this accounts for only a very limited number of activities. Most of us who inertly listen to inventive music do not then use our cerebral ideas to generate our own music afterward: we may never get involved in inventing music during our lifetime. If we suddenly start, we cause suspicion, since we may not exhibit the right credentials to be a "composer," i.e., credentials to be inventive. Society licenses people to be creative, and without the right license we may meet with intense opposition and censorship. Not many people in the UK know, for example, that they could, in theory, gain access to an inexpensive video camera and generate their own TV program and transmit it nationwide, via "public" TV. Provided the camera is attached to a swivel and a support (such as a shopping cart), anyone from about two and one half years old can generate TV images for transmission and, unlike written language (and in common with most visual communication), there is little vocabulary to learn to become literate. Video literacy, like drawing with a pencil, is very natural to children. The difference is that drawing and communicating with a pencil are legal, while freely "drawing" with a video camera and transmitting or receiving its images over the air are not.

This ability to create, whether with video or with sounds, pictures, words, or three-dimensional material, is often considered a *childlike activity*. Artists and creative scientists are frequently childlike in their behavior, often because of a simple behavioral fact, that they *enjoy themselves while working*. A classic education profile of such people shows them to be childlike when actually a child, inert in their youth, and then, amazingly, they "surface" from inertia to become creative again. There is, however, little evidence for this flow of events, since we are not quite sure whether they really were ever truly inert, for we did not watch them carefully. Perhaps they were active all the time, seemingly inert; or perhaps there is a structural, electrical, or biochemical reason why we become inert around the age of eleven, thus explaining our inert secondary schools. Later on in life we may undergo another biological change, and surface as artists. However, if this is so, the credentialed people who imprison children in the secondary schools have surely been unsuccessful in stating the biological argument!

If, from the point of view of the user, we accept that environments may be of two main types, inert and inventive, then
where do these occur, and which of us occupy which type at
which stages of our lives?

Here are some examples:

Contrasting situations and environments:

Inventive	*Inert*
Artist's workshop	Artist's exhibition
Mobile open classroom	Classroom for teacher teaching
Beach	Sand in an adventure playground
Natural environment	Zoo
Two-way video	One-way TV
City center that evolves	City center designed by an architect
Synthesizer	Performing classical score
Grass	Astroturf
Alphabet	Book of poems
People's park	Concrete plaza
Making own clothes (polyform)	Uniform
Face-to-face conversation	Memo

If inventive environments exist for children (such as mobile
open classrooms) and inert ones for adults (such as concrete
plazas), under what circumstances do we allow for the behavior
of the inventive or childlike adult (e.g. the artist) or for the
behavior of the inert (adultlike) child or non-artist? Or, are
we all latent artists of one sort or another?

These questions raise some fundamental doubts about the
way present-day environments are generated. First of all, most
of our environment (whether inventive or inert) is generated
by adults. Children are not permitted to invent any part of the
environment—are not considered equal to adults in this respect,
in any sense. Second, even if inert people invade inventive peo-

ple's territory (an example might be an adult credentialed and certified environment builder trying to design a free school), the converse never occurs, in which children are free to invent an environment for the education of adults. *What would happen, for example, if children between the ages of five and ten could take over all the decision-making regarding the future of Covent Garden and Piccadilly?* Second, we know from experience what it is like to live in an inert society, but we have no experience of its opposite, a world of constantly evolving and changing variables where active and creative decisions are being made all the time by people. What would it be like?

We might witness all kinds of changes, such as decentralization of decision-making; the decline of the elite professions and licensed environment builders; the disuse of fossilized art galleries, arts councils, and the parasitic critics of the creativity of others. We might see the end of secrecy, information might become public, and communications be accessible to all; we might see the decline of compulsory education so that education, as well as art, would become a natural lifelong activity for everyone. And we might see the evolution of a great number of different types of community and individual, resulting in different behaviors and life-styles that would be reflected in a great diversity of three-dimensional forms: clothing, building, traveling, communicating, and all other activities would evolve differently in different places. The *catalytic* theory of design and social change would largely disappear, because in a society where all can be creative, the need for "passive" action by communication experts, credentialed architects, and social scientists to initiate social change by catalytic action would no longer occur.

Such a world would be the exact opposite of the master-planned monocultural educational schemes proposed by each of the major political parties of today and is therefore science fiction. But it is a world that I believe would be spontaneously generated by children if children were allowed equality and to be themselves, and allowed to think about and have ideas about the environment and learn by being able to generate their own lives.

There is evidence that many of the desirable qualities in the environment are achieved with simplicity by children but with difficulty by adults. Is this why children are suppressed and imprisoned? Above all, if child-generated environments exhibit qualities that are important to children, *do such environments exhibit qualities of importance to all humans?*

The popular way of disposing of this last question is to state that solving environmental problems is so complicated that only people over the age of eighteen can do it, and even then it is better if one is over forty, since people are then supposed to show good judgment, i.e., are capable of being good judges. This is a myth with little evidence to support it. There are a great many examples now of children being in situations in which they have been free to be planners. For example, the recent project in West Los Angeles, at the Webster Junior High School Learning Center, where children planned and developed a pond ecosystem, desert biome, and organic gardens, as a part of their ecological and environmental planning project. The environmental parameters at Webster High were quite complicated, and could be handled by eighth-grade students (ages twelve to thirteen).

In another example, at Elliot School, Putney (London), children had access to portable video cameras and recorders in order to develop design projects and express their ideas about their school environment. The results showed that much of their environment was invisible to most adults in the school (including both visitors and staff) and that the "invisible" features were almost certainly invisible to the architect also. Schools simply would not be built the way they are, for example like Elliot, if those who used them, made them.

In Oxford we have been experimenting with city planning with children of ages seven to eleven. The children have shown an almost instant understanding of such problems as "partially pedestrianized" streets (Cornmarket, Queen Street) and of the environmental impact of bus lanes on cyclists and pedestrians, which accredited planners have been slow to realize. Planning decisions in Oxford, as in other cities, are never made by children.

It would not be difficult—no more difficult than the examples above—to allow children access to information, legal and planning data, ordinances, maps, codes, communications, printing, video, radio, and exhibitions from (at the latest) school-entrance age in an area or community in the UK as an experiment. It used to be thought that to plan environments for children was the "answer." Now, finding this often does not work, should not children plan their own?

Postscript

The following is an extract from the diary of Lucy Blackmar, describing a member of the "zoo group" at Webster High:

"To offer Darrell anything—either academically or culturally enriching—placed a tremendous challenge upon the Webster Junior High School. He was one of the blacks bused in from the Crenshaw District to achieve a racial balance at Webster— essentially a foreigner in the West Los Angeles school and away from all his neighborhood friends. But this didn't seem to matter to him personally, as school didn't matter to him personally. He operated with an 'air' of confidence—always getting by because he was too darn bright and clever not to get by, but never really getting ahead. He didn't find most of the other Learning Center students very exciting or most of their projects very worthwhile. His teachers often found him lovable, but most despaired of ever really motivating him.

"One day, several weeks after I had begun working at Webster, he drifted out to the pond site to observe the commotion of pond-building (planning and measuring and digging and clearing, etc.). He immediately pitched in and stayed to contribute substantially to the final project. He was one of the first Blacks to get actively involved in the project—his cohorts had been conspicuously absent from the planning phases of the project. A 'real' pond right outside the classroom has enough of a fanciful flare to be worth a bit of time—and mornings out in the sun were infinitely preferable to being cooped up in classes.

"Through the pond project, Darrell got more involved in the Learning Center. He seemed to thrive on recognition of his work on the pond project. He loved making suggestions to me personally about how the project ought to be run, though he didn't seem as anxious to share his thoughts with his classmates. One day he spontaneously presented a map he had drawn of the pond area; and another time he wrote a proposal to the principal for repairing a broken fence on the ecology site. He appeared to take tremendous personal pride in such individual efforts.

"We talked a lot. Darrell needed a friend who could listen with a non-judging ear so that he could make some sense of it all just by hearing it. And I needed 'educating' on 'how to beat the system.' His topics ranged from 'how to be truant and not get caught' to 'how to pick a padlock and keep the alarm from sounding' to 'how to steal a minibike and sell it on the black market.' His grasp of the cultural environment that was his everyday world surpassed that of his fellow students. Indeed, he demonstrated such a sophisticated understanding of his personal environment and a self-designed set of values for acting therein, that it seemed ironical to think of the school as offering him any 'Environmental' or social learning.

"As an individual, Darrell thrived. But one couldn't help wonder where he'd find a social rôle. Maybe he wasn't made for any school, but at least an open-type classroom seemed to provide him some of the freedom he demanded. It increased the chance that he might accidentally fall into a worthwhile project; it reduced the pressure for conformity; it somehow respected his restlessness. And the enthusiasm with which he responded to the pond project—an action project in the school —offered a convincing case that he was more alive in a flexible, unstructured program than in a traditional classroom."

Simon Nicholson and Barbara Katherina Schreiner. *Community Participation in City Decision Making*. (Open University Press, DT201/22, June 1973)

Charles W. Rusch, MOBOC: *Mobile Open Classrooms*. (12361 Deerbrook Lane, Los Angeles 90049)

Lucy Blackmar, *The Social Learning Process in Theory and Practice: Some Effects of Group Structure on Participatory Planning and Action Explored in an Open Education Setting.* (UCLA School of Architecture and Urban Planning, July 1973)

Pat Crowley and Shelley Surpin, "The High School Video Workshop," in *Big Rock Candy Mountain.* (Portola Institute, Menlo Park, California, 1971)

"Access to Communications as a Generator of Design," ½″ Sony Videotape by children at Elliot Comprehensive School, Putney. (The Open University Oxford Research Unit, Oxford, 1972)

Roger M. Downs and David Stea (eds.), *Image and Environment: Cognitive Mapping and Spatial Behavior.* (Chicago: Aldine, 1973)

Edward de Bono, *Children Solve Problems.* (Allen Lane, The Penguin Press, 1972)

"Allowing young people to be advocates in institutions that are meant to serve them will not only benefit these youths directly. It will also bring new vitality to the institutions. . . ." Donald Cohen and Catherine V. Richards, writing in Children Today, *give cogent reasons for the encouragement of youth advocacy projects and also state their concern that many of the adults working with the young aren't mature enough to encourage independent participation.*

Youth as Advocates
DONALD COHEN, M.D., AND
CATHERINE RICHARDS

An accepted principle in relation to advocacy groups is that *the advocate optimally attempts to transform those institutions which shape his own life.* This is far less clearly applied to youths, whose advocacy is often channeled by adults toward more distant, and sometimes abstract, causes. It is more consistent with psychological development and our social principles to allow youths to fully participate as advocates in shaping the institutions which, in turn, shape their lives. Giving the vote to eighteen-year-olds was one step in the direction of giving youths a voice in shaping major institutions.

Outside of the family, a major social institution that affects the personal development of children and youths is the school, which society entrusts to convey its highest values and beliefs about the democracy, equality, and freedom on which this nation is founded. Yet schools have often become ineffective in conveying social values, at best, and dangerously oppressive, at worst.

One reason for the difficulties of educational institutions is the separation in schools between the schooled and the schoolers, between the taught and the teachers, and between the school and the community. There were times when these divisions were considerably more narrow. Socrates learned from the questions and assertions of his students, with whom he argued. The questions of a youthful friend and student inspired Maimonides to write his *Guide for the Perplexed.* To what degree today do elementary and high school teachers feel comfortable in discussing ideas with students, admitting ignorance, or in showing that they, too, are still studying and learning? To what extent are advocates invited into the school, or are students asked to consider matters of mutual concern in the community?

Socrates might say that the only programed instruction from which a student could really learn—in a way that changed his character—was a program that the student himself helped to write. It is in this way that advocacy and instruction intersect. The renewal of educational institutions requires dramatic changes in the quality of school social relations. By advocating for the principles and causes that affect them, students can help create educational institutions of new vitality. To make this possible, however, the adults must feel secure enough about their own competence and personal worth to be able to acknowledge personal doubts, needs, and values. Today, the preconditions for advocacy are not met in most schools, for there is little coming together between adults and young people.

This analysis of schools is equally applicable to social institutions that affect youth: community centers, boys and girls clubs, youth organizations, athletic centers, sites of employment, churches, etc. The value of these institutions for the people they are meant to serve has often been reduced by the division between the provider and those provided for. Allowing young people to be advocates in institutions that are meant to serve them will not only benefit these youths directly. It will also bring new vitality to the institutions that serve them now and in which they will participate as adults in the future.

This small selection of excerpts from FPS, *the magazine of young people's liberation published by the Youth Liberation News Service, attests to some of the interests and official responses to youthful attempts at action.*

Items from FPS
YOUTH LIBERATION NEWS SERVICE

San Diego. About two dozen children, ages seven to eleven, held a protest against the local ice-cream man, who, they said, had been treating them rudely. They carried signs with slogans like YOU KID HATER and WE CAN DO WITHOUT YOU. The ice-cream man, who said he wasn't being mean but was just reacting to harassment, didn't show up at the protest. *October 1971*

John Malachowsky, twelve, was annoyed by a four-cent hike in the cost of model-airplane paint. He wrote a postcard complaining to the Internal Revenue Service. The Justice Department filed a $150,000 suit against the paint manufacturer, citing Malachowsky's complaint. *December 1972*

Pamela Gross, who is nine years old, recently wrote a letter to President Nixon complaining that she could "smell the sewage" and suggesting that he do something about it. She received a letter back from the Department of Health, Education, and Welfare suggesting that she "Pay attention to your own learning activities and let the President take care of decisions on national and international affairs." *February 1972*

New Orleans. Two students at Warren Easton High School have been suspended indefinitely because their mother insulted the principal and refused to publicly apologize. The mother has been critical of the school's policy forbidding girls to wear slacks. The suspension action was taken under a school-board rule allowing children to be suspended or punished if their parent or guardian was "offensive" toward a teacher or administrator, unless the parent apologized. The American Civil Liberties Union has said it will file suit against the school board. *February 1972*

In addition to reporting on actions being taken by youth and against youth, the FPS magazine also reviews books about children and youth, keeps readers up to date on court decisions regarding student and youth rights, and provides suggestions for organizing and running school newspapers and protest meetings. It also runs articles by young people criticizing the material used in the schools and school practices. One article worth quoting from was written by Avedon Carol, the science fiction reviewer, who "was once diagnosed as 'hyperactive.'"

"The brief article *Curing Hyperactivity*, in the March FPScope pages, quoting Dr. Sydney Walker, still misses the point, I feel, that everything on the subject manages to avoid.

"Just what is hyperactivity? Although it is often described as a learning disability, research shows that most complaints leveled against hyperactives are disciplinary. Hyperactives tend to question their environment, thereby causing disruptions in the normal flow of home or classroom activities, where the adult authority expects unquestioning obedience.

"The average I.Q. score of hyperactives is higher than the norm. By the schools' standards, this means that they have more academic ability than the average student. However, hyperactives seem to do worse scholastically than less academically gifted students. It is possible that the learning-motivated student may find classroom teaching inconsistent with whatever it is she wants to learn. Most classroom teaching is composed of drill and 'going over' old material, as well as homework, which is just a rehash of the same thing the student has been listening to all day.

"According to Dr. Paul Wender, a leading 'expert' in the field and a major proponent of drug treatment for hyperactivity . . . children respond differently than adults do to amphetamines. Speed makes children more tractable, and lengthens their attention span to the degree that they will do whatever busywork their teachers give them. . . .

"Apparently, Wender hasn't spent much time with speed freaks. Contrary to popular belief, speed freaks do not spend all of their time being intractable and fidgety. In fact, the reverse is true. A room full of amphetamine users bears a striking resemblance to a classroom. Speed, for anyone, will actually make enjoyable those tasks which are normally so uninteresting that they drive one to distraction. That's why people take it."

To engage the issue of "ageism," a group of middle-school students in Hawthorne, New York, meet with old people. Teacher Bob Stauf tells about it.

Young Meet Old
ROBERT STAUF

A hip young Puerto Rican of fifteen years yelps happily how "slick" and "far out, man" it is to see some pictures in a local journal of recognizable aged citizens from a nursing home not far from Hawthorne Middle School. Several youngsters travel southward to the Ethical Culture Center in order to rap with the Gray Panthers about their ideas on child advocacy, rights of the old, the mutual exclusion and segregation of both groups by the mainstream of American society. Students of junior-high age spontaneously give a standing ovation at a Celebration of Community conducted at their school where a presentation to the young is made from the residents of the Hebrew Home for the Aged in Riverdale—average age proudly noted by them as eighty-three years.

The scroll, entitled *Together*, is a poetic reminder written by staff member Amber Harris; "society has shelved us both you see, or pigeon-holed us out of blind insensitivity." It optimistically expressed the expectation that they might "one to one and each to each, through knowing each other extend society's reach." The key to the underlying spirit of the newly launched intergenerational program could be gleaned from reflection on the final stanza:

> For all of us can teach and all can learn
> And all, degrees that really count can earn
> And those who watch us will most surely be
> Startled by the strength in our unity.

A presentation from the students of a framed picture of a bridge that travels easily from Hawthorne Middle School in Yonkers to the Hebrew Home for the Aged in Riverdale serves also to symbolize "The Generation Bridge," so named by the participants in this intergenerational program. Words communicate weakly what it is like to experience the cohesiveness that comes only from a free and open sharing between the octogenarian, whose sense of self was long ago established, and the newly arrived adolescent, whose identity search takes on a fresh meaning. Both appear unusually sensitive, driven by a near compulsion for involvement, committed to a sense of community, acutely aware of the uniqueness of their own situation in life, anxious to touch the personhood that makes persons special.

Approximately seventy students and residents, from the Hebrew Home for the Aged in Riverdale and an eighth-grade team from Hawthorne Middle School in Yonkers, meet every three weeks. (Residents and students agreed this was "just not enough time" to develop their creative talents.) Older folks reminisce to the delight of the young, and together they anticipate a play written and produced by them that serves to call to mind the days that were and will never be again. Nostalgia trips, sugar-coated a bit by the desire to keep alive mostly what was good, give much pleasure to the young, whose flights of fancy become stimulated by what it must have been like in the land of the yesterdays.

A poignant example of the impact such participation had on one youngster was written one month after school had closed. Addressed to all the residents, a note from Nadina Simon reported that her grandfather, "seventy-four years and a wonderful man," had just passed away and that this was her first experience with death of a beloved one. She wrote to illustrate how much she enjoyed the program and to exhort her old friends "not to be disgraced because you are in an old-age home, or you are sick, or any other problem. . . . Just be glad you are alive and with love and care." She closed by stressing she had "gotten a load off my chest."

The newspaper group happily trades off journalistic views of their cross-generational experiences. A letter is read by one of the residents, written to a great-grandson who may not experience, it is feared, the magnificently moving presence of such a sensitive grandmother. A totally impressed student, Dave Wasserman, reported that "Everyone was crying. It really

made you feel good inside." Dawn Cavaluzzi writes in an open
letter to all elderly people an apology for "having put you down.
. . . I'm very sorry for it. I guess it is because I've realized
you're being put in the same spot as young people . . . being
put down for not knowing anything. . . . We can open new
doors and open more eyes to the strengths we have. . . . Soon
if we work and try really hard we'll both be able to live in society, not outside of it."

The book-review group agrees as to how books are still one's
good friends. The invasion of the video has not yet totally
blinded the imagination that seems to increase only from the
reading of a fascinating book. All talk of books they enjoyed
and those they want to read. All promise to come back to consider what literature has raised the aesthetic experiences of
their lives. Over and over, back in the classroom during reaction
sessions, the students, however, agree enthusiastically: the rap
sessions with the old teach more than any book they can remember studying.

Some young fellows initially approach the arts-and-crafts
scene with some apprehension. They are relieved to know that
they, too, can experience great joy in what had been previously
stereotyped as a task "for ladies only." As time goes by they are
able to offer with the old their own craftsmanship and to consider what innovative additions can be made in the construction of what becomes a joy forever.

Memories of these experiences will fade quite slowly in the
hearts and minds of the residents if one reads from the June–
July 1975 *Resident's Voice*, the journal of the Hebrew Home.
Rose Tamres, who wrote the letter to the newborn grandson,
writes "To the Hawthorne Middle School students who at-
tended our meetings of the newspaper group" to assert that
"We all enjoy your presence whenever we meet . . . how everyone impressed me at our first meeting."

Lena Rouda, whose energy level at eighty-three ought to be
bottled and injected into anyone who fears the coming of age,
writes, "A group of students work with us, play with us, socialize, send us flowers on Mother's Day, and we enjoy them im-

mensely. . . . The older generation should listen to the young and try to understand them, as the youngsters must try to understand the elders. . . . Hopefully we have made a lasting impression on the boys and girls, and so when they go out into the world they will remember what they learned here."

Comments from students on a final English exam suggest such hopes are not in vain. Nicky Vece dreamed the dream that "with young people's energy and the elderly people's knowledge society may function a little more civilly." Annette Schnaufer, a mild-mannered girl made a bit more militant by this consciousness-raising this year: "Both young and old are misplaced in society. By working together we can fight for our rights and prove to society that we could both play an important role." Harlan Pincus, who greeted the program with a jaundiced eye, felt satisfied with his opportunity to voluntarily participate. He asserted that the young and old hardly have any rights and are "kicked around like a football." All were involved in an intergenerational discussion group that attempted to see another social ill, ageism, from a dual perspective, and noted some fascinating parallel concerns.

Such an experience in human relations brought about interesting behavior changes in the young participants as well. Janet Udis, whose reputation for finding just about everything in life boring was legion, described the residents as "very intelligent, creative, and talented . . . a pleasure just to sit and listen to them but they're also great fun to talk to." Barbara Torhan echoed this feeling, adding, "I realized they have feelings and ideas that I never realized were there. Nobody has the right to put these feelings aside." Belinda Alphonso, an unusually introverted youngster, seemed to blossom during these experiences. She discovered, "I found out they only want to be independent and don't want to be babied."

Steve Huvane, a new student whose prior regimentation had been book-centered, felt "they should bring them into the community and let them become part of the community for their sake and ours." Jeff Kalpack, building on a strong capacity to

relate, noted authoritatively that "they are a people who can
love and be loved. . . . There are no barriers on love."

The students are experiencing in their time ongoing exposés
of corruption and scandals in the nursing homes. They learn,
too, that neglect of and disrespect for the aged is a blight on
so many of us who took so long to consider in any serious way
what growing old is all about—the joys and sorrows. We can
only look ahead to anticipate the possibility of the ultimate in
long-range impact of a program on the young. I dream of the
year 2045, when in my scenario a knowledgeable senior citizen
enjoys his eighty-third birthday by continuing a most productive and active life "smiling wistfully that he first prepared for
this experience seventy years ago."

"The Generation Bridge" evolved because of combined spirit
and resolve from several quarters. Ella Drucker, a young social
worker from the Home, reacted with instant approval and ex-
citement. Her genuine warmth permeated her exploratory visit
with our students, some of whom were understandably somewhat apprehensive. Adrienne D'Amato, an attractive and caring girl, pressed on in class discussion with the importance that
such a program would have ("service . . . student morale . . .
doing something meaningful"). Resident Syd Hoch joined
Lena Rouda in the first meeting, proclaiming over and over
there is no such thing as a generation gap.

The devotion of both to the cause soon won over the hearts
of all. Administration and personnel of the Home co-operated
in every way, and seemed deeply moved by the instant chemistry that occurred, a ready responsiveness that both groups
gave to this mutual sharing. My principal cautioned that this
might be my "heaviest undertaking." It was, but not so because
of the possible turn-off he thought might occur. Still, he never
said we shouldn't test the idea—and I was grateful.

At first I had to sell the idea to the members of my teaching
team. The science teacher was dubious, the social-studies
teacher noncommittal, the math teacher non-receptive—I began to sense a team of experts ought to be hired to make this
sales pitch. Acceptance became possible after assuring the team

that volunteer students would have to "make up every bit of missed work." The math teacher needed to know that she would not be obliged, with the schedule changes, to teach what she felt would be "two slow classes in a row."

Ever perceptive, my principal then wrote, "I felt that there were so many worthwhile projects that you wanted the class to work on, and so many things that you wanted us to see, but that hassles you encountered from other teachers on the team, kept you from letting us. I just wanted you to know that I appreciate the work that you went to, and I hope that next year you are teamed with teachers who are more responsive to your way of thinking." I gulped hard at this, the kind of message that keeps a teacher's adrenalin going. Too, I knew that next year I would be able to learn so very much more, for I had been transferred to a newly formed team, all who had already offered much in sensitivity and expertise to their students.

Finally, Bob Vega, a Puerto Rican boy who had lost a couple of years in transferring to an American school, made certain no class was dull. He was capable of blocking all sorts of communication or giving up an evening to translate for me what was happening at a Spanish PTA. He had initiated the idea of chipping in for flowers for the "old folks at the Hebrew Home for the Aged," had devised ways of getting more students involved, and at other times drove teachers to cite him as a "royal pain."

His parting review of the year seemed to sum up what Room 211 was about:

1. I learned to communicate with people a little better.

2. I learned how to show love and consideration toward others.

3. I learned how to gain respect and friendship from teachers (at least some).

4. I learned to control my attitude just a little more.

5. I learned to gain respect from older and younger people.

6. I learned how to listen and think before I speak (still need more practice, though).

7. I learned that you will never get everything you will want the way you want it all the time.

8. I have learned that I am someone who is worth something and that is loved by others.

9. I have learned to follow directions more easily than I used to.

10. I have learned big words.

"The reason I think they are meaningful to me is because this is all life. If you can't do most of the things I have up here, I think you are in trouble. I think you need a lot of respect, love, kindness, and most of all you need interest to live a true life like this."

There are those who see the "back to the basics movement" in education as a kind of salvation of the system. I submit that Bob, in his own free way, understood a great deal more of what the basics in life truly are.

The significant actions of young people don't have to be organized or institutionalized to be important. Here British writer Leila Berg evokes beautifully some ways that the children she has lived among act, in their relations to each other, more morally than do adults.

Personal Actions
LEILA BERG

I stand by the railings in Battersea play park and watch. In front of me is the brow of a green hill, littered with large play bricks. A boy comes into view, from the left, about six years old. With some very definite purpose, he seizes a wheelbarrow full of bricks and starts to trundle it away. Just then, over the hill comes a three-year-old. He sees the older boy, and the wheelbarrow, and is riveted with the force of a lightning conclusion. Then his paralysis ends. He hurls himself at the other boy, kicks him, pummels him, tears at him. The older child is astonished. He drops the handle of the barrow, and does not know what to do. He is also very angry. He makes a decision. He strides purposefully toward a crate of bricks, with a porter's truck lying alongside. Grimly, resolutely, with his back to the small one, he begins to fill the truck with bricks from the crate and from the grass.

Again the little one is riveted, appalled. Again, after a minute's paralysis, he hurls himself, thundering over the grass, at the older one, and kicks him savagely, tearing at his clothes. And again the older one is furiously angry. His teeth are set, his face is black with murderous hate. He does not know what to do. Life has never brought him this problem before. He has tried to deal with it forbearingly, for after all he is not a baby; he has done his best, but it is unavailing. In a second he will turn on the little one and bring a brick crashing down on his head, annihilating him. But within that second the little one, quite unaware of doom, is suddenly entranced by the movement of the boy's hands, still grimly, fightingly, going from the crate to the truck, the crate to the truck; and caught up in the movement, in the rhythm of it, in the satisfying creative result of it, his flailing arms stop in mid-air . . . waver . . . and then swing also into the crate and the truck, the crate and the truck.

The older boy is amazed. But he says nothing. No recognition of any kind passes between them. He goes on filling the truck, and the little one does the same, puffing a little with exertion. When it is full, the older one straightens up, grips the handles, and wheels it off.

The small one stands up, startled again. A flicker of doubt passes over his face as he sees the boy and the truck and the bricks disappear. He had not foreseen this. He stands watching, uncertain, poised. Then with a sudden sturdy acceptance he turns, and trudges chubbily back over the hill, on some quest of his own.

Throughout the whole episode not one word has been spoken. Neither has acknowledged the other. It has only been movement—appearance, conflict, co-operation and exit—like ballet.

Now, that was an extraordinary thing. I was ready to cry out —or, rather, because the moment had that knife-edge delicacy when a sudden cry might bring catastrophe—I was on the point of calling with tensely gentle reassurance to both of them, "It's all right." But I held back. And it *was* all right. More all right than I could ever have made it.

Yesterday Richard sat on the floor with me and we played picture dominoes. I hadn't met him before; he's four. I showed him how you stand your dominoes up so that only you can see them. He picked the game up immediately. Then, at one point, several of my dominoes fell over. I hurriedly started to pick them up. But then I saw Richard was looking at them intently. So I took my hand away and let them lie; I even managed to knock over several more in doing so. He gazed, very thoroughly. Then he chose a domino from his own pile.

Authoritarians would assume he chose one that would block me. Also, they would say he was cheating. And also that I had encouraged him to cheat. They would say, "Man is naturally competitive," and that is why we have to try to teach him not to cheat, because if we didn't he would destroy civilization; and so on.

But Richard didn't block me. He deliberately chose a domino that would enable me to continue the game.

He did it not because he was altruistic, or self-sacrificing, but because he needed the game to continue, he wanted our relationship—our co-operation—to continue. To win—that is, to destroy this pleasant relationship-in-existence—was an idea quite alien to him. But an authoritarian adult would have taught him to win—and to destroy what was important to him, and ultimately to believe that winning was what he wanted.

I met Elizabeth and Judy for the first time at tea, Elizabeth nearly two, Judy four. They sat at the table, and they each took a cream cracker. I offered Elizabeth the butter dish. She took some butter with her knife, an enormous lump. She put it on her plate, then picked it up in her hand and squashed it, squeezing it through the cracks between her fingers, gazing at it gravely, very much caught up in its texture and the crackle it made as it ballooned through.

I offered Judy the butter dish. She also took a very large lump with her knife. Made slightly apprehensive by Elizabeth, I half put out a hand to dissuade her, then stopped. She spread all her butter on one cream cracker, using her large knife very deliberately and carefully and with great pleasure. It lay very thick. Then she stretched her knife toward the butter dish again. "But that's enough!" I started to say—and again I stopped. Carefully and skillfully she was scraping off the surplus butter from her knife against the side of the dish; then she scraped carefully and delicately and skillfully all over her cream cracker, removing more surplus butter, and returned that to the butter dish . . . and went on and on repeating this process till her cream cracker had a thin but absolutely smooth layer of butter on it. Sitting with great enjoyment bolt upright, and crooking her little finger, she nibbled with flamboyant style.

Elizabeth at two, sensuously exploring her material. Judy at four, carefully controlling a tool and practicing a technical skill and a social skill. Neither of them was primarily interested in eating. If I had thought they were, I would have interfered and stopped them growing.

We are always extraordinarily sure that all that children are interested in is food—perhaps because that is all we are sure we can give them. And we can patronize them and ridicule them while we give it—oh, in the nicest possible way—which makes us feel doubly secure. But even very deprived children are not *primarily* interested in food. I once knew some children like this, so deprived at three they did not even respond to their own names. One day—drawn by the activity of another child—they became absorbed for the first time in a game, pouring out water from a child's tiny tea set and pretending it was tea. But they were expected by adults to be having real food and drink, because they were half starved. And eventually, very gently, the make-believe tea was taken away from them (it had to be *taken* away, because the children would not give it up) and real food was set before them. They turned their faces away and would not eat.

Up till that day when they played their first game, they had wolfed the food down. Now they had found something deeper —and had it taken away from them. They ate nothing that day.[1]

A friend told me recently that she was watching a child build a sand castle and not succeeding and found herself very surprised the child didn't lose her temper; almost she decided to help the child. Much later, still thinking about the child's surprising self-control, she suddenly realized that the child wasn't building a sand castle at all—but that she, the adult, assumed that was what she was doing, and therefore that she was failing. If we look at children from the height of the little hill we have captured, they are bound to seem unsuccessful adults. Unfortunately we have the power to act on our arrogant and mistaken assessment of the situation, and generally do so.

So we hurry on, desperately trying to organize the chaos that is building up in our own untranquil mind, listening only to what the child would mean if he were adult and not to what the child is saying.

I was once sitting in the garden at Neill's Summerhill, and a little girl of four or five came up to me and asked what time it was. "It's nearly twenty-five past three," I said. She still stood there. A few seconds later she said, "What time is it?" Somewhat surprised, I repeated my answer. Still she stood there, and a few seconds later she asked me again. "But I told you," I said gently. "It's nearly twenty-five past three." "But what time *is* it?" she said.

The penny dropped. Her sweet patience and persistence had

[1] I have described these children and this incident in more detail in *The Tram Back* (Allen Lane, The Penguin Press, autumn 1972, written with Pat Chapman).

far more guts than mine. I said humbly: "It's twenty-three and a half minutes past three," and she smiled and went away.

I've just met Mark. Brenda, who lives nearby—aged four, like Mark—was at the table. She had been "invited." Mark, already angry for private reasons, was indignant even to see her.

She placidly took a cake. "If you take that cake, I won't like you!" She bit it. "If you take that cake, I won't let you come in my house!" She took another bite and beamed. "If you take that cake, I won't let you sit in my chair!" She took another bite. "If you take that cake, I—I—I'll—!" then in a more resigned but still intense tone, "Greedy guts." She gave him a ravishing smile and said calmly, "I'm not a greedy guts" . . . and went on eating.

She ate up all the little cake while he stood watching, beside himself with rage. She took another, nibbled all the icing off, then put it back on the dish, smiling sweetly at Mark. In fury, Mark took all the little sweets off the top of the big cake. Brenda placidly picked up her spoon and pushed some green jelly round the plate. It melted as it circled. Mark watched with beetling brows. "I don't like you!" Brenda, compliantly playing rather than retaliating, smiled happily and said, "I don't like *you*"—and went on pushing the jelly. Mark scowled even more furiously.

He got under the table, and didn't actually kick her—his family is strong on good manners—but he made threatening kicking movements. Brenda, above the table, took no notice at all, just went on pushing the jelly. After a sizable demonstration of menace, Mark very cautiously put his head up to see the results. Brenda, looking up from a spoonful, caught sight of him and shrieked with laughter—a lovely, relaxed, earth-mother laugh—then seriously concentrated on the jelly again.

Puzzled, Mark withdrew under the table. He thought about it, then cautiously peeped out again. Same thing—a wonderful, gurgling scream of laughter. Mark frowned, menaced, and shot down again. Once more he peeped up. And again that laughter. Now dawning on his face was the realization that the laughter was *for* him. His anger became pride, then delight. And he began to pop up and down, up and down, up and down. Brenda became completely hysterical with laughter and almost fell off her chair.

Mark, exhausted, rested for a moment under the table, then put his fingertips over the edge to pull himself up again. Brenda leaned over and tickled his fingers. Instantly Mark took umbrage. "You scratched me!" Brenda was calmly eating jelly again, unconcerned. His mother had just come in and said in her quiet way, "No, she tickled you." "Did she? Oh." He thought about it.

At that moment his two boy friends came marching in with packets of sweets. He scrambled out, and they gave him some. "Give some to Brenda!" he commanded.

"Who's Brenda?"

"My friend," he said in a lordly way, putting his arm round her.

She lifted her face from her plate of jelly to give them her beautiful smile, took a sweet, and got on with the jelly again.

I sat outside a "one o'clock club" in a London play park and watched a small girl of about three grab a hefty wooden baby carriage and start pushing it over the bumpy grass, concentrating hard. Eventually, yanking, thrusting, forcing it over the threshold, she managed to push it inside the inner area of a small jungle gym that other children were playing on; there somehow she managed the even more difficult feat of turning it around, thrusting, yanking, forcing it out again. As soon as it was out—plonk! a larger, black girl was seated in it. The two stared at each other, the first amazed, the second bold. At such a time you can almost hear children growing; they tick like small clocks. Just as time was moving toward some momentous resolution, a mother hurtled into the situation—"Get out of it, will you!"—and dragged the second child out of the carriage and righteously pushed the first on her way.

I consoled myself. In one o'clock clubs lonely mothers meet other lonely mothers and then turn their backs on their children. The situation would be played out again—without interference.

Five minutes later I saw the child again, sloped at 45 degrees to the grass, head down, a larger child in her carriage. In desperate spurts, then in a gradually accelerating conquering trot, she pushed the carriage over the grass to the far end, then turned it. As she began to push it back, the larger child suddenly leaped out and ran off to some other game, and she continued her serious trundling alone. Neither of them had spoken. Each had carried out her own movement incommoded by the other's. Neither had stopped for the other. Neither had come to grief.

Muscles had been used, apprehension had dissolved, an undemanding temporary relationship had been made; a child had grown a little. And the mother, having made a friend, had not come between.

This is what nursery schools are for. They are not for aiming at the A stream, for learning politeness and conforming to adults' demands. They are a place where the child can *live exploringly*—in his own rhythm, undisturbed by anxious adults.

My favorite state nursery school in this part of the country is in a tough working-class area. It is not one of those trendy, easy-to-supervise places, built with the head and not the heart, where every child can be seen at a glance from the head's glass office and there are no private worlds. It is a large old house. The children clamber of their own accord up the stairs, go into a room and close the door and play in privacy if they want to. People have said, "But isn't this dangerous?" Yet there has never been an accident. The kitchen is the warm, scented heart of the place, and the cook is chosen for the solace and mothering she offers, not only for good cooking. (Indeed the meal place and the lavatory are places where young children ask their most important questions and older ones hold many of their most important conversations. Yet they are the two specific places where orthodox teachers recoil from duty.) Two large trees grow in the garden—the council originally sent men to cut them down, but the head stopped them, saying the children would need them. The days are filled with music and painting, and when you sit in the head's study the ceiling booms and thunders with the jumping, dancing feet overhead, and little girls gravely set a picnic for themselves on the carpet, and from behind the settee on which you are sitting comes the rustle of a little boy, hidden, looking at books.

In this nursery school a new mother is encouraged, and helped, to sit still. I have watched so many new mothers in other nursery schools, wandering around with the child, making bright, too-bright conversations, showing him this, exclaiming at that, putting pressure without consciously meaning to, anxious to reach as quickly as possible the approved goal of child-settled-in-school. Here, a mother sits still and tranquilly waits. She takes out knitting, or looks at a magazine, a quiet base. The child clings at first to her lap, casting looks that perhaps he does not want to feel are noted, at the other children. And after a while, in little sallies of his own choosing, he begins to move out. Other children draw him. Music draws him. Stories being read draw him. Always he casts a glance back to the mother still sitting there, still quiet and unalarmed . . . until, of his own choice and in his own time, and of his own finding, he has become involved in a new, creative community.

Of course, not all my local nursery schools are like that one. I read about one in the local paper where a kind elderly couple had made a wendy house for the children. The paper said that the children were so pleased with it that the kind couple said they were going to "make another one for the boys"! I turned from this disconcerting text to an equally disconcerting photograph, where the little girls with neat bows in their hair and frilly dresses peeped coyly out of the doors of the wendy house, and leaned waving out of the windows; and it looked like nothing so much as a brothel.

Lea has just started at primary school.
She is lively, intelligent, talkative, and sociable. "Did you like school?" I asked her. "Yes, it was lovely." "What did you like

best?" . . . The new teaching methods? The paintings on the walls? The story writing? The young teacher? "What I liked best was . . . two lovely juniors. They're called Martin and Terry. They came in our playground." "Is that allowed?" "No. And Martin gave me a bottle of perfume."

"What did he say?"

"He said, 'It's for you.' "

"And what did you say?"

"I said, 'Is it really! I can't believe it!' . . . I like Martin best, but they're *both* lovely." She went on drawing a picture. "That's what was best."

5.
Bills of Rights

People interested in advancing the interests of children have begun recently to shift from talking about young people's needs to speaking of their rights. The shift is subtle but important. "A need and a right both may refer to the same phenomenon, such as adequate nutrition or education of high quality," writes the *Harvard Educational Review*. "But a need connotes dependency, and it is not clear whose responsibility it is to correct the situation, the individual's or the state's. A right, on the other hand, implies equality, as in the equal protection of those whose inalienable rights are guaranteed by the Constitution. If a right is abridged, this is an injustice which the institutions of the state must correct."

Moreover, as Margaret Mead has pointed out, we have tended to err on the side of protecting children, often to the degree of infringing on their rights. Our historic pattern is to remove or insulate children from situations in the society in which they are endangered or their needs are not being met, rather than to rectify those situations or provide the wherewithal to meet children's needs and thereby allow the children to remain. (We even do this when it costs more: we regularly remove children from deprived families and place them in residential care that costs far more than would support of the family to make it economically viable.) Dr. Mead notes that this policy removes the humanizing influence that the presence of children might have on our institutions, while at the same time isolating children from much of reality. Shut away from the horrors of the adult world, the children may often benefit, but they also may suffer from being at the mercy of their keepers as well as from knowing they must grow up into a society unwilling to face its real problems.

A question often raised about polemical statements on the rights of children is whether they ignore their distinctive needs. But no one is proposing that children simply be treated as completely and always equal and the same as adults for all purposes and in all situations. Our public policies regarding children, as with all people, should respect and if possible meet their particular needs. But the basis of correct thinking is children's basic equality as human beings. Without that, we will continue to treat all children badly in some ways, and we will certainly continue to treat individual children whose capacities are unusual as if they were incapable. The point here is that treating anyone in a restricted way simply because he or she is below a certain age is likely to lead to abuse. The justification should be apparent in each individual case if it is indeed defensible. We have made too much of the categories of childhood and youth. Our policies and practices must be rethought, around individuals rather than abstractions.

The impulse to affirm that the young have rights, rather than merely needs, has resulted in a number of powerful and useful statements. Some are official, such as the UN Declaration of the Rights of the Child, some personal, such as John Holt's. Some apply to special areas such as sexual rights, others are designed to give grounds for broad social action, such as Shirley Soman's proposed constitutional amendment. But among them will be found a cogent expression of the requirements for the full enfranchisement and recognition of the young as fullfledged human beings, if not in every capacity and attribute, in their essential humanity and innate dignity.

John Holt would like young people to have available to them, not imposed upon them, the rights, privileges, duties, and responsibilities of adults. He explains in detail how and why he thinks such a system would work to benefit children, and society.

Why Not a Bill of Rights for Children?
JOHN HOLT

I propose that the rights, privileges, duties, responsibilities of adult citizens be made *available* to any young person, of whatever age, who wants to make use of them.

Some of the rights, much more than others, are linked to and depend on other kinds of change, in law, custom, or attitudes. Thus, we are likely to give young people of a given age—say, fourteen—the right to drive a car sometime before we give them the right to vote, and we are likely to allow them to vote for some time before we give them the right to marry or to manage their own sex lives. And we are not likely to give young people the right to work at all in a society that tolerates massive unemployment and poverty. A country would have to make a political decision, as Sweden and Denmark have, to do away with severe poverty and to maintain a high level of employment before adults would even consider allowing young people to compete for jobs. By the same token, no society is likely to give to young people the right to equal treatment before the law

if it denies this right to adult women or to members of racial
or other minority groups. . . .

People who feel that they understand children and want to
defend them often speak about them in a way that I used to
agree with but now find more and more often confused, sentimental, or misleading. They tell us that a child needs "to be
allowed to be a child" or "the freedom to be a child" or "to
experience childhood." They say that a child needs "time to
grow" or that he should live in a "child's world" so that he
may experience himself as "a human being in his own right."
They speak of people trying to "destroy childhood" or "take
childhood away from children."

What is wrong with such words and ideas is that much of
what they imply about children and childhood is not true, and
what is true applies just as much to adults as to children. To
whatever extent children really need what these words say they
need, so do all the rest of us, young or old. To whatever extent
we adults are denied those needs by the society and culture in
which we live, so much will children be denied them. When
we say of children's needs, as of their virtues, that they belong
only to children, we make them seem trivial, we invalidate
them. What is more important, we insure that they will not
be met. For no amount of sentimentalizing or preaching will
make a society provide for its young people a better quality of
life than it provides for its adults. We fool ourselves if we think
ways can be found to give children what all the rest of us so
sorely lack.

"A child's world." "To experience childhood." "To be allowed
to be a child." Such words seem to say that childhood is a time
and an experience very different from the rest of life and that
it is, or ought to be, the best part of our lives. It is not, and
no one knows it better than children. *Children want to grow
up.* While they are growing up, they want, some of the time,
to be around the kind of adults who like being grown-up and
who think of growing up as an exploration and adventure, not
the process of being chased out of some garden of Eden. They

do not want to hear older people say, as many people in the alternative-school movement so often do, "These are the best years of your life; we are going to save them for you and keep the wicked world from spoiling them." What could be more discouraging? For they are going to grow up, whether they want to or not. They would like to think that this is something to look forward to. What they want to hear from the older people is that it gets better later. They want the kind of message my best friend sent to me on my thirtieth birthday: "The best is yet to come." He was right, it was, and I still feel that way. . . .

Much is said and written these days about children's "rights." Many use the word to mean something that we all agree it would be good for every child to have: "the right to a good home" or "the right to a good education." As I noted above, I mean what we mean when we speak of the rights of adults. I urge that the law grant and guarantee to the young the freedom that it now grants to adults to make certain kinds of choices, do certain kinds of things, and accept certain kinds of responsibilities. This means in turn that the law will take action *against* anyone who interferes with young people's right to do such things. Thus, when the law guarantees me the right to vote, it is not saying I must vote, it is not *giving* me a vote. It only says that if I choose to vote it will act against anyone who tries to prevent me. In granting me rights, the law does not say what I must or shall do. It simply says that it will not allow other people to prevent me from doing these things.

This would not be true of the right to receive a guaranteed income. Here we speak of *requiring* the government or state to do something. To say that people have the right to a guaranteed minimum income means that the state is required by law to assure that all citizens have at least this much income. To grant this right to children would mean that whatever income the state made available to adults it must make equally available to the young.

There is no use telling the state to guarantee what it does not have and cannot provide. The state has money, and so can provide it. The state can promise to take action against people who in certain ways prevent a citizen, young or old, from choosing and acting. But the state cannot guarantee every child a good home and a good family. It does not have these things to give and cannot make or get them. What are its options if it tries to order everyone to make a good home for his child? In the first place, who decides, and on what grounds, whether the home is good? In one case reported in *Life* magazine the state took children away from their parents, whom they loved and wanted to stay with, because some psychologist had decreed the parents did not have a high enough I.Q. to raise a family—though they had been raising it. In other cases the state has taken unwilling children away from their parents because the neighbors and the community did not approve of the parents' life-style or politics. The state can decide things for very peculiar reasons. And if it has been decided, somehow, that the home is not good, what does the state do next? Take the child away? Has it other good homes to offer in place of this one? Suppose the child does not want to leave the home, bad as the state thinks it may be? Suppose he likes the old home better than the one the state has provided for him? Suppose he refuses to stay in the "good" home and keeps going back to the old home the state decided wasn't good enough? What happens now is that the state sends the police after him, to take him by force to the home of its choice. Or, if the state does not want to, or cannot, take the child away from a home that it considers bad, does it say to the parents, "This home is bad, make it good." And if they do not or cannot, what does the state do? Punish them? Will this make the home better?

What we can and should do is leave to the child the right to decide how good his home seems to be and give him the right if he does not like it to choose something else. The state may decide to provide or help provide some of these other choices. But it should not make these choices compulsory. It should allow the child to make choices other than the ones it has provided. It should give the child the right to say no to *it* as well as to his parents.

Children, of any age, should have the right to work for money and to own and use, spend or save, the money they earn. This right . . . could be granted to young people even if no other adult rights were granted. . . .

There are many reasons why many children would like to work and why it would be good for them to be able to. They need or want the money they could earn to buy things they like, to save up for the future. Perhaps most important, in a consumer society such as ours, to be without money makes most people feel left out, a non-person; to have one's own money, even when not a matter of need, is a matter of self-respect. . . .

Work is novel, adventurous, another way of exploring the world. Many defend the boredom and drudgery of the schoolroom by saying that we have to teach children what work is like. Why make the schoolroom dull in order to do that, when most children *want to find out* what work is like and for a while at least would not find it dull at all? Many children, often the most troublesome and unmanageable, want to be useful, to feel that they make a difference. Real work is a way to do this. Also, work is a part of the mysterious and attractive world of adults, who work much of the time. When a child gets a chance to work with them, he sees a new side of them and feels a part of their world. He also sees a glimpse of his own future. Someday he too will be big and will work most of the time; now he can find out what it will be like.

Some rights, to be effective, depend very much on the other rights being available; others are more able to stand alone. But even so, as we have found in the case of adults, these rights tend very much to go together. If all the rights I propose were available, many young people might not necessarily choose to use all of them at once; they might only choose one or two. But they would probably not be able to use effectively the rights they wanted to use unless in a pinch they could use some of the others.

Take for example the right to leave home, to travel, to make one's own home. On the whole this right has no meaning unless the young person also has a right to earn money, to receive from the state a minimum income, and to be legally and financially responsible—to open a bank account, write checks, and so forth. But a young person in such a position will not be able to protect himself against cheating and exploitation (hard enough for adults right now) unless he can have the full use and protection of the law. This in turn is not likely to mean much unless he can vote. So perhaps the right to vote is most important and must come first. As a practical matter young people can probably get this right before they get others, and they will probably have to get it in order to get others. But even the right to vote can perhaps not be fully meaningful to a young person unless he can protect himself from undue pressure from his parents to vote the way they want. Society and the law might help him do this. But these can only be effective up to a point as long as the young person cannot get away from home and has no other place to go.

In the same way, the right of a young person to manage his own learning is a right that could and should be granted, and could be used more or less independently of others. There is no reason why a child, living in every other way as a dependent of his parents, could not and should not have (like everyone else) the right to decide what he wants to learn and when and how much of it he wants to learn in school, and in what school, and how much time he wants to spend doing it. But, again, this right will not be fully effective unless he has some way of resisting or escaping whatever pressures his parents may put on him.

It seems likely that if the young gain these rights, they will do so only as a result of a long series of laws and court decisions, many of them affecting only one right at a time. But people working to gain these rights for the young will be wise to understand that no one of them, *by itself*, is likely to be very effective or to make a great deal of difference in the lives of the young people. If we care very much about some of them we will probably have to work for some of the others.

1. The right to equal treatment at the hands of the law—i.e. the right, in any situation, to be treated no worse than an adult would be.

2. The right to vote and take full part in political affairs.
3. The right to be legally responsible for one's life and acts.
4. The right to work, for money.
5. The right to privacy.
6. The right to financial independence and responsibility—i.e. the right to own, buy, and sell property, to borrow money, establish credit, sign contracts, etc.
7. The right to direct and manage one's own education.
8. The right to travel, to live away from home, to choose or make one's own home.
9. The right to receive from the state whatever minimum income it may guarantee to adult citizens.
10. The right to make and enter into, on a basis of mutual consent, quasi-familial relationships outside one's immediate family—i.e. the right to seek and choose guardians other than one's own parents and to be legally dependent on them.
11. The right to do, in general, what any adult may legally do.

"Birthrights" are what psychologist Richard Farson, president of the Esalen Institute, calls these reforms that he believes are necessary for the liberation of children, including his own five youngsters.

Birthrights
RICHARD FARSON

A Child's Bill of Rights

1. THE RIGHT TO SELF-DETERMINATION. *Children should have the right to decide the matters that affect them most directly.* This is the basic right upon which all others depend. Children are now treated as the private property of their parents on the assumption that it is the parents' right and responsibility to control the life of the child. The achievement of children's rights, however, would reduce the need for this control and bring about

an end to the double standard of morals and behavior for adults and children.

2. THE RIGHT TO ALTERNATIVE HOME ENVIRONMENTS. *Self-determining children should be able to choose from among a variety of arrangements: residences operated by children, child-exchange programs, twenty-four-hour child-care centers, and various kinds of schools and employment opportunities.* Parents are not always good for their children—some people estimate that as many as 4 million children are abused annually in the United States, for instance, and that a half million children run away each year.

3. THE RIGHT TO RESPONSIVE DESIGN. *Society must accommodate itself to children's size and to their need for safe space.* To keep them in their place, we now force children to cope with a world that is either not built to fit them or is actually designed against them. If the environment were less dangerous for children, there would be less need for constant control and supervision of children by adults.

4. THE RIGHT TO INFORMATION. *A child must have the right to all information ordinarily available to adults—including, and perhaps especially, information that makes adults uncomfortable.*

5. THE RIGHT TO EDUCATE ONESELF. *Children should be free to design their own education, choosing from among many options the kinds of learning experiences they want, including the option not to attend any kind of school.* Compulsory education must be abolished, because the enforced, threatening quality of education in America has taught children to hate school, to hate the subject matter, and, tragically, to hate themselves. Children are programed, tracked, and certified in a process of stamping out standardized educated products acceptable to the university, military, business and industry, and community. Education can change only through the achievement of new rights for those exploited and oppressed by it—the children themselves.

6. THE RIGHT TO FREEDOM FROM PHYSICAL PUNISHMENT. *Children should live free of physical threat from those who are*

larger and more powerful than they. Corporal punishment is used impulsively and cruelly in the home, arbitrarily in the school, and sadistically in penal institutions. It does not belong in our repertoire of responses to children.

7. THE RIGHT TO SEXUAL FREEDOM. *Children should have the right to conduct their sexual lives with no more restriction than adults.* Sexual freedom for children must include the right to information about sex, the right to non-sexist education, and the right to all sexual activities that are legal among consenting adults. In fact, children will be best protected from sexual abuse when they have the right to refuse—but they are now trained *not* to refuse adults, to accept all forms of physical affection, and to mistrust their own reactions to people. They are denied any information about their own sexuality or that of others. We keep them innocent and ignorant and then worry that they will not be able to resist sexual approaches.

8. THE RIGHT TO ECONOMIC POWER. *Children should have the right to work, to acquire and manage money, to receive equal pay for equal work, to choose trade apprenticeship as an alternative to school, to gain promotion to leadership positions, to own property, to develop a credit record, to enter into binding contracts, to engage in enterprise, to obtain guaranteed support apart from the family, to achieve financial independence.*

9. THE RIGHT TO POLITICAL POWER. *Children should have the vote and be included in the decision-making process.* Eighty million children in the United States need the right to vote, because adults do not vote in their behalf. At present they are no one's constituency, and legislation reflects that lack of representation. To become a constituency, they must have the right to vote.

10. THE RIGHT TO JUSTICE. *Children must have the guarantee of a fair trial with due process of law, an advocate to protect their rights against the parents as well as the system, and a uniform standard of detention.* Every year, a million children get into trouble with the law. One out of every nine children will go through the juvenile court system before the age of eighteen. At any given time, about one hundred thousand children are

in some kind of jail. Some are held illegally, many have not committed any kind of crime, most have done nothing that would be considered a crime if done by an adult, and none has been given a fair trial with due process of law. The juvenile justice system was designed to protect children from the harsh treatment of the adult justice system—but it is more unfair, more arbitrary, and more cruel.

Only each child can decide what rights are most important personally. A reader of Ann Landers' column sent her his, and she responded. The emphasis in this particular person's statement on autonomy in interpersonal relations is interesting, as are the implications of his ten points about his family and community.

One Kid's Own Bill of Rights
FROM ANN LANDERS' COLUMN

Dear Ann Landers: Us kids have rights, too. Too few adults are willing to recognize this fact. I hope you will print the Bill of Rights for Kids so every parent who reads your column can see it. It's time we were treated like people.

1. I have the right to be my own judge and take the responsibility for my own actions.

2. I have the right to offer no reasons or excuses to justify my behavior.

3. I have the right to decide if I am obligated to report on other people's behavior.

4. I have the right to change my mind.

5. I have the right to make mistakes and be responsible for them.

6. I have the right to pick my own friends.

7. I have the right to say, "I don't know."

8. I have the right to be independent of the good will of others before coping with them.

9. I have the right to say, "I don't understand."
10. I have the right to say, "I don't care."
                    —A Reader Since Childhood in Las Vegas

Dear Reader: Here's your Bill of Rights. Some of them I buy, especially numbers 4, 5, 6, and 9.
Number 2 is off base, and number 3 I would accept—to a point.
As for number 8. I don't dig it.
Number 10: of course you have the *right* to say you don't care, but that doesn't mean you *shouldn't* care.

Youth Liberation, an Ann Arbor-based group (see Section 6 for a fuller account of their activities, publications, and services), has issued a fifteen-point program "to put together truth about what is wrong with our present situation and to lay out changes that must be made. . . . If our program strays from the specific needs of youth, it is because we know that we are not free until all people are free and the earth is a healthy place to live."

Youth Liberation Program
YOUTH LIBERATION OF ANN ARBOR

Youth Liberation Program

Every day, it becomes clearer that we might be the last generation in the experiment with living. The problems facing humanity are so huge that some of us think working for change is futile. We of Youth Liberation, however, will not be led either to the treadmill or to the slaughterhouse like "good Germans." We know there is a basic decision to make: either we stay quiet and become part of a system of oppression, or we seize control of our lives, take risks, and struggle to build something new. We believe that problems have causes and that by studying these causes we can learn solutions. We know that young people have power if we take it and use it. We must liberate ourselves from the death trip of corporate America. We must take control of our lives, because within us is the seed of a new reality—a seed that cannot grow until our lives are our own. It is a reality of ecstasy, made up of love, justice, freedom, peace, and plenty.

The Youth Liberation Program is an attempt to put together truth about what is wrong with our present situation and to lay out changes that must be made. This process never ends. To win, we must know very clearly what we want and what we reject. We are learning to struggle together. If our program strays from the specific needs of youth, it is because we know that we are not free until all people are free and the earth is a healthy place to live.

1. WE WANT THE POWER TO DETERMINE OUR OWN DESTINY.

2. WE WANT THE IMMEDIATE END OF ADULT CHAUVINISM. We believe ideas should be judged on their merit and people on their wisdom or kindness. Age *in itself* deserves no recognition. Adults who want to support youth struggle or "improve communication" should show their concern by providing concrete resources. Words alone are not enough. Age might once have led to wisdom, but the old have proved themselves unable to deal with present reality. If the human species is to survive, the young must take the lead.

3. WE WANT FULL CIVIL AND HUMAN RIGHTS. We believe young people are necessary participants in democracy. We must have complete freedom of speech, press, assembly, and religion, and the right to vote. We believe that all people are created equal and are endowed with certain unalienable rights; among these are life, liberty, and the pursuit of happiness.

4. WE WANT THE RIGHT TO FORM OUR EDUCATION ACCORDING TO OUR NEEDS. We believe compulsory education is a form of imprisonment and must be abolished immediately. Grades and all forms of tracking must end, because they stimulate competition, divide us, and make us work for other people's ends. All discipline procedures must be decided democratically within

the school community. No school staff should be hired or fired without the democratic consent of students and teachers. Students and the community must have the right to use school facilities whenever they feel it is necessary.

5. WE WANT THE FREEDOM TO FORM INTO COMMUNAL FAMILIES. We believe that the nuclear family is not in the best interest of the people involved. Young people are now considered property —to be molded in the image of their parents. Since we demand self-determination for our lives, this is intolerable. In communal families children can grow in the company of many people, both peers and adults. They can learn the co-operation of community rather than the oppression of ownership. Until communal families are a reality, some healthy provision must be made for young people whose present conditions of life force them to become cultural refugees.

6. WE WANT THE END OF MALE CHAUVINISM AND SEXISM. We believe women must be free and equal. We recognize that sexism is all-pervasive and often subtle and demeans the humanity of everyone. All forms of sex-role stereotyping must end. Macho must go. Abortions must be free and legal. We consider the women's movement our natural ally since both young people and women are systematically oppressed by male-supremacist society.

7. WE WANT THE OPPORTUNITY TO CREATE AN AUTHENTIC CUL-TURE WITH INSTITUTIONS OF OUR OWN MAKING. We believe western culture is decadent and we refuse to continue it in our lives. People's appearance must not affect their civil rights. All drugs must be legalized, as we see that it is not laws that govern people's use of drugs, but societal conditions. We hope to create a society in which people will not need death drugs. Our music and cultural gatherings must be allowed to flourish in peace. We must be set free to begin living in the new age and begin to accept a responsibility for developing plans and examples of institutions that build joy, justice, and a respect for life.

8. WE WANT SEXUAL SELF-DETERMINATION. We believe all people must have the unhindered right to be heterosexual, homosexual, bisexual, or transsexual.

9. WE WANT THE END OF CLASS ANTAGONISM AMONG YOUNG PEOPLE. We believe that those in power cultivate elitism and class divisions among youth which only serve to weaken us. The survival of young people of all classes and races is threatened by the few who run this world. We condemn academic tracking, honors, and all other class divisions imposed upon us.

10. WE WANT THE END OF RACISM AND COLONIALISM IN THE UNITED STATES AND THE WORLD. We believe America is an imperialist country. America uses over 50 per cent of the world's resources for less than 7 per cent of the world's population. Racism in schools is severely damaging to students, particularly minority students. Students must eliminate racism and stop fighting each other. We must unite to fight the real enemy until we have education that meets the needs of all races. We support the liberation struggles of colonized people of all colors everywhere.

11. WE WANT FREEDOM FOR ALL UNJUSTLY IMPRISONED PEOPLE. All young people in juvenile homes, training schools, detention centers, mental institutions, and other penal institutions for minors must be set free. They did not receive a trial before a jury of their peers, and the society they offended is itself criminal. Young people must never receive discriminatory treatment before the law, whether in the courtroom, going to a movie, buying alcohol, or leaving home. The military draft must be abolished and the military made democratic.

12. WE WANT THE RIGHT TO BE ECONOMICALLY INDEPENDENT OF ADULTS. We believe we are entitled to work or to unemployment benefits. Child-labor laws and extended schooling now force youth into the status of a dependent colony.

13. WE WANT THE RIGHT TO LIVE IN HARMONY WITH NATURE. We believe that to survive we must have clean air to breathe, pure food to eat, water fit to drink, products built to last, free medical care, and an end to population growth. Life exists in balance and harmony, but greed and stupidity have now sent us disastrously out of balance with our environment and earth death seems certain. Each person must learn to live a sound ecological life, and all people together must change the eco-

nomic structure of the world until the needs of the earth and
its people are met.

14. WE WANT TO REHUMANIZE EXISTENCE. We believe that to
do this we must recognize and deal with the invisible dictator-
ship of technocracy and bureaucracy. We are the crown of creation, and we announce that it is not our destiny to become
robot parts of the Great Machine.

15. WE WANT TO DEVELOP COMMUNICATION AND SOLIDARITY
WITH THE YOUNG PEOPLE OF THE WORLD IN OUR COMMON STRUG-
GLE FOR FREEDOM AND PEACE. We believe national boundaries
are artificial and must inevitably be abolished. In the new
world, all resources and technology must be used for the benefit of all people.

Youth will make the revolution. Youth will keep it young!

*It is essential that we view the rights of children in a world
perspective. While it is entirely fitting that we, as Americans,
address ourselves in the first instance to the oppression and
destruction of children in this country, we should not forget
that the vast majority of the world's children live short and
painful lives. To alleviate such conditions must be an unremitting concern and ultimate objective of any open-eyed commitment to children.*

The UN Declaration of the Rights of the Child
UNITED NATIONS

The Need for a Declaration of Children's Rights

Sometimes progress is so complete that its beneficiaries take
it for granted and are unaware of the strenuous efforts that
were once necessary to achieve it.

In places where child labor has long been abolished, where

children are effectively protected from all forms of degrading slavery, where such horrors as infanticide and legally sanctioned cruelty to children are unknown, where medical help is widely available, where free and adequate education is provided, many people may not realize that there is any need to define or defend the rights of children.

One hundred years ago, however, most people saw nothing wrong in the fact that young children had to earn their own living (and often a very meager one, providing the barest minimum of food and clothing) by working long hours under difficult conditions. They took for granted the fact that more than half the children born would die before reaching adulthood.

The vast majority of children have, in fact, always lived short and painful lives. They have been doomed to ignorance and horrifying poverty—and, although many people in prosperous parts of the world are so fortunate they find it hard to realize, this is still the fate of the majority of children today.

Three quarters of the children born this year face short lives that will be afflicted by chronic illness and hunger. In some parts of the world, children still receive no medical attention, enjoy no educational or recreational facilities, and have no legal protection.

History of Earlier Declarations of Rights

The peace for which all mankind yearns is much more than the mere absence of armed conflicts—that is simply its foundation. True peace means the opportunity to enjoy life and its blessings.

Therefore, when the nations of the world, after the holocaust of the First World War, hopefully established the League of Nations, they attempted also to establish standards according to which nations would be pledged to live, to help build a truly peaceful and happy society.

On the twenty-sixth of September, 1924, the Assembly of the League of Nations adopted the Geneva Declaration of the

Rights of the Child. In 1939, however, world war broke out once again, and rendered the League powerless. Its declarations became mere "scraps of paper."

In 1946, a year after the United Nations was formed, it was recommended to the Economic and Social Council of the United Nations that the Geneva Declaration be revived to "bind the people of the world today as firmly as it did in 1924."

Two years later, in 1948, the United Nations General Assembly approved the adoption of a Universal Declaration of Human Rights. In this declaration the freedoms and rights of children were implicitly included, but it was thought that this was not enough: the special needs of children justified an additional, separate document.

Summary of the Declaration

The Preamble states that the child, because of his physical and mental immaturity, needs special safeguards and care, both before and after birth, and that individuals and groups should strive to achieve children's rights by legislative and other means. Mankind, it says, owes the child the best it has to give.

In ten carefully worded principles, the declaration affirms that all children are entitled to

1. the enjoyment of the rights mentioned, without any exception whatsoever, regardless of race, color, sex, religion, or nationality;

2. special protection, opportunities, and facilities to enable them to develop in a healthy and normal manner, in freedom and dignity;

3. a name and nationality;

4. social security, including adequate nutrition, housing, recreation, and medical services;

5. special treatment, education, and care if handicapped;

6. love and understanding and an atmosphere of affection and security, in the care and under the responsibility of their parents whenever possible;

7. free education and recreation and equal opportunity to develop their individual abilities;

8. prompt protection and relief in times of disaster;

9. protection against all forms of neglect, cruelty, and exploitation;

10. protection from any form of racial, religious, or other discrimination, and an upbringing in a spirit of peace and universal brotherhood.

Finally, the General Assembly resolved that governments, non-governmental organizations, and individuals should give this declaration the widest possible publicity as a means of encouraging its observance everywhere.

United Nations Declaration of the Rights of the Child

A five-point Declaration of the Rights of the Child was stated in 1923 by the International Union for Child Welfare, with 1948 revisions in a seven-point document. The League of Nations adopted the IUCW declaration in 1924. The following Declaration of the Rights of the Child was adopted by the United Nations General Assembly in 1959.

DECLARATION OF THE RIGHTS OF THE CHILD
PREAMBLE

Whereas the peoples of the United Nations have, in the Charter, reaffirmed their faith in fundamental human rights and in the dignity and worth of the human person and have determined to promote social progress and better standards of life in larger freedom,

Whereas the United Nations has, in the Universal Declaration of Human Rights, proclaimed that everyone is entitled to

United Nations, General Assembly Resolution 1386(XIV), November 20, 1959, published in the *Official Records of the General Assembly, Fourteenth Session, Supplement No. 16*, 1960, p. 19.

all the rights and freedoms set forth therein, without distinction of any kind, such as race, color, sex, language, religion, political or other opinion, national or social origin, property, birth, or other status,

Whereas the child, by reason of his physical and mental immaturity, needs special safeguards and care, including appropriate legal protection, before as well as after birth,

Whereas the need for such special safeguards has been stated in the Geneva Declaration of the Rights of the Child of 1924, and recognized in the Universal Declaration of Human Rights and in the statutes of specialized agencies and international organizations concerned with the welfare of children,

Whereas mankind owes to the child the best it has to give,

Now therefore,

The General Assembly

Proclaims this Declaration of the Rights of the Child to the end that he may have a happy childhood and enjoy for his own good and for the good of society the rights and freedoms herein set forth, and calls upon parents, upon men and women as individuals, and upon voluntary organizations, local authorities, and national governments to recognize these rights and strive for their observance by legislative and other measures progressively taken in accordance with the following principles:

PRINCIPLE 1

The child shall enjoy all the rights set forth in this declaration. All children, without any exception whatsoever, shall be entitled to these rights, without distinction or discrimination on account of race, color, sex, language, religion, political or other opinion, national or social origin, property, birth, or other status, whether of himself or of his family.

PRINCIPLE 2

The child shall enjoy special protection, and shall be given opportunities and facilities, by law and by other means, to enable him to develop physically, mentally, morally, spiritually, and socially in a healthy and normal manner and in conditions of freedom and dignity. In the enactment of laws for this purpose the best interests of the child shall be the paramount consideration.

PRINCIPLE 3

The child shall be entitled from his birth to a name and a nationality.

PRINCIPLE 4

The child shall enjoy the benefits of social security. He shall be entitled to grow and develop in health; to this end special care and protection shall be provided both to him and to his mother, including adequate prenatal and postnatal care. The child shall have the right to adequate nutrition, housing, recreation, and medical services.

PRINCIPLE 5

The child who is physically, mentally, or socially handicapped shall be given the special treatment, education, and care required by his particular condition.

PRINCIPLE 6

The child, for the full and harmonious development of his personality, needs love and understanding. He shall, wherever possible, grow up in the care and under the responsibility of his parents, and in any case in an atmosphere of affection and of moral and material security; a child of tender years shall not, save in exceptional circumstances, be separated from his mother. Society and the public authorities shall have the duty to extend particular care to children without a family and to those without adequate means of support. Payment of state and other assistance toward the maintenance of children of large families is desirable.

PRINCIPLE 7

The child is entitled to receive education, which shall be free and compulsory, at least in the elementary stages. He shall be given an education which will promote his general culture, and enable him on a basis of equal opportunity to develop his abilities, his individual judgment, and his sense of moral and social responsibility, and to become a useful member of society.

The best interests of the child shall be the guiding principle of those responsible for his education and guidance; that responsibility lies in the first place with his parents.

The child shall have full opportunity for play and recreation, which should be directed to the same purposes as education; society and the public authorities shall endeavor to promote the enjoyment of this right.

PRINCIPLE 8

The child shall in all circumstances be among the first to receive protection and relief.

PRINCIPLE 9

The child shall be protected against all forms of neglect, cruelty, and exploitation. He shall not be the subject of traffic, in any form.

The child shall not be admitted to employment before an appropriate minimum age; he shall in no case be caused or permitted to engage in any occupation or employment which would prejudice his health or education, or interfere with his physical, mental, or moral development.

PRINCIPLE 10

The child shall be protected from practices which may foster racial, religious, and any other form of discrimination. He shall be brought up in a spirit of understanding, tolerance, friendship among peoples, peace and universal brotherhood, and in full consciousness that his energy and talents should be devoted to the service of his fellow men.

6.
Resources
For Consciousness-Raising
And Action

Best Further Reading to Become More Capable of Helping Children and Young People

THE EDITORS

This is our selection of the most important and readable books that have been published in the field, mostly during the past five years. Almost all are available in paperback, and we have listed the paperback publishers.

We have not included technical and reference books such as those on the juvenile justice system. Nor have we included the voluminous literature on what's wrong with schools or how they might be improved—an overview of this field is provided by the two previous anthologies of ours, which are listed. We have also kept the list as short as possible by being highly selective and by listing only one title of each author, as a sampling of his or her work, from which the interested reader will find it easy enough to get led to other writings. Thus such prolific authors as Robert Coles, Erik Erikson, and Edgar Friedenberg are represented by the book of theirs that we think makes a good start.

Adams, Paul; Berg, Leila; et al. *Children's Rights: Toward the Liberation of the Child.* Introduction by Paul Goodman. New York: Praeger Publishers, 1971.

Reichian essays on the need to give children freedom and autonomy if they are to grow up whole and free.

Ariès, Philippe. *Centuries of Childhood: a Social History of Family Life.* Tr. by Robert Baldick. New York: Random House, 1962.

The highly influential revisionist history of childhood in Western culture, showing that our contemporary image was a distinct invention and not "natural."

Bakan, David. *Slaughter of the Innocents: a Study of the Battered Child Phenomenon.* Boston: Beacon Press, 1971.

A speculative rather than definitive book, with the extraordinary thesis that "child abuse is an evolutionary mechanism associated with population-resource balance."

Berends, Polly Berrien. *Whole Child/Whole Parent: a Spiritual and Practical Guide to the First Four Years of Parenthood.* New York: Harper's Magazine Press, 1975.

"Even our littlest children are seeking everywhere the same goals we are" is the premise of this holistic approach to child-rearing.

Berg, Leila. *Look at Kids.* Baltimore: Penguin Books, 1972.

Sensitive but bitingly realistic portrayals and observations of city children, by a brilliant British writer.

Blishen, Edward, ed. *The School That I'd Like.* Baltimore: Penguin Books, 1969.

Based on a British newspaper competition for secondary school youngsters, and eloquent in the writers' demand for a say in the processes of their own education.

Blum, Jeffrey D.; and Smith, Judith E. *Nothing Left to Lose.* Cambridge, Mass.: Sanctuary Press, 1972.

One of the best books on runaways; sympathetic and profound.

Bock, R.; and English, A. *Got Me on the Run.* Cambridge, Mass.: Sanctuary Press, 1973.

Compassionate and understanding treatment of runaways.

Bremner, Robert H., ed. *The Legal Rights of Children: an Original Anthology.* New York: Arno Press, 1974.

Some important papers on the major topics in the field.

Chase, Naomi Feigelson. *A Child Is Being Beaten: Violence Against Children, an American Tragedy.* New York: Holt, Rinehart and Winston, 1975.

Says it all about how society fails to provide for the tens of thousands of children abused by their parents, often consigning them to conditions even worse than those from which they have been removed.

Children's Defense Fund. *Children Out of School in America.* Cambridge, Mass.: Children's Defense Fund, 1974.

A model of what child advocacy can accomplish: rigorous but committed, a compelling exposé and a brief for change.

Clark, Ted. *The Oppression of Youth.* New York: Harper, 1975.

Documents the subordination of youth in the society, in the family, in schools, and in the realm of sexual expression, and contends that "the opposite of oppression—letting young people be, guiding and assisting them but not violating their integrity as human beings . . . will at least give them a fighting chance to deal with the real problems of living. . . ."

Coigney, Virginia. *Children Are People Too: How We Fail Our Children and How We Can Love Them.* New York: William Morrow, 1975.

A fine, rage-filled book about our depredations against the young: treating them as property, demanding that they worship us, disrespecting their feelings, controlling them for our convenience rather than for their own good.

Cole, Larry. *Our Children's Keepers: Inside America's Kid Prisons.* New York: Grossman Publishers, 1972.

Brief, vivid, scathing exposé of what are usually called "training schools," "youth guidance centers," and "juvenile centers," but are really chaotic and brutal jails for youngsters.

———; and Ralph, Pauli, Eddie, & Charlie. *Street Kids.* New York: Grossman Publishers, 1970.

Written largely by kids themselves, this book powerfully evokes the life of the urban ghetto.

Coles, Robert. *Uprooted Children: the Early Life of Migrant Farm Workers.* New York: Harper & Row, 1971.

"Nobody else knows about children as precisely and movingly as Robert Coles," Edgar Friedenberg has written, and this inexpensive little volume provides a fine introduction to this author's immeasurably commendable work.

Cottle, Thomas J. *The Abandoners: Portraits of Loss, Separation, and Neglect.* Boston: Little, Brown, 1972.

"Cottle knows the difference between facing a problem and facing a face," said a reviewer, accurately, about this superb set of vivid profiles of youngsters.

Cuban, Larry, ed. *Youth as a Minority: an Anatomy of Students' Rights.* Washington: National Council for the Social Studies, 1974.

Good overview of this field for teachers.

De Francis, Vincent; and Lucht, C. L. *Child Abuse Legislation in the 1970's.* Denver: American Humane Association Children's Division, 1972.

Excellent summary of legal standing, state by state.

DeMause, Lloyd, ed. *The History of Childhood.* New York: Harper & Row, 1975.

A pioneering and shocking exploration of this neglected area, revealing how Western civilization has amounted to an unremitting war on children for most of its history.

Denzin, Norman K., ed. *Children and Their Caretakers.* New York: E. P. Dutton, 1973.

Documentation of the atrocities committed regularly in schools, day-care centers, and other institutions.

Elizabeth Cleaners Street School. *Starting Your Own High School.* New York: Random House, 1972.

Written mainly by the students who did it, and demonstrating the degree to which they could and did take command of their own lives and education.

Erikson, Erik H. *Identity: Youth and Crisis*. New York: W. W. Norton, 1968.

Successor to *Childhood and Society*, this hard but rewarding volume is a masterwork by the foremost psychiatrist student of young people's development.

Farson, Richard. *Birthrights*. New York: Macmillan, 1974.

Detailed discussion of a platform for a movement to liberate children—and parents. More oriented to broad social change than the comparable volume by Holt described below.

Forer, Lois G. *No One Will Lissen: How Our Legal System Brutalizes the Youthful Poor*. New York: John Day, 1970.

Devastating detailed exposé of the juvenile "justice" system by a dedicated lawyer who has for years given legal counsel to poor and minority-group children caught in the coils of the law.

Foster, Henry H., Jr. *A "Bill of Rights" for Children*. Foreword by Judge Justine Wise Polier. Springfield, Ill.: Charles C. Thomas, 1974.

A superb brief for a new set of guidelines for the encounters of children and youth with the legal system.

Friedenberg, Edgar. *The Dignity of Youth and Other Atavisms*. Boston: Beacon Press, 1965.

Friedenberg's revision of the highly influential views, put forward in the earlier *The Vanishing Adolescent*, on why young people can't grow up as complete human beings in this culture.

Gerzon, Mark. *A Childhood for Every Child: the Politics of Parenthood*. New York: E. P. Dutton, 1973.

A compelling argument that American society, far from being supportive of parents' efforts to bring up their children, interferes destructively with the process of healthy growth at every stage.

Goldstein, Joseph; Freud, Anna; and Solnit, Albert J. *Beyond the Best Interests of the Child*. New York: Free Press, 1973.

Argues correctly, against the customary legal favoritism to "natural" parents, in favor of the child's need for the psychological sustenance that may best be provided by foster parents.

Goodman, Paul. *Growing Up Absurd: Problems of Youth in the Organized System.* New York: Random House, 1960.

A prophetic and still-relevant book that argued, fifteen years ago, that "youth problems" reflect defects in our social, economic, and political system, and that therefore social change is needed to give young people a decent world to grow up into.

Gottlieb, David, ed. *Children's Liberation.* Englewood Cliffs, N.J.: Prentice-Hall, 1973.

Excellent essays documenting that "American children are in too many instances victims of indifference, intimidation, abuse, exploitation, and vengeance."

Gross, Ronald; and Gross, Beatrice; eds. *Radical School Reform.* New York: Simon & Schuster, 1970.

Writings by the major radical critics of the schools: John Holt, Paul Goodman, Herbert Kohl, A. S. Neill, Jonathan Kozol, etc.

Gross, Ronald; and Osterman, Paul; eds. *High School.* New York: Simon & Schuster, 1972.

Writings by high school students, teachers, and radical critics, and case studies of innovative programs.

Hamilton, Russel; and Greene, Stephanie, eds. *What Bothers Us About Grownups.* New York: Avon Books, 1973.

One of the few books of materials by young children, and therefore worth a critical reading despite its cutesiness.

Harrison-Ross, Phyllis; and Wyden, Barbara. *The Black Child: a Parent's Guide to Raising Happy and Healthy Children.* New York: Berkley Publishing, 1974.

Fine step-by-step guide, endorsed by Dr. Spock.

Harvard Educational Review. *The Rights of Children.* Cambridge, Mass.: Harvard Educational Review, 1974.

In-depth monographs on the legal conception of children's rights, issues and developments in children's advocacy, and proposed new social policies affecting children.

Haskins, Jim. *Children Have Rights, Too.* New York: Hawthorn Books, 1975.
Good introduction to the whole field.

Hemmings, Ray. *Children's Freedom: A. S. Neill and the Evolution of the Summerhill Idea.* New York: Schocken Books, 1973.
The first extended critical evaluation of the life and thought of A. S. Neill, relating his achievements to the current thinking of Marcuse, Laing, and Illich.

Holt, John. *Escape from Childhood.* New York: E. P. Dutton, 1974.
Straightforward, lucid explanation of why and how young people should have access to the rights, privileges, duties, and responsibilities of adult citizens on demand.

James, Howard. *Children in Trouble: a National Scandal.* New York: Pocket Books, 1969.
Fine journalistic treatment of the subject, a little dated but still well worth reading.

Joseph, Stephen M. *Children in Fear.* New York: Holt, Rinehart and Winston, 1974.
The author of *The Me Nobody Knows* talks about some terrible fears we teach children, and how parents can do better.

Kahn, Alfred J.; Kamerman, Sheila B.; and McGowan, Brenda G. *Child Advocacy: Report of a National Baseline Study.* Washington: U. S. Office of Child Development, 1973.
A useful though naturally somewhat dated national survey of what was going on around the country under the rubric of child advocacy.

Keniston, Kenneth. *Youth and Dissent: The Rise of the New Opposition.* New York: Harcourt Brace Jovanovich, 1971.

Perhaps the most successful attempt to probe the significance of the sixties revolt of America's privileged youth against their society.

Keyserling, Mary Dublin. *Windows on Day Care*. New York: Council of Jewish Women, 1972.

Report of findings by volunteer researchers on day-care needs and services in their local communities—a model of what a voluntary organization can accomplish in finding out what's going on and promoting progress.

Klein, Carole. *The Myth of the Happy Child*. New York: Harper & Row, 1975.

Designed to reassure parents of young children by making them aware that childhood is a time of considerable anger, aggressiveness, and unhappiness—much of it not the parent's fault.

Lauter, Paul; and Howe, Florence. *The Conspiracy of the Young*. New York: World Publishing, 1970.

Based on the authors' personal involvement with young people's movements for social change in the sixties, this radical interpretation rightly stresses the healthfulness of those impulses and their possible continuation in adult life.

Levine, Alan H.; with Carey, Eve; and Divoky, Diane. *The Rights of Students: the Basic ACLU Guide to a Student's Rights*. New York: Discus/Avon, 1973.

Chapters on the right to an education itself, and rights of free speech, personal appearance, due process, law enforcement, corporal punishment, discrimination, tracking and classification, marriage-pregnancy-parenthood, school records, grades, and diplomas.

LeShan, Eda J. *The Conspiracy Against Childhood*. New York: Atheneum Publishers, 1973.

"It is my belief that this is a *terrible* time to be a child," the author asserts, "and if this is so despite the child-centeredness of our lives, then surely we must be doing *something* wrong!"

Loeb, Robert H., Jr., in consultation with Maloney, John P. *Your Legal Rights as a Minor.* New York: Franklin Watts, 1974.

Covers driving, business, sex, work, school, parents, drugs, arrest, medical treatment, and holding public office.

Mirthes, Caroline; and the children of P. S. 15. *Can't You Hear Me Talking to You?* New York: Bantam Books, 1971.

Ghetto school children describe their world, harshly but with great affirmation of life.

National Commission on Resources for Youth. *New Roles for Youth in the School and the Community.* New York: Citation Press, 1974.

The best single source of information about youth-run projects of all kinds, all around the country.

National Commission on Resources for Youth. *What Kids Can Do.* New York: National Commission on Resources for Youth, 1974.

Brief but complete and useful case studies of projects that have worked in the fields of community service, medicine, legal help, crisis intervention, ecology, day care and teaching, and the arts.

National Council of Jewish Women. *Children Without Justice.* Foreword by Justice William O. Douglas. New York: National Council of Jewish Women, 1975.

Most recent survey of juvenile justice at the grass-roots level, with excellent case histories and recommendations.

Nelson, Jack. *Captive Voices: The Report of the Commission of Inquiry into High School Journalism.* New York: Schocken Books, 1974.

Reveals how one of our most basic freedoms—freedom of speech and of the press—is pervasively denied to young citizens in high schools.

Panel on Youth of the President's Science Advisory Committee. *Youth: Transition to Adulthood.* Chicago: University of Chicago Press, 1974.

The "Coleman Report," a key statement on the need to rectify our overemphasis on schooling by broadening the options for young people.

Peck, Ellen; and Senderowitz, Judith. *Pronatalism: the Myth of Mom & Apple Pie*. New York: Thomas Y. Crowell, 1974.
Explores the social pressures to have children, and argues that this decision should be individual, not abstract, and made in the light of each adult's needs, preferences, and abilities.

Pepper, William. *The Self-Managed Child: Paths to Cultural Rebirth*. New York: Harper & Row, 1973.
An idiosyncratic but provocative volume advancing the concept that the human being from infancy is a functional entity that can, and does, make her or his own essential decisions, and that we should therefore maximize the self-determination of children.

Schorr, Alvin L., ed. *Children and Decent People*. New York: Basic Books, 1974.
A long-time leader in the fight for greater state subvention of children in need, Schorr has gathered a fine collection of essays on major child-welfare programs.

Schrag, Peter; and Divoky, Diane. *The Myth of the Hyperactive Child*. New York: Pantheon Books, 1975.
Brilliant polemic against the newly fashionable ways of controlling, labeling, conditioning, and drugging children into conformity and passivity.

Sexton, Brendan John; and Sexton, Patricia Cayo. *Reaching Out: Helping Young People in Trouble*. New York: Agathon Press, 1975.
A collaboration between a professor of sociology and her "stepson," based on the latter's experiences as a founder of a non-residential therapeutic community for young people in trouble.

Soman, Shirley Camper. *Let's Stop Destroying Our Children*. New York: Hawthorn Books, 1974.

Shocking documentation of the destruction of children through graphic case histories of injuries, abuse, neglect, and abandonment.

Strouse, Jean. *Up Against the Law: the Legal Rights of People Under 21.* New York: Signet Books, 1970.
The most readily available inexpensive guide to the legal rights of young people.

Talbot, Nathan B. *Raising Children in Modern America: What Parents and Society Should Be Doing for Their Children.* Boston: Little, Brown, 1976.
Based on a Harvard interdisciplinary seminar, this volume distills the most enlightened expert opinion and research findings revealing the condition of American children. The author makes sound recommendations on such specific topics as fighting exploitive advertising, day care, school curricula, and child rearing as moral teaching. Concludes that we need a universal child-family screening and support program centered around a national health plan.

White House Conference on Children. *Profiles of Children.* Washington: Government Printing Office, 1970.
Prepared for the 1970 White House Conference, a classic and useful portrayal.

White House Conference on Children. *Report to the President.* Washington: Government Printing Office, 1971.
Classic and still-relevant (so few of its recommendations were ever actuated) examination of the issues and problems.

Wilkerson, Albert E., ed. *The Rights of Children: Emergent Concepts in Law and Society.* Introduction by Justine Wise Polier. Philadelphia: Temple University Press, 1973.
A most comprehensive treatment of the subject.

Yankelovich, Daniel. *The New Morality: a Profile of American Youth in the 70's.* New York: McGraw-Hill, 1974.
A well-done opinion survey, supported by no less than four

different foundations, revealing the general shift, away from the radicalism of the sixties, toward conventional attitudes with strong impulses toward personal security through secure jobs.

Youth Liberation of Ann Arbor. *Youth Liberation: News, Politics, and Survival Information.* Washington, N.J.: Times Change Press, 1972.
Some of the best materials that this group has published, by and for young people.

Young, Leontine. *Life Among the Giants.*
Superb evocations of what life is like for "little people."

Videotapes and Films

The following excellent tapes and films of young people engaged in creative and productive activities are available for borrowing or purchase from the National Commission on Resources for Youth, 36 West 44th Street, New York, N.Y. 10036. Write them for prices and terms.

FILMS

The Enfield Social Studies Lab (16mm)
Shows how to start and operate a program in which high school students develop slide/tape presentations about subjects of interest to them. 15 minutes, color.

It Begins with a Camera (16mm)
Documents the struggles, successes, and failures of four young filmmakers as they try to bring their feelings and ideas to life in film. 20 minutes, color.

Pretending (16mm)
Children at a day-care center engage in various kinds of make-believe play which helps them learn about social interaction and the world around them. Adults or youth, as facilitators, enrich the play experiences and help children work out occasional problems that arise. 16 minutes, color.

Share and Repair (16mm)

Describes a project in which young people and adults share the work of fixing up the homes of their neighbors. A social-studies class makes the work of the project part of its course of study. The film is full of the barn-raising spirit of neighbors working together to solve a real community problem, culminating in a grand end-of-work celebration. 12 minutes, color.

With Time to Share; The Sonoma Youth Project (16mm)

Describes a project in California in which high school students do sophisticated physical therapy with children and adults in a home for the retarded. It also shows the training and communal-living situation the students set up for themselves. 30 minutes, color.

Youth Tutors Youth (16mm)

A documentary based on a Youth Tutoring Youth summer program in Philadelphia. 20 minutes, black-and-white.

VIDEOTAPES
(all ½ inch, reel-to-reel, black-and-white)

The Museum of the Hudson Highlands

Teen-agers initiated and maintain a natural-science museum that has become a tremendous resource for schools in upper New York.

The Ramapo School and Community Service Programs

Teen-agers receive school credit for working in a great variety of community-helping agencies. The school provides seminars related to their service work, and individual counseling.

Students Concerned with Public Health

High school students use a variety of imaginative strategies such as puppet shows and scientific demonstrations to teach elementary school children about public-health problems such as alcoholism and VD.

The Unwinding Room

Girls at a parochial school in South Philadelphia counsel

their peers on serious personal problems. The girls are trained
by a professional counselor; a school room closed to adults is
the setting for this program.

The Fourth Street i
Puerto Rican teen-agers from New York's Lower East Side
publish a magazine about their Puerto Rican culture. Now the
magazine is being used as a reading resource in the public
schools.

The High School Archaeology Project
High school students in Atlanta perform primary archaeologi-
cal research, digging up the remains of an ancient Indian settle-
ment. Students identify, date, and catalog all artifacts. They
do this work as an independent study project and receive full
course credit from the Atlanta schools even though, while they
are working, they spend no time in school.

Foxfire
High school students produce a magazine about the culture
of elderly residents of Appalachia. They are preserving an aspect
of American culture that would otherwise be lost. The Smith-
sonian Institution has tapes and records of this project.

City Arts Workshop
Teen-agers from various ethnic groups have painted murals
depicting their heritages on walls of neighborhood buildings.
This tape shows how a group of Jewish youth planned and
painted one mural.

The following excellent films on juvenile delinquency and the
juvenile justice system are available as indicated.

Busted (1972), 17 minutes. Distributor: Oxford Films, 1136
North Las Palmas Avenue, Hollywood, Calif. 90038

Juvenile Court (1973), 144 minutes. Distributor: Zipporah
Films, 54 Lewis Wharf, Boston, Mass. 02110

Locked Up: Locked Out (1973), 30 minutes. Distributor: Car-
ousel Films, 1501 Broadway, New York, N.Y. 10036

A Second Chance (1971), 25 minutes. (Volunteer training film for working with juveniles) Distributor: National Audiovisual Center, General Services Administration, Washington, D.C. 20409

This Child Is Rated X (1971), 52 minutes. Distributor: NBC Educational Enterprises, 30 Rockefeller Plaza, New York, N.Y. 10020

Vandalism: What and Why? (1973), 11½ minutes. Distributor: Film Fair Communications, 10900 Ventura Boulevard, Studio City, Calif. 91604

The following films recommended by the federal Office of Youth Development are available on a free-loan basis from RHR Filmedia, Inc., 48 West 48th St., New York, N.Y. 10036.

After Awareness, What?
This is a 28-minute, 16mm film in color that examines the way in which one community is dealing with the problem of a communications gap between youth and adults. The film is available with a discussion guide.

Challenge, Action, Change
This is a 16mm film in color that shows how three communities—Philadelphia; Boise, Idaho; and Placentia, California—have developed community-based programs to divert young people from the juvenile justice system.

Where to Get Help, Materials, and Information
DEAN CALABRESE

The number of individuals and groups working on behalf of children and youth is growing rapidly at every level, from the national to the grass-roots. They are highly diverse, but all united in the cause.

The Children's Defense Fund, for example, is one of the nation's leading advocacy groups, essentially a corps of lawyers operating through the courts. The Carnegie Council on Children is a research and study project—academic experts seeking more humane guidelines for public policy.

But this field is too important to be left to professionals and experts. Action for Children's Television and Parents for Responsibility in the Toy Industry are groups of ordinary citizens concerned about children and focused on specific institutions of the society that must be changed. Still another kind of action is self-help, as represented here by Parents Anonymous and, in a different way, by such youth-staffed enterprises as the Children's Rights Organization, the National Youth Alternatives Project, and Youth Liberation of Ann Arbor.

Perhaps the most significant actions for youth are the actions *by* youth that can be found in virtually every community. The National Commission on Resources for Youth gathers and disseminates information about such projects at the grass-roots level.

These are the major national organizations we have been able to identify in this field. We do not know many of them at first hand, so each reader will have to make his or her own judgment, from materials obtained from the source, whether a given organization is useful for a particular purpose.

A few of the entries are especially full, such as the Children's Defense Fund, National Youth Alternatives, and the National Commission on Resources for Youth. This reflects our estimate of the importance of these organizations, though in a few other cases equally important groups are described only briefly, either because only that much information was available about them or because their work could be adequately described in brief.

We have not included the many organizations in the field of school reform. A listing of this "teachers' underground" can be found in our *Will It Grow in a Classroom?* available in paperback. The best single source of more up-to-date information is the New Schools Exchange, Pettigrew, Arkansas 72752, a longtime national network of free-school teachers and students.

To find *local* organizations, one of the best sources is the

People's Yellow Pages, which are published in many big cities, frequently by women's groups; these directories usually list the best child-care, health, educational, and other services.

At the end is an additional list of just the names and addresses of organizations that either seemed marginally relevant, and thus not worth a full entry from our particular point of view, or about which no further information was forthcoming in response to our survey.

Action for Children's Television, 46 Austin Street, Newtonville, Mass. 02160

ACT was founded in 1968 by a small group of parents, teachers, physicians, and television professionals who sought to eliminate the abuses of commercialism and lack of diversity that they believed characterized most profit-making children's programs. Since then, ACT has grown to a national advocacy group with about five thousand members and has attracted the support of many organizations concerned with children.

Working on behalf of ACT's goals are over ninety contacts, or representatives, who distribute information prepared by ACT and who co-ordinate the efforts of other individuals dedicated to improving programing in their own communities.

ACT's most significant achievements have occurred since its 1970 petition to the Federal Communications Commission requesting the elimination of all host selling and commercialism from children's programs. As a result of massive public response to the FCC's invitation to comment on the issue, the National Association of Broadcasters (NAB) ruled that advertising on weekend children's television should be reduced from 16 to 9½ minutes per hour by December 1975 and that hosts on children's programs should not sell products to their young viewers.

ACT submitted petitions to the Federal Trade Commission to eliminate all advertising for toys, food, and vitamins from children's programs. Though the FTC has not yet acted, the major drug manufacturers have voluntarily withdrawn their

vitamin ads from programs directed to children, and the NAB
has introduced more-rigid guidelines regulating toy and food
ads.

American Child Guidance Foundation, 18 Tremont Street,
Boston, Mass. 02108
ACGF assists welfare agencies, clinics, schools, and other
institutions and groups in prevention and control of childhood
emotional and behavioral disorders.

American Civil Liberties Union, 22 East 40th Street, New
York, N.Y. 10016
The ACLU "champions the rights of man set forth in the
Declaration of Independence and the Constitution: Freedom
of inquiry and expression—speech, press, assembly, and religion—for everybody; due process and fair trial for everybody;
equality before the law—for everybody—regardless of race, color,
national origin, political opinion, or religious belief." Its activities include test court cases, opposition to repressive legislation,
public protest on every inroad of rights. Maintains a library of
more than five thousand volumes. Publications: Policy statements, reprints, pamphlets, and *Civil Liberties* (9/year)

Big Brothers of America, 220 Suburban Station Building, Philadelphia, Penna. 19103
BBA is a federation of local agencies composed of volunteer
laymen who, under the supervision of professional social workers, give guidance through friendship on an individual basis to
fatherless boys. Publications: *Big Brother Ambassador* (quarterly)

Black Child Development Institute, 1028 Connecticut Avenue,
N.W., Washington, D.C. 20036
In 1970, national headquarters of BCDI were set up in
Washington to serve as the advocate for black children across
the nation. Development in black communities of quality child-
care programs is the main thrust of BCDI.

Carnegie Council on Children, 285 Prospect Street, New
Haven, Conn. 06520

The Carnegie Council was established by the Carnegie Corporation of New York in mid-1972 and has received over a million dollars in funding since that time. Headed by Professor Kenneth Keniston of M.I.T., with a membership of eleven persons with diverse experience or interests in the area of child welfare and development, the council has been undertaking critical reviews of existing attitudes, knowledge, and public policy with regard to the current position of children in American society.

"We are a small, private commission," says Keniston, "a group of women and men chosen not to represent particular constituencies, professions, or groups, but because we have a common concern with the needs of American children and their families. We are not a blue-ribbon group, but simply a dozen individuals from diverse backgrounds, fields, and perspectives, most of us in our thirties and forties, most of us parents. Assisted by an able young staff, we have not been doing original scientific research but, rather, attempting to learn, from the experience, action, and studies of others, where children fit today in America, what are the unmet needs and problems of American children and families, and which of these problems most urgently deserve our response."

Starting in 1976 the commission will report its findings and recommendations on such vital topics as children's health and rights, the role of the family, early child care and education, the problems of minority children, disabled and handicapped children, the impact of the media, and other crucial influences in a child's life. Three studies and a final report, to be accompanied by thorough analyses of the meaning of their recommendations in economic and human terms, will be widely disseminated to scholars, the public, and to policymakers through books of various kinds, articles, seminars, press conferences, and possibly television.

Catholic Big Brothers, 1011 First Avenue, New York, N.Y. 10022
CBB's aim is to prevent and control juvenile delinquency. It helps boys between the ages of eight and fifteen, generally

fatherless boys who have a need for male relationships and have
been referred through courts, schools, parishes, and individuals.
Publications: *Newsletter* (quarterly)

Center for Law and Education, Harvard University—Larsen
Hall, 14 Appian Way, Cambridge, Mass. 02138
As part of the Office of Economic Opportunity's legal services program, the function of the center is to promote reform
in education through research and action on the legal implications of educational policies. It has participated in school desegregation suits, evaluation of tracking practices, special education, and other methods of pupil classification, efforts to help
parents to gain a greater say in the spending of federal school
funds, the development of bilingual education, and the exploration of educational vouchers and alternative schools. Other
center activities include the promotion of students' personal
and political rights and assistance to welfare-rights organizations, Mexican-Americans, and American Indians who are seeking to improve their children's education. Publications:
Inequality in Education (quarterly); assorted manuals and materials on students' rights, the use of sedative drugs to quiet
school children, and other subjects.

Child Abuse Listening Mediation, P.O. Box 718, Santa Barbara, Calif. 93102
CALM's objective is to reach parents "who feel that they
cannot cope with their problems and frustrations and who may
be in danger of taking out these feelings on their children."
They provide telephone listening services twenty-four hours a
day, referrals to other organizations, and other resources services. CALM volunteers are available to go into the home, to
act as "compassionate listeners and friendly neighbors" to help
in various ways in situations of crisis. They conduct a program
of public information and education. CALM maintains a resource library on the battered-child syndrome. Publications:
Keeping Up with CALM (newsletter—sporadic), bibliography
on the battered-child syndrome, an untitled report on the organization's work.

Child Development Associate Consortium (CDAC), 7315 Wisconsin Avenue, Suite 601—East, Washington, D.C. 20014
National associations whose concern is early childhood education and child development. Competency-based developmental project focusing on personnel working with three-to-five-year-old children in early-childhood setting. Seeks to improve the quality and effectiveness of the care and education provided for young children by developing a competency-based assessment system (a set of procedures to assess an individual's proficiency in skills considered essential for working with young children) and by developing appropriate credential procedures to provide individuals who are assessed as competent Child Development Associates (CDA's) with a permanent record of proficiency. Publications: *Communiqué,* 6–9/year; also publishes numerous brochures, pamphlets, directories, reprints. Convention meeting: annual.

Child Study Association of America, 50 Madison Avenue, New York, N.Y. 10010
The CSAA is an educational and training organization concerned with family mental health. It conducts training programs for professional and paraprofessional workers in parent education and for parent participation in Project Head Start; offers assistance to community groups and agencies; holds workshops, institutes, and conferences for educators, social workers, psychologists, nurses, and others concerned with mental health and family life; reviews books on child development and publishes annotated lists of the most helpful; reviews current books for children, prepares book lists and exhibits; compiles anthologies of children's stories for different age groups; and maintains a library of four thousand volumes on family life. Publications: *Children's Books of the Year* (annual); *Recommended Reading About Children and Family Life* (annual); and an extensive list of pamphlets and books for parents and educators.

Child Welfare League of America (CWLA), 67 Irving Place, New York, N.Y. 10003
Federation of public and private child-care agencies seeking

to raise standards of child care. Conducts research, provides consultation and information, conducts surveys of agency or community services, publishes professional literature, works with national and international organizations, provides legislative groups with information necessary for the passage of "sound legislation," develops standards for child welfare services (child protection, day care). Publications: *Child Welfare*, 10/year; *Newsletter*, quarterly; *Directory*, annual; also publishes books and monographs.

Childhood Sensuality Circle, P.O. Box 20163, El Cajon, Calif. 92021

This organization is concerned with children's liberation, particularly in the area of sexual freedom. Publications: *CSC Newsletter* (bimonthly—4/1/75 was the first issue); and many pamphlets and booklets on children's sensuality, children's liberation, and children's rights.

Children, Inc., P.O. Box 5381, Richmond, Va. 23220

This is an international organization concerned with the mental, physical, and spiritual needs of children. Currently involved in twenty-seven countries and assisting thirteen thousand children. It provides food, clothing, medical and school supplies, and personal necessities. It also aids (financially) the establishments that serve the children. Funds are raised largely through sponsors. Publications: *CI News*, semiannual; *Children—Their Needs* (booklet); *Children—Their Friends* (booklet).

The Children's Defense Fund, 1746 Cambridge Street, Cambridge, Mass. 02138

What is the Children's Defense Fund?

The Children's Defense Fund (CDF) is a national nonprofit organization created in 1973 to provide long-range and systematic advocacy on behalf of the nation's children. It is funded by a number of private foundations and staffed with lawyers, federal policy monitors, researchers, and community liaison people dedicated to reforming institutions, policies, and practices affecting the lives of children.

CDF PROGRAM PRIORITIES

CDF's program areas include:
— the right to an education for children who have been excluded or misclassified,
— the protection of children's right to privacy of records kept by various social agencies, with particular attention to guidelines for data banking and information-retrieval systems,
— the protection of children from medical experimentation or other harmful research techniques and the right to treatment for institutionalized children,
— the right to adequate health care for children,
— the right of children to receive fair and humane services under the juvenile justice system, and
— the rights of children to comprehensive child development services.

In each of these areas, CDF will seek to act in co-operation with other agencies and groups to bring about specific reforms.

Children's Division, American Humane Association, P.O. Box 1226, Denver, Colo. 80201

The Children's Division of the American Humane Association is a national association of individuals and agencies (state and local social services, public and voluntary agencies, courts, probation services, welfare councils, schools, medical services, etc.) working to prevent neglect, abuse, and exploitation of children. It is involved in research and surveys as well as a consultation service offered with the intention of stimulating the organization of new programs or to improve standards in existing child protective services. Guidelines for legislation to strengthen child protective services are prepared by the Children's Division. It surveys state laws and makes comparative studies of existing legislation to point out areas that need change. (Most recent emphasis has been in relation to laws for the mandatory reporting of child-abuse cases.) Publications: the C.D. prepares and publishes books and pamphlets on child protective services. The current list of publications contains more than thirty titles and may be obtained by writing directly to the national office, in Denver, Colorado.

The Children's Foundation, 1028 Connecticut Avenue, N.W., Suite 614, Washington, D.C. 20036

A charitable organization that supports projects designed to bring about change and improvement in areas such as child nutrition and health, day care, education, and public information. Works with local organizations and representatives of low-income families to "eliminate inequities in tax-supported child-feeding programs, such as school lunches."

Children's Rights, Inc., 3443 17th Street, N.W., Washington, D.C. (202) 462-7573

A lobbying organization and clearinghouse to promote legislation protecting parents who have had a child abducted by its other parent in violation of court orders and/or visitation rights, a surprisingly commonplace occurrence. At present there is no law against this, and the perpetrators are rarely punished. The founder of CRI, Arnold Miller, a victim of this practice himself, plans to expand its activities into the areas of child abuse and constitutional rights for children.

Children's Rights Organization, 17 65th Avenue, Plaza Del Rey, Calif. 90291

This group is run both by and for youth. They provide information and other services to youth, families, and other interested people. They advocate for the rights of youth; have been active in the investigations into juvenile halls and foster-homes services; provide youth and family with counseling, consultation, information, and literature; and also have speakers on these subjects on call. CRO also makes referrals to appropriate agencies and professionals. Publications: tape cassettes (on open childhood, legal rights of youth, CRO, etc.); Litera-

ture Package (Bill of Rights, Research Report and Questionnaire, Child Slavery, etc.)

Citizen's Committee for Children of New York, 2 Park Avenue,
New York, N.Y. 10016
An advocate body for the children of New York. Its program
consists of research, investigation, and reports in the fields of
health, mental health, education, child welfare, and children's
rights. They conduct two 16-week seminars per year entitled
"Course in Community Leadership." Issues (erratically) numerous reports.

Citizens Committee for Constitutional Liberties, 22 East 17th
Street, Room 1525, New York, N.Y. 10003
CCCL works to "expose and defeat repressive legislation
through education and action programs." Works to stop any
form of "preventive detention and repressive measures in laws
or government policies." It is also involved in pushing for the
passage of a law to bar unconstitutional surveillance, dossiers,
data banks, and blacklists. CCCL provides leaders for seminars
and classes on civil liberties topics for schools and groups. Publications: *Liberty* (quarterly); *Concentration Camps U.S.A.*
(booklet); *F.B.I. Listing; The Conspiracy Tactic;* and other
booklets.

Community Service Volunteers, 237 Pentonville Road, London,
England
This group is concerned with aiding adults and young people
in developing community-service projects. Publications: *School
and Community Kits* (bimonthly), pamphlets, and other assorted kits and goodies.

Day Care and Child Development Council of America, 801
North Fairfax Street, Alexandria, Va. 22314
The DCCDCA believes that quality child-care services are
the right of every child, every parent, and every community.
The goal of this organization is to promote the development
of a locally controlled, publicly supported, universally available
child-care system. A catalog of publications and audio-visuals

for 1975 entitled *Resources for Child Care* is available upon request. This catalog contains numerous publications on background of child care, public policy, administration and costs, day-care manuals, developmental activities, licensing, and care of children.

Drop-outs Anonymous, 3876 East Fedora Avenue, Fresno, Calif. 93726
This is a telephone information service that provides limited counseling and supportive assistance to youth who are contemplating dropping out of school and to youth and adults who wish to return to school. It occasionally provides small temporary loans to these students. DOA operates on a twenty-four-hour basis and serves the Fresno and San Joaquin Valley areas.

Feminists on Children's Media, P.O. Box 315, Grand Central Station, New York, N.Y. 10017
FOCM's aim is to combat sexism in children's literature. It has compiled a list of articles on sex discrimination in children's books and a bibliography of children's books with positive attitudes toward women.

High School Student Information Service, 1000 Wisconsin Avenue, N.W., Washington, D.C. 20007
Those who participate in HSSIC are high school students interested in changing the nature of the school systems, and high school student unions. Their purpose is to exchange information concerning activities in educational reform in high schools and to aid individuals and organizations in making the changes they feel will significantly improve education. Conducts research on the "educational power structure" and on innovative school programs. Publications: *National High School Publication* (monthly); information packets (monthly); and a literature list.

National Association for Child Development and Education, 500 12th St., S.W., Suite 810, Washington, D.C. 20024
Privately owned child-care centers (both multiple units and individual, family-owned units). Purposes are to give to the

private child-care provider a voice in an arena now dominated by the tax-sustained operator, and to ensure to the private provider representation in the policymaking and administration activities of the Department of Health, Education, and Welfare and similar entities. Conducts seminars and training sessions in administration and education. Publications: *Chalk Talk* (newsletter), monthly; *Membership Directory*, annual.

National Center for Child Advocacy, Children's Bureau, Office of Child Development, Box 1182, Washington, D.C. 20013

In May 1971 the National Center for Child Advocacy was authorized to be established in the Children's Bureau. Its major functions are to provide a central point of information on child development, services, and programs, as well as a voice for children within the federal government. Essentially the center is a back-up center of information for advocates throughout the country. It provides information in advocacy programs, publishes a quarterly, *Advocacy for Children*, and provides consultation as requested, especially to national and state agencies and organizations.

National Child Labor Committee, 145 East 32nd Street, New York, N.Y. 10016

This is the parent organization of the National Committee on the Education of Migrant Children and the National Committee on Employment of Youth. Publication: *New Generation Magazine* (quarterly).

The National Commission on Resources for Youth, 36 West 44th Street, New York, N.Y. 10036

The National Commission on Resources for Youth was established because of the increasing difficulty young people find today in making the transition from adolescence to constructive adult life. In earlier periods the home, the local community, and the place of employment furnished a variety of opportunities for youth to work, to make helpful contributions to family and community, and to associate in other ways with adults. As they grew older, this enabled them to participate more and more in adult activities and to assume an increasing degree of responsibility. In this way they gained both competence and assurance that they were moving successfully into adulthood.

This situation has changed. The specialization of contemporary society, the reduction, and in many cases the elimination, of home chores, limitations placed on youth employment, greater emphasis upon youth protection rather than production, and the high degree of age stratification in urban activities have greatly isolated adolescents from the adult world and blocked the pathways through which the young move into mature roles in society.

The National Commission's purpose is to find and make widely known examples of successful programs that have overcome these blockades and enabled young people to participate in productive adult activities and to assume real responsibility for what they do. To accomplish this objective, it has developed a network of people, largely volunteers, and organizations that are on the lookout for promising programs. As these are identified, the commission seeks to obtain impartial external appraisals of their effectiveness and their potential usefulness in other communities. In some cases, programs validated in this way have become demonstration projects, such as Youth Tutoring Youth and Youth Helper in Day Care; the responsibility for the demonstration is undertaken by the commission. To disseminate information about projects, the commission publishes *Resources for Youth*, a newsletter with a wide circulation.

Within the limits of its resources, the commission also provides technical assistance to community groups that wish to adopt and adapt a program for their own use. This assistance includes such things as suggestions on ways of getting the program sponsored, advice about organizing and administering it, and help in training personnel for the new activities involved.

The National Commission on Resources for Youth was created in 1967 as a kind of spontaneous action by a group of educators, social scientists, judges, and businessmen who had long been concerned with the well-being of youth. The decision to form a small organization was made as they discussed the difficulties young people face in making a constructive transition to adult life. They believed that such an organization could be of significant help in opening the channels for youth development by working with major institutions such as the schools and voluntary agencies in developing, improvising, and expanding programs in which young persons can find more opportunities to participate actively and responsibly in the world around them.

The director of the commission is Judge Mary Conway Kohler, who works with a small staff, a larger group of part-time associates, and a much larger band of volunteers. This kind of organization is particularly effective in making firsthand contact with promising programs and providing a variety of personal observations as well as more formal descriptions and appraisals. This type of organization is necessary because the United States is a very large country, and it is not surprising that dozens of promising programs are brought to the attention of the commission every month. Although most communities have not thus far broken the blockades that interfere with the transition of their youth into responsible adulthood, a few have, and they are to be found in all areas of the nation. *Ralph W. Tyler*, Chairman

National Committee for Prevention of Child Abuse, 836 West Wellington Avenue, Chicago, Ill. 60657

Operates the Child Abuse Prevention Program, a hospital-based, controlled study to develop, apply, and test techniques useful in screening and identifying parents who are "at risk" with respect to abusing and/or neglecting their infant or young child, and to develop and apply interventions effective in preventing the victimization of an infant or child "before the fact" as well as early intervention in suspected or actual cases to prevent recurrence and untoward consequences. Sponsors the annual National Symposium on Child Abuse. Developing a national media campaign. Maintains a library. Publications:

National Directory of Child Abuse Services and Information, annual; also publishes *Bibliography of Child Abuse Literature* and various reports.

National Council of Jewish Women, 1 West 47th Street, New York, N.Y. 10036

The NCJW is a national membership agency of Jewish women who are dedicated to work for disadvantaged children, youth, and the aged, and to seek to improve the quality of life for all people through programs of education, social action, and community services. Two of its publications are *Windows on Day Care,* a report on day-care needs and services by Mary Dublin Keyserling; and *Children Without Justice,* based on the council's findings and with a foreword by Justice William O. Douglas, each available for two dollars.

National Council of Juvenile Court Judges, P.O. Box 8978, University of Nevada, Reno, Nev. 89507

Judges with juvenile jurisdiction and others with a professional interest in the nation's juvenile justice system. To further more effective administration of justice for young people through the improvement of juvenile-court standards and practices. Beginning in 1962, the council has been developing a continuing education program for judges with juvenile jurisdiction, and other court-related personnel. The judicial training programs consist of summer colleges in Reno, Nevada, as well as regional institutes, conferences, and seminars. Compiles statistics. Publications: *Juvenile Court Digest,* monthly; *Juvenile Court Newsletter,* bimonthly; *Juvenile Justice,* quarterly; *Directory,* annual.

National Council of Organizations for Children and Youth, 1910 K Street, N.W., #404, Washington, D.C. 20006

A private, non-profit umbrella group representing over two hundred organizations and individuals interested in children and youth. NCOCY acts as a clearinghouse of information and a convener and mobilizer of organizations around various issues. Members participate in cluster groups on day care, health, foster

care/adoption and youth development. NCOCY publishes a
monthly newsletter, *FOCUS*, available without charge to
NCOCY members and to non-members for twenty-five dollars
a year. *FOCUS* provides up-to-date information on all executive, legislative, and judicial actions in Washington affecting
children and youth, as well as monthly columns by experts in
and out of government.

National Council on Crime and Delinquency, Continental
Plaza, 411 Hackensack Avenue, Hackensack, N.J. 07601
Social workers, prison officials, judges, and others interested
in probation, parole, juvenile and family courts, detention services, and the prevention, control, and treatment of crime and
delinquency. Furnishes legislation and legal advisory service.
Sponsors professional training institutes. Maintains library of six
thousand volumes, information files of thirty thousand items.
Maintains two centers: Research Center, Davis, Calif., Information Center, Hackensack, N.J. Publications: *Criminal Justice
Newsletter*, biweekly; *Crime and Delinquency*, quarterly; *Crime
and Delinquency Literature*, quarterly; *Journal of Research in
Crime and Delinquency*, semiannual; *Probation and Parole Directory of the U.S. and Canada*, every two to four years; also
publishes *Directory of Detention Institutions*, books, pamphlets, forms, and training materials.

National Emergency Civil Liberties Committee, 25 East 26th
Street, New York, N.Y. 10010
NECLC strives "to re-establish in full the traditional freedoms guaranteed under the Constitution and the Bill of Rights.
We stand uncompromisingly for civil liberties for everyone and
every variety of dissent." The legal staff handles "test cases" in
the courts, without charge to clients. Also functions as an information service. Publications: *Rights* (bimonthly).

National Foundation—March of Dimes, 1275 Mamaroneck
Avenue, White Plains, N.Y. 10605
The mission of the National Foundation is preventing birth
defects, ameliorating their consequences, and improving the

outcome of pregnancy. The March of Dimes has a wide variety of publications, films, and exhibits on birth defects and prenatal care which are available to the general public. Printed materials cover various subjects relating to birth defects and are published in Spanish and in English for educators and the general public.

National Institute on Crime and Delinquency (NICD), c/o Library, National Council on Crime and Delinquency, 703 Market Street, 1707, San Francisco, Calif. 94103

Not a membership organization. Conducts annual national institute in the field of crime and delinquency to promote professional growth, encourage research, and disseminate information on new knowledge and techniques. Institute includes workshops, delivery of papers, and general sessions of interest to all disciplines operating in the various programs relating to the administration of justice. Sponsored by National Council on Crime and Delinquency, National Association of Training Schools and Juvenile Agencies, and five regional correctional associations.

National Legal Aid and Defender Association, 1155 East 60th Street, Chicago, Ill. 60637

NLADA is a central clearinghouse for local organizations providing legal-aid and defender services to persons without means to pay lawyers' fees. It provides a directory of legal aid and defender facilities in the United States and Canada. It also compiles statistics on cases handled by legal-aid and defender services, costs, fund sources, and population covered. Publications: *Washington Memo* (monthly), *Briefcase* (bimonthly), and *Directory of Legal Aid and Defender Services* (annual).

National Student Volunteer Program Action, 806 Connecticut Avenue, N.W., Washington, D.C. 20006

ACTION publishes and disseminates information about community service and youth volunteer programs in the United States. Publications: *High School Student Volunteers* (booklet) and *Synergist* (3/year—articles about youth volunteer projects in the United States and abroad).

National Youth Alternatives Project, 1830 Connecticut Avenue, N.W., Washington, D.C. 20009

The National Youth Alternatives Project (NYAP) is a non-profit organization dedicated to the development of a variety of alternative social services, particularly those which include client participation in the design and provision of service. Funded through grants and donations, NYAP offers technical assistance to groups attempting to organize innovative programs aimed at meeting the needs of young people who have, in general, been treated paternalistically or ignored by traditional social-service institutions.

NYAP has specific experience in the development of runaway houses, group foster homes, hotlines, crisis-intervention centers, drug centers, alternative job placement, free schools, and the training of paraprofessional workers in the field of youth counseling. NYAP operates several programs. They are (1) the Youth Alternatives Clearinghouse, (2) training programs for youth workers, (3) mobilizing alternative agencies to impact public policy, (4) the preparation and distribution of various publications designed to aid youth workers in alternative social-service fields.

The Youth Alternatives Clearinghouse gathers and disseminates information on alternative social-service programs and on the activities of federal, state, and local departments of government, foundations, and private agencies that directly affect youth and youth workers. NYAP welcomes contact with new and ongoing programs to facilitate coalition building, information sharing, and mutual aid among alternative youth-serving agencies.

The training program includes a series of regional conferences for paraprofessionals and professionals working in alternative youth programs as well as other specialized conferences, and a research and demonstration program in support of alcohol-problem counseling for youth and their parents.

In addition, NYAP has played a key role in organizing the National Network of Runaway and Youth Services. The National Network originated in an effort to inform Congress and the Department of HEW of alternative agencies' perspectives in the development of a federal program for runaway youth. NYAP is currently providing technical support for the National Network's operations.

Current publications available from NYAP include: *National Directory of Runaway Centers* ($3), *Runaways and Runaway Centers, a Bibliography* (free), *Stalking the Large Green Grant,* a basic manual on methods of obtaining funds for alternative social-service projects ($3), and *Youth Alternatives,* a monthly newsletter ($6 per year). NYAP also helps publish the bimonthly *C/O: The Journal of Alternative Human Services,* available from Community Congress of San Diego, 621 Fourth Avenue, San Diego, Calif. 92101 (annual subscription: $6 for individuals, $12 for agencies, or whatever you can afford).

New Schools Exchange, Pettigrew, Ark. 72752

The NSE is a national clearinghouse for the exchange of ideas and information about alternatives in education. Their primary purpose is to continue and expand communication/co-operation among schools and individuals at all levels of alternative education. Publications: *New Schools Exchange Newsletter* and the "Only annual directory of alternative schools in the U.S. and Canada. This directory is published as a regular edition of the newsletter and is provided free to subscribers."

Operation: Peace of Mind, P.O. Box 52896, Houston, Tex. 77052

POM maintains a seven-day-a-week, round-the-clock, toll-free hotline for youthful runaways. It serves as a means for these runaways to contact their family and/or friends and to let them know that they are well (without the risk of having their whereabouts found out). The toll-free number in Texas is 800-392-3352; out of state it is 800-231-6946. No information is given to the relatives other than that which the caller wishes divulged, and no attempt is made to trace the location of the caller. POM also maintains a referral service for callers in need of the services of runaway houses, drug-crisis centers, health clinics, and counseling centers. Again, no attempt is made to discover the location or identity of the caller.

Parents Anonymous, Inc., 250 West 57th Street, Room 1901, New York, N.Y. 10019

Parents Anonymous is a self-help group of parents who offer immediate relief to parents who feel that they are abusing or neglecting their children. They are a non-profit group offering free services, privacy, and confidentiality. Their primary objective is the rehabilitation of damaged relationships between parents and children. PA offers a twenty-four-hour telephone hotline at 212-765-2336 to the troubled parents for the release of their angers, frustrations, and tempers on the telephone (as opposed to "on their children").

Parents Anonymous, 2009 Farrell Avenue, Redondo Beach, Calif. 90278

"Adults who have abused their children" and others interested in child-abuse problems. Aim is to rehabilitate child abusers and to insure the physical and emotional well-being of their children. Program includes voluntary group and intergroup participation (e.g. weekly or daily phone calls or visiting contacts among the members). Members seek "total involvement in helping ourselves and other members to become constructive, loving parents." Provides speakers for various groups. Child abuse—physical or emotional—is estimated to affect over six hundred thousand children a year.

Parents for Responsibility in the Toy Industry—PACT, 38 West 9th Street, New York, N.Y. 10011

PRTI, a New York-based group that has as its aim the elimination of toys that reflect and perpetuate the violence in our society. It was formed in 1966 by representatives of churches and local PTA's joining with Women Strike for Peace and the Women's International League for Peace and Freedom. The organizers were people who felt a special responsibility since they were raising their families within a mile of 200 Fifth Avenue, the center of the toy industry. And some toys should never reach store shelves, especially since one third of those purchased are bought by children themselves.

In 1971, together with members of NOW, PRTI was successful in a campaign to convince Nabisco to discontinue the torture kits made by their subsidiary, Aurora. During 1974, a letter-writing campaign contributed to the decision of Quaker Oats to drop the Marx gun line.

For the past two years, PRTI has been able to become much more effective as a member of the Public Action Coalition on Toys, a group of organizations united to encourage the toy trade to take a more socially responsible position toward the children who play with their products.

Student Coalition for Relevant Sex Education, 300 Park Avenue South, 5th floor, New York, N.Y. 10010, or c/o Michael Blumenfeld, Board of Education, 110 Livingston Street, Brooklyn, N.Y. 11201

A group of high school students devoted to devising a new sex-education program in an attempt to counteract the growing rate of pregnancy and venereal disease among teen-agers. In each high school a panel of specially trained students would dispense confidential information on birth control and venereal disease to students upon request. Students with special problems would be referred to appropriate agencies.

U.S. Youth Council, 1221 Connecticut Avenue, N.W., Washington, D.C. 20036

National youth and student organization. To provide a unifying, co-ordinating force among youth and student groups and to promote activities by them in the fields of human rights and social justice in this country and international co-operation abroad. Represents U.S. youth organizations at international seminars and regional conferences. Conducts research on international youth movements. Sponsors youth voter-education project, Frontlash. Sponsors international youth leadership exchanges; conducts training programs for youth-serving organizations in developing countries. Publications: *Minutes,* semiannual; also publishes occasional reports.

World Union of Organizations for the Safeguard of Youth, 28 Place Saint-Georges, Paris 9ème, France

Individuals and organizations united to help national organizations for the care of maladjusted children to study their technical and administrative problems at the international level. Purposes are to seek a solution to the many problems of juvenile maladjustment; to promote co-operation in each country between state-organized and -administered departments and private agencies; and to facilitate co-operation among scientific, technical, or professional specialists and workers, with special emphasis on the multiprofessional team. Publications: *Bulletin*, quarterly; *Proceedings of International Conferences*, triennial; *Reports*, irregular.

Young Filmmakers Foundation, 4 Rivington Street, New York, N.Y. 10002

This association encourages media production as recreational, educational, and vocational experience for young people. Its services include a 16mm Film Club in which 15–21-year-olds learn the arts of sound recording, animating, editing, budgeting, acting, filming, scriptwriting, directing, and showing movies; Film Club Super 8mm, which teaches basically the same skills (although at a much more elementary level) to 8–13-year-olds; Media Teacher Intern Training, which teaches the art of teaching media to children, teen-agers, and community groups and operates teaching workshops for other interested parties; the Media Equipment Resource Center, which lends film, videotaping, and other film-oriented equipment and facilities to non-profit organizations and individual artists; and Community-Action-Newsreel, which serves as a production and training center for the Lower East Side of New York City, co-produces with community groups tapes and films documenting issues and events pertinent to the neighborhood, and holds regularly scheduled showings of these films at local hangouts. Publications: various books and documentary films.

The Youth Law Center, 693 Mission Street, 2nd floor, San Francisco, Calif. 94105

The lawyers and law students here do chiefly major-impact litigation and advocacy in behalf of people under the age of eighteen. The center also provides general information about the law as it affects young people. Its services are provided at no cost to people who cannot afford private lawyers, but the center can take only cases that have significant law-reform potential.

Youth Liberation, 2007 Washtenaw Avenue, Ann Arbor, Mich. 48104

Its purpose is to help young people who are oppressed by discriminatory laws, compulsory schooling, the family, and the church, and to give all young people more control over their own lives. YL maintains a library of independent and underground high school papers. They operate a Youth Liberation News Service (FPS), which provides news and graphics to high school papers, both official and underground, and publishes articles on the technical and political aspects of organizing young people, young people's struggles across the country, analysis of youth oppression, and other important national issues. CHIPS (Co-operative Highschool Independent Press Syndicate), which provides help for students who have started, or who want to start, independent papers in their schools, is another function of YL. Publications: *FPS* (monthly—four issues annually are specifically devoted to education and schooling), pamphlets, kits, posters and other odds and ends.

Index